Social Status and Psychological Disorder:
A Causal Inquiry

WILEY SERIES ON PSYCHOLOGICAL DISORDERS

IRVING B. WEINER, *Editor*
School of Medicine and Dentistry
The University of Rochester

Social Status and Psychological Disorder:

A Causal Inquiry

BRUCE P. DOHRENWEND
College of Physicians and Surgeons
Columbia University

BARBARA SNELL DOHRENWEND
The City College of the City University of New York

WILEY-INTERSCIENCE   A Division of John Wiley & Sons
New York · London · Sydney · Toronto

Library of Congress Catalogue Card Number: 72–88310

SBN 471 21752 2

Printed in the United States of America

To our parents

Series Preface

This series of books is addressed to behavioral scientists concerned with understanding and ameliorating psychological disorders. Its scope should prove pertinent to clinicians and their students in psychology, psychiatry, social work, and other disciplines that deal with problems of human behavior as well as to theoreticians and researchers studying these problems. Although many facets of behavioral science have relevance to psychological disorder, the series concentrates on the three core clinical areas of psychopathology, personality assessment, and psychotherapy.

Each of these clinical areas can be discussed in terms of theoretical foundations that identify directions for further development, empirical data that summarize current knowledge, and practical applications that guide the clinician in his work with patients. The books in this series present scholarly integrations of such theoretical, empirical, and practical approaches to clinical concerns. Some pursue the implications of research findings for the validity of alternative theoretical frameworks or for the utility of various modes of clinical practice; others consider the implications of certain conceptual models for lines of research or for the elaboration of clinical methods; and others encompass a wide range of theoretical, research, and practical issues as they pertain to a specific psychological disturbance, assessment technique, or treatment modality.

University of Rochester
Rochester, New York

Irving B. Weiner

Preface

This book reports research executed and theory developed as part of a program aimed at solving some basic issues concerning the causes of psychological disorder. We hope that we have made a start in the right direction in the propositions we have developed concerning, for example, the relation of stressful social environments to psychological symptoms. How right or wrong we are will be decided by our own current and planned field experiments and, we hope, by empirical research of others based on these propositions.

Bruce P. Dohrenwend
Barbara Snell Dohrenwend

New York, New York
May, 1969

Acknowledgments

This work has been supported in part by Grants OM-82, MH 07327, MH 07328, MH 10328, and MH 13356 from the National Institute of Mental Health, U. S. Public Health Service. It has also been supported in part by Grant U1053 from the N. Y. C. Health Research Council to the Community Population Laboratory of Columbia's School of Public Health and Administrative Medicine.

Several of the chapters include in revised and expanded form material that appeared earlier in the following articles: Bruce P. Dohrenwend and Barbara Snell Dohrenwend, "The Problem of Validity in Field Studies of Psychological Disorder," *Journal of Abnormal Psychology,* **70,** 1965, 52–69; Barbara Snell Dohrenwend and Bruce P. Dohrenwend, "Field Studies of Social Factors in Relation to Three Types of Psychological Disorder," *Journal of Abnormal Psychology,* **72,** 1967, 369–378; and Bruce P. Dohrenwend, "Social Status and Psychological Disorder: An Issue of Substance and an Issue of Method," *American Sociological Review,* **31,** 1966, 14–34. Grateful acknowledgment is made to the American Psychological Association and the American Sociological Association, who publish these journals, for their permission to use this material. We should also like to express our gratitude to George Allen & Unwin Ltd. for their permission to quote material from Leo Eitinger, *Concentration Camp Survivors in Norway and Israel.*

Some of the data in this book come from epidemiological studies conducted by other researchers in different parts of the world. Sometimes our attempts to analyze these data were confronted by translation problems. Especially formidable were the studies that were published in Japanese. We are very grateful to Robert J. Smith and Yorihiko Kumasaka for their help with the Japanese studies.

Other data presented here were collected in personal interview studies of samples of residents of Washington Heights, a section of Manhattan in

New York City. These studies were greatly facilitated by Columbia's Community Population Laboratory, whose staff conducted a Master Sample Survey in 1960–1961 on behalf of researchers at the Columbia-Presbyterian Medical Center and in several New York City agencies. We are most grateful to Jack Elinson, the director of the Population Laboratory, and to Regina Loewenstein, its statistician, for their help and advice.

Still other data come from a study of psychiatric patients. For their assistance in facilitating the selection and interviewing of these patients we should like to thank the following physicians: Elizabeth B. Davis of Harlem Hospital, Roger MacKinnon and Joseph Snyder of Vanderbilt Clinic of the Columbia-Presbyterian Medical Center, and Jack Sheps, formerly of Jewish Memorial Hospital.

With regard to their very able help with the processing and analysis of the data from both the community sample and the patients, special thanks are due to Edwin Chin-Shong and Robert Hill, who, at the time, were graduate students in Columbia's Department of Sociology. Our thanks go also to the psychiatrists who, as students in courses that one of us taught in Columbia's Division of Community and Social Psychiatry and at the William Alanson White Institute, kindly gave us their ratings of the "social desirability" of a number of the symptom items that we used.

We owe a very special debt to our co-workers in Columbia's Community Psychiatry Research Unit. While the work reported here was underway these were, in addition to Edwin Chin-Shong, psychiatrists DeWitt L. Crandell and Gladys Egri. They have influenced our thinking more than they can possibly know.

Others of our colleagues whose advice and criticism have helped us in important ways with this book are John Colombotos, Elizabeth Davis, Jack Elinson, Ernest Gruenberg, Lawrence Kolb, Thomas Langner, John Rainer, and Joseph Zubin. It is a pleasure to have this opportunity to express our deep gratitude.

We should also like to express our appreciation to the office staff of The City College Psychology Department for their cheerful help in preparing the manuscript: Mrs. Minna Fuchs, Mrs. Pearl Friedman, Mrs. Rose Bogdansky, and, especially for her many long hours at the typewriter, Mrs. Joan Stern. In this regard special votes of thanks are due also to Office Staff at Columbia: to Mrs. Aida Rosa who not only helped with the typing of the manuscript but participated as well in the fieldwork of the Washington Heights studies, in which she proved indispensable, and to Mrs. Karen Goodman for her valuable help in constructing the name index for this book.

Finally, we should like to take this opportunity to thank the people, both patients and nonpatients, of Washington Heights and adjacent areas who have come into our study samples. They have given generously of their time to answer our questions. In doing so they have contributed most to our education on relations between social status and psychological disorder.

B.P.D.

B.S.D.

Contents

CHAPTER 1

Introduction

For more than 100 years researchers have been reporting that social status is related to psychological disorder. An early instance is Jarvis' finding, in 1856, that the "pauper class" in Massachusetts furnished proportionately 64 times as many cases of "insanity" as the "independent class" (Sandifer, 1962). Among the numerous later investigators reporting similar results (Dunham, 1955; Mishler & Scotch, 1965), a classic example is the research of Faris and Dunham (1939) on the distribution of admissions to mental hospitals from Chicago. Finding the highest rates of disorder in the central slum section, these investigators suggested that the social disorganization characteristic of areas of this type might be causing psychological disorder.

However, in his introduction to Faris and Dunham's 1939 monograph, Ernest Burgess reminded his readers that an empirical relationship is one thing; its interpretation, quite another. Therefore, critics argued, although it might be that high rates of disorder were being produced by conditions of slum living, Faris and Dunham's finding could be explained equally well in terms of the social selection of previously ill persons into slum sections of the city (e.g., Meyerson, 1940). In this view, social status is seen not as a cause but as a consequence of psychological disorder. The disturbing reality, unfortunately, is that correlations such as those reported by Jarvis, by Faris and Dunham, and by more recent investigators have been promiscuous where theories are concerned, lending themselves equally well to social causation or social selection interpretations (e.g., A. H. Leighton, Lambo, Hughes, D. C. Leighton, Murphy, & Macklin, 1963, p. 280; D. C. Leighton, Harding, Macklin, Macmillan, & A. H. Leighton, 1963, pp. 343–346; Michael, 1962).

THE QUESTION OF ETIOLOGY

It is possible, of course, to view correlations between social status and psychological disorder in terms of the problems they present for social policy and planning psychiatric services (e.g., Joint Commission on Mental Illness and Health, 1961; Kolb, Bernard, & Dohrenwend, in press; Susser, 1968). In this case the direction of the relationship need not be resolved for the fact of it to be useful. We are interested, however, in the roles of poor heredity and unfavorable environment in etiology, a fundamental theoretical question that is still unanswered for most types of disorder. For this reason, we must be concerned about the issue of social selection versus social causation of lower-class cases of psychological disorder.

In this controversy, the hypothesis that lower-class cases of disorder are due to exposure to an unfavorable environment is usually intended to implicate the social rather than the biological environment. This ruling out of the biological environment from the issue results, first, from the fact that in certain disorders, such as general paresis resulting from syphilitic infection, the organic etiology is so well established as to be beyond controversy. Second, where controversy does exist concerning the role of biological processes, for example, the role of metabolic disturbances in producing schizophrenia (e.g., Kety, 1965; Pauling, 1968; Throne & Gowdey, 1967), these disturbances are conceived as possibly resulting either from biological environmental deficits, such as poor nutrition, or from hereditary handicaps (e.g., Heath, 1965; Pauling, 1968).

Therefore, although we must be aware of the possible involvement of the biological environment in etiology, it will not be the focal problem for our study. Rather we will be concerned mainly with the issue that underlies most of the theoretically oriented studies of relations between social status and psychological disorder: the part played in etiology by poor heredity as compared to unfavorable social environment.

THE PROBLEM OF DEFINITION

To begin our inquiry into relations between social status and psychological disorder, let us consider two questions of definition: What is social status? What is psychological disorder? The former question we shall answer immediately and firmly. The latter we shall answer gradually, and tentatively to the end.

Social Status

The social statuses with which we are concerned are objective conditions of life that vary with such characteristics of the individual as sex, age, and social class. We know, for example, that a male in our society is, in certain respects, treated differently by others from a female; an adult has rights, duties, and obligations that differ from those of a child. Objective social statuses consist of such normative reactions by others, which define what rights and duties are appropriate for an individual on the basis of his apparent innate or acquired characterics.

Note that this formulation of social status is defined independently of an individual's own conception of his position or "place." Our reason for using this type of definition is that reliance on the individual's subjective definition of status would leave the problem with which we are concerned hopelessly confused. To illustrate, does a person identify himself as lower class because he is depressed, or is he depressed because he feels that he occupies a lower-class status? Or are these merely two expressions of some more basic psychological state? Without independent measures of social status on the one hand, and psychological disorder on the other, we would run the risk of finding built-in relationships that would defy clear interpretation.

Age, Sex, Ethnicity, and Class as Bases for Social Status. Of the four statuses that we will investigate, two present no special problems of objective identification. These are age and sex. An individual's chronological age and genetically determined sex are adquate indicators of the age and sex statuses to which he is assigned in the social order. What is not so clear, however, are the bases for assignment to ethnic and class statuses.

In their description of social stratification in a major city in the Deep South before World War II, Davis, B. B. Gardner and M. R. Gardner (1958) wrote as follows of the distinction between the white and Negro castes:

"The 'caste line' defines a social gulf across which Negroes may not pass either through marriage or those other intimacies which Old City calls 'social equality.' A ritual reminder is omnipresent in all relationships that there are two separate castes—a superordinate white group and a subordinate Negro group" (p. 371).

Within each of these two castes, the investigators pointed out, there were further distinctions:

"As one becomes acquainted with the white people of Old City, he soon realizes that they are continually classifying themselves and others. There are 'Negroes' and 'whites'—the caste groups—a relatively simple dichotomy. There are also 'leading families,' 'fine old families,' 'the four hundred,' 'the society crowd,' 'plain people,' 'nice respectable people,' 'good people, but nobody,' 'po' whites,' 'red necks,' etc." (pp. 371–372).

The importance of these distinctions, both within and between the two main castes, the investigators made clear, is that they described conceptions people had of "place" in society and that, moreover, people tended to act in terms of these conceptions.

Let us distinguish more formally between the conception of "class" as we shall be using the term and other bases for "place" in society. Max Weber used the term "class situation" to describe the individual's ". . . typical chance for a supply of goods, external living conditions, and personal life experiences, insofar as this chance is determined by the amount and kind of power or lack of such, to dispose of goods or skills for the sake of income in a given economic order" (Gerth & Mills, 1946, p. 181).

In addition to his formulation of the concept of class situation, Weber developed the idea of "status situation." He wrote: "In contrast to the purely economically determined 'class situation' we wish to designate as 'status situation' every typical component of the life fate of men that is determined by a specific positive or negative estimation of *honor*" (*ibid.*, pp. 186–187). As he pointed out, this honor or prestige may be connected with any quality shared by a plurality. Class is one such quality; ethnicity, especially as it is based on race, is another that in our own society rivals class in importance.

The differences in such factors as class and ethnicity that determine differences in status situations are accompanied by differences in what Weber termed "styles of life"—including place and type of residence, formal and informal associations, reading habits, leisure time activities, and, in some degree, beliefs and values. Note, then, that what Weber meant by "status groups," that is, persons in similar status situations, is quite similar to what some other students of social stratification such as Warner (Warner, Low, Lunt, & Srole, 1963, pp. 36–37) have meant by "social class." Following Weber, we will keep conceptually distinct the notions of "class situation" and "status situation," with the latter the more inclusive term. In this way, we shall be able to analyze the contributions of both class and ethnicity to the individual's status situation and to the likelihood that he will develop psychological disorder.

With ethnicity we shall be concerned with distinctions commonly made on the basis of various combinations of skin color, religion, language, and national origin. Thus we will compare Negroes to whites, as well as investigating differences among such groups as Jews, Puerto Ricans, and persons of Irish background.

In connection with class we shall be concerned with differences associated with indicators such as occupation, education, and income. We will, at many points, make only the gross distinction between middle and lower class. Although there may be important intraclass differences, particularly between upper-lower and lower-lower classes (e.g., Cohen & Hodges,

1963), the available data do not always permit a consistent breakdown at this more refined level. This is particularly true when we distinguish, as we shall, between classes within races. Moreover, in many instances the contrasts between middle and lower classes are sufficiently complex and extensive to justify the grosser analysis even if some intraclass differences are lost.

The Problem of Directionality. Objectifying the concept of social status assures that we are not stating a mere redundancy when we describe a relationship with a psychological condition. However, objective identification of a status does not completely solve the problem of the direction of the relationship for all types of status. Clearly it does so for relationships between psychological disorder and such statuses as age and sex. As objective characteristics, neither of these statuses can be dependent on the individual's psychological condition. The same is true of ethnicity since we conceive of this status as ascribed to the individual on the basis of such antecedent characteristics as skin color and religious, linguistic, or national heritage.

The problem of directionality remains, however, for social class. It is as conceivable that a man's occupation, education, or income results from his psychological condition as the other way around. Although some leverage on the problem is gained by investigations of relations involving the social class of the subject's family of origin, rather than his own social class, the problem remains a tricky one that poses a major challenge for studies of the relationship between social status and psychological disorder.

Psychological Disorder

Most studies of social status and psychological disorder have defined disorder in terms of admission to psychiatric treatment. Although operationally the clearest definition of a "case," this is also one of the most limited. The limitations are especially evident when research focuses on the possible significance of social factors in etiology (e.g., Faris, 1941; Owen, 1941). As Dunham (1961) and others (e.g., Felix & Bowers, 1948; Gruenberg, 1955; Mishler & Waxler, 1963) have pointed out, treatment rates presumably vary, for example, with the availability of treatment facilities and with public attitudes toward the use of available facilities. Either factor could be responsible for spurious relations between social statuses and rates of disorder measured by number of cases in treatment.

The importance of these criticisms of defining disorder in terms of admission to treatment has been vividly underlined by research findings. Consider, for example, the experience of Eaton and Weil (1955) in their study of the Hutterites, an ethnic enclave with a population of about

8500 persons living in 93 settlements in western portions of North America. This stable sect, with its secure agrarian economy and theocratic social organization, had a strong reputation, on the basis of earlier, non-psychiatric studies and anecdotal accounts, for a virtual absence of psychological disorder. And Eaton and Weil (1955) reported, "If we had used the operational definition of most official statistics—'persons admitted to a mental hospital'—or of the New Haven Study of Psychiatric Disorders—'persons under treatment by a psychiatrist'—no Hutterites would have been counted as 'ill' at the time our field work was done" (p. 215). However, more intensive study, using direct interviews with Hutterites and unofficial reports, revealed an appreciable number of cases of psychological disorder.

Nor had these instances of disorder escaped psychiatric treatment because they were all mild in nature. The investigators found 53 cases that they judged to be psychotic. Of these, only 4 had ever been in treatment (p. 233). Eaton and Weil concluded that Hutterite society, contrary to previous opinion, did not immunize its population against the development of psychological disorder.

The small proportion of Hutterite cases ever in treatment is a function, at least in part, of the unusually supportive attitude of the community toward its mentally ill (Eaton & Weil, 1955, p. 163f). One might, therefore, expect problems of psychological disorder in New York City to be more likely to come to the official attention of the mental health professions. Yet here, too, the findings of the Midtown Study indicate that the rates of untreated disorder are much higher than those of treated disorder. Only about a quarter of those judged to resemble psychiatric cases in this interview study had ever been in treatment. Furthermore, even among the most seriously ill of these—persons judged to be incapacitated—only a little more than a third had ever been in treatment (Srole, Langner, Michael, Opler, & Rennie, 1962, p. 147).

Clearly, then, treated rates are grossly inadequate as evidence of the amount of psychological disorder in general populations. Our interest, however, is in relations between social status and psychological disorder. If, therefore, treated and untreated rates of disorder were found to show similar relations with a particular social status in which we were interested, we would be justified in using treated rates for investigating the nature of the relationship. The evidence is, however, that such similarity cannot be assumed for most types of psychological disorder.

Thus, for example, the New Haven Study (Hollingshead & Redlich, 1958) found the highest prevalence of treated psychological disorder in the lowest social class. By contrast, the Midtown Study in New York City, using a broadly similar definition of treated disorder, found the highest rate of treated cases in the highest social class. Unlike the New Haven Study, however, the Midtown Study developed measures of disorder that were independent of treatment status and, when these measures were used, found a strong inverse relationship between social class and psychological disorder. Apparently, therefore, relations between class and treated rates were strongly affected by such factors as the greater availability of private psychiatrists to high-income groups in Midtown New York City and the relatively favorable orientation to psychiatric treatment in Midtown New York, as compared to New Haven (Srole et al., 1962, pp. 240–252).

Nor is the problem limited to relations between social class and treated disorder. As Pasamanick (1961) noted of his research in Baltimore, ". . . the extraordinarily high rates of hospitalization of Negroes in . . . Baltimore are almost certainly due to the inability of the community and the family, particularly, to care for the individuals at home. I think this accounts for our finding that the rate of psychoses in the noninstitutionalized Negro is extraordinarily low . . ." (p. 362). And Fink, Shapiro, Goldensohn, and Daily (1969) showed that Jews are more likely than non-Jews to secure psychiatric outpatient treatment on the basis of their stronger tendency to utilize medical care of all kinds rather than on the basis of either higher rates of psychological disorder or greater ability to pay for the treatment.

Clearly, then, we cannot assume that an empirical relation between social status and rate of psychological disorder based on treated cases necessarily reflects the true relationship. For this reason, we shall rely for the most part on the growing number of studies that have attempted to assess the rate of untreated as well as the rate of treated psychological disorder in general populations to determine how social status is related to psychological disorder. We shall, moreover, begin our inquiry by accepting at face value the definitions of disorder used by the investigators themselves to see how far their cumulative results will take us in our search for consistent findings.

SUMMARY

Concern with the nature of relations between social status and psychological disorder is generated to a considerable extent by questions about the role of heredity versus social environment in the etiology of these disorders. However, to date, investigations of relations between social status and psychological disorder have not resolved the etiological issue for at least two reasons. One is that correlational studies have yielded results that are ambiguous with respect to theoretical interpretation. The second reason is that studies utilizing treated cases to determine rates of psychological disorder have not yielded reliable results concerning relations with social status, because these rates are influenced by extraneous factors. We shall, therefore, utilize studies including untreated as well as treated psychological disorder to investigate the empirical relation between objective social status and psychological disorder.

CHAPTER 2

Etiological Leads from Epidemiological Studies

In epidemiological studies investigators attempt to relate the distribution of psychological disorders to population characteristics. One value of such research is the leads that it provides to etiology. When a high rate of disorder is found to be associated with a particular population characteristic, a possible implication is that this characteristic, or something that accompanies it, contributes to producing the disorder.

The etiological leads that epidemiological studies provide are by no means unbiased, however, since the design of a study usually reflects the investigator's hypothesis concerning the roles of heredity and social environment in producing psychological disorder. For example, if he favors the social environmental hypothesis, he is likely to do epidemiological studies focused on social statuses such as social class. In contrast, investigators who prefer the genetic hypothesis are likely to study the relation between rates of disorder and geneological or familial connections.

This theoretical leaning may also influence the investigator's decision as to how to measure rates of disorder. In principle, it is possible to measure either the incidence of disorder, that is, the number of new cases coming into existence during a specified time period, or the prevalence of disorder, the number of cases in existence during a specified period regardless of their time of origin. In practice, incidence studies of psychological disorder are rare because of the difficulty of establishing retrospectively the point in time at which a disorder began. Exceptional is Hagnell's (1966a) study, which, following up a previously surveyed population after 10 years, measured incidence by counting the number of persons classified as cases on the second but not on the first survey.

Prevalence studies can be divided into those measuring the prevalence of disorder during a limited time period, usually no more than a few years, and those measuring lifetime prevalence, that is, the number of persons suffering from psychological disorder at any time in their lives. Perhaps reflecting a greater interest in contemporary external influences, social environmentalists are more likely to measure short-term prevalence. Genetically oriented investigators, on the other hand, usually assay lifetime prevalence since it is theoretically possible that genetic disposition to psychological disorder will express itself only late in life.

Thus, recognizing that procedures are usually designed to focus a study on either social environmental or genetic factors, let us see what etiological leads these investigations provide. In this chapter, we will review epidemiological studies concerned with relations between social statuses and psychological disorder. In Chapter 3 we will turn to studies designed to test hypotheses concerning the role of heredity.

SOCIAL STATUSES AND PSYCHOLOGICAL DISORDER

At least 35 different investigators or teams have attempted to count untreated as well as treated cases of psychological disorder in 44 different studies of the relation of various social statuses to rates of psychological disorder.* Excluded from consideration are studies that have reported scores measuring symptomatology but have not indicated what is to be considered a case (e.g., Gurin, Veroff, & Feld, 1960; Kellert, Williams, Whyte, & Alberti, 1967; Langner, 1965; Parker & Kleiner, 1966).

Typically, the whole population in a specified geographical area has been included in investigations of untreated as well as treated cases. In the few studies that have relied on sample estimates, the n's have usually been large; for example, probability samples of 1660 in the Midtown Study (Srole, Langner, Michael, Opler, & Rennie, 1962) and 1010 in the Stirling County Study (D. C. Leighton, Harding, Macklin, Macmillan, & A. H. Leighton, 1963).

In most of the studies, the rates we have extracted represent prevalence during a period of a few months to a few years. Most of the exceptions— studies by Helgason (1964), by Lin (1953), and by Rin and Lin (1962), and a summary by Strömgren (1950) of 18 small studies, counted as one study here—presented lifetime prevalence rates. In addition, Hagnell (1966a) gave 10-year incidence rates.

Psychological Disorder in General

Table 2-1 shows that the range in the rates reported in these studies is from less than 1 per cent to over 60 per cent, suggesting that variation

---

* Since our first analysis of these community studies (Dohrenwend & Dohrenwend, 1965), and even with additions included in our later follow-up of this analysis (Dohrenwend & Dohrenwend, 1967), a number of new studies have been published or, previously missed, have come to our attention. These are included in the expanded analyses reported in this book.

Table 2-1. Percentage of Psychological Disorder Reported According to Geopolitical Area and Rural Versus Urban Study Site

Site	North America	Northern Europe	Asia	Africa
Rural	1.7 (Eaton & Weil, 1955)	1.1[a] (Kaila, Study II, 1942)	0.8 (Uchimara et al., 1940)	40.0 (A. H. Leighton et al.,[d] 1963)
	1.9[a,b] (Rosanoff, 1917)	1.3 (Brugger, 1931)	0.8[a] (Rin & Lin, Ami, 1962)	
	6.9 (Roth & Luton, 1943)	1.3 (Kaila, Study I, 1942)	0.8[a] (Rin & Lin, Paiwan, 1962)	
	18.0 (Trussel et al., 1956)	3.5[a] (Brugger, 1937)	1.0 (Lin, small town, 1953)	
	27.5 (Phillips,[d] 1966)	4.2 (Strömgren, 1950)	1.1 (Lin, village, 1953)	
	50.0+[c] (D. C. Leighton et al.,[d] 1963)	7.5 (Brugger, 1933)	1.2[a] (Rin & Lin, Saisait, 1962)	
	64.0 (Llewellyn-Thomas,[d] 1960)	9.0 (Mayer-Gross, 1948)	1.9[a] (Rin & Lin, Atayal, 1962)	
		11.9 (Fremming, 1951)	2.7[a] (Akimoto et al., 1942)	
		12.4[a] (Piotrowski et al.,[d] 1966)	54.0 (Rin et al., in press)	
		13.2 (Primrose,[d] 1962)		
		13.6[a] (Essen-Möller, 1956)		
		14.8[a] (Strotzka et al., 1966)		
		15.6[a] (Hagnell, 1966a)		
		23.2 (Bremer,[d] 1951)		
		28.6 (Helgason, 1964)		

Table 2-1. (Continued)

Site	North America	Northern Europe	Asia	Africa
Urban	1.8[a] (Lemkau et al., 1942)	1.0[a] (Kaila, Study I, 1942)	1.1 (Lin, city, 1953)	11.8 (Gillis et al.,[d] 1965)
	2.3 (Cohen et al., 1939)	1.1[a] (Kaila, Study II, 1942)	2.4[e] (Dube,[d] 1968)	
	3.4 (Manis et al.,[d] 1964)	15.5[a] (Piotrowski et al.,[d] 1966)	3.0[a] (Tsuwaga et al., 1942)	45.0 (A. H. Leighton et al.,[d] 1963)
	10.9 (Pasamanick et al., 1959)	20.6 (Hare & Shaw,[d] 1965)		
	23.4 (Srole et al.,[d] 1962)	33.0 (Taylor & Chave,[d] 1964)		
	32.0[a] (Cole et al.,[d] 1957)			

[a] Calculated by B. S. Dohrenwend.
[b] Includes urban minority not reported separately.
[c] " . . . Our conclusion from all the available information is that at least half of the adults in Stirling County are *currently* suffering from some psychiatric disorder defined in the American Psychiatric Association *Diagnostic and Statistical Manual*" (p. 356).
[d] Age range limited.
[e] Includes rural minority not reported separately.

in rates may be associated with social factors that differ between studies. As we see, however, when the studies are grouped according to the geopolitical area in which they were conducted, and according to whether the study site was rural or urban, these contrasts in setting do not account adequately for the variation in rates. Although all but one of the studies done in Asia yielded very low rates, suggesting the possibility of a difference between Western and Asian populations, the rate reported in the one exception (Rin, Chu, & Lin, in press) is so high that it argues against this interpretation. There is no indication of especially low rates in Africa, since two figures reported for this continent are near the top of the range found in North American and northern European studies. Moreover, within North America and northern Europe, there is no evidence that the study site is associated with the rate of disorder, almost the full range of rates being represented within each of four categories: North American rural, North American urban, northern European rural, and northern European urban.

Another possible explanation of differences in rates is the age range included in the study. As indicated in Table 2-1, 14 studies covered a limited age group. In all of these, the youngest ages, in which the minimum rate is usually found (see Table 2-2), are excluded. With two exceptions, (Dube, 1968; Manis, Brawer, Hunt, & Kercher, 1964), the rates reported for these age-restricted studies range from moderate to high. Since one of these exceptions, the study by Manis and his colleagues, included the same range as the Midtown Study by Srole et al. (1962), 20 through 59 years, the low rate reported by the former investigators underlines the fact that elimination of the youngest age group is not a sufficient explanation of high reported rates.

Statuses investigated within studies sufficiently frequently to show a pattern of relationship to rates of judged psychopathology include age, sex, race, and social class. The age groups for which minimum and maximum rates have been reported are shown in Table 2-2. With only five exceptions, the minimum rate was in the youngest age group reported. However, Table 2-2 does not show a consistent pattern for the age at which maximum rates were found. In 5 of the studies, the maximum appeared in adolescence, in 12 in the middle years, and in 7 in the oldest age group studied. No clues to etiology seem evident in such discrepant results.

Sex comparisons, shown in Table 2-3, likewise do not present a clear picture. Although 18 studies reported higher rates for women, and only 12 reported higher rates for men, this difference is not large enough to establish a clear trend.

Also, there is no evidence of a difference in the studies comparing

Table 2-2. Minimum and Maximum Rates of Psychological Disorder Reported According to Age

	Minimum		Maximum			
	Age	%	Age	%	d	Author(s)
	Maximum in Adolescence					
Minimum	0–5	0.03	11–15	1.88	1.85	Brugger, 1931
in	0–4	0.4	10–14	4.0	3.6	Cohen et al., 1939
youngest	0–5	0.0	11–15	7.5[a]	7.5	Brugger, 1937
group	0–4	2.6	10–14	11.4	8.8	Roth & Luton, 1943
studied	0–5	0.2[a]	11–15	14.1[a]	13.9	Brugger, 1933
	Maximum in Middle Years					
	0–10	0.01	41–50	2.0[a]	2.0	Uchimara et al., 1940
	5–14[c]	1.2[a]	35–54	4.6[a]	3.4	Dube, 1968
	0–10	1.6[a]	61–70	7.2[a]	5.6	Tsuwaga et al., 1942
	0–14	0.8	15–34	14.8	14.0	Pasamanick et al.,[b] 1959
	10–19[c]	13.9	40–49, 50–59	28.1	14.2	Bremer, 1951
	0–15	3.2[a]	21–45	20.9[a]	17.7	Strotzka et al., 1966
	15–24[c]	35.1[a]	25–34	83.3[a]	48.2	Llewellyn-Thomas, 1960
	Maximum in Oldest Group Studied					
	20–29[c]	15.3	50–59[d]	30.8	15.5	Srole et al., 1962
	16–24	15	65+	32	17	Hare & Shaw, 1965
	Under 39	46.3[a]	60+	63.7[a]	17.4	D. C. Leighton et al.,[e] 1963
	16–24[c]	27.5[a]	65+	48.1[a]	20.6	Taylor & Chave,[f] 1964
	18[c]	3.1	59[d]	26.4	23.3	Gnat et al., 1964
	0–4	0.9	80+	49.1	48.2	Essen-Möller, 1956
	0–9	6.8[a]	80+	72.3[a]	65.5	Hagnell, 1966a
	Maximum in Middle Years					
Minimum	60+	38.1[a]	40–59	40.5[a]	2.4	A. H. Leighton et al., 1963
in other						
than	60–69	2.2[a]	70–79	5.4[a]	3.2	Akimoto et al., 1942
youngest	45–49	8.2[a]	25–29	15.7[a]	7.5	Gillis et al., 1965
group	30–39	23.2	50–59	39.5	16.3	Phillips, 1966
studied	40–44	8.7[a]	50–54	27.4[a]	18.7	Primrose, 1962

[a] Calculated by B. S. Dohrenwend.

[b] Excludes "other mental, psychoneurotic, and personality disorders" included in total rates.

[c] Youngest group reported.

[d] Oldest group reported.

[e] Results reported in A. H. Leighton et al. (1963, p. 152).

[f] Based on survey data without supplementary physicians' reports included in total rate.

Table 2-3. Rates of Psychological Disorder Reported for Males and Females

Rate for Males Higher (%)

Male	Female	d	Author(s)
1.1[a]	1.0[a]	0.1	Kaila, Study II, 1942
1.3[a]	1.2[a]	0.1	Kaila, Study I, 1942
11.9	11.8	0.1	Fremming, 1951
1.4[a]	1.2[a]	0.2	Brugger, 1931
1.0[a]	0.6[a]	0.4	Uchimara et al., 1940
2.8	1.9	0.9	Cohen et al., 1939
3.4[a]	2.0[a]	1.4	Akimoto et al., 1942
7.9	6.0	1.9	Roth & Luton, 1943
4.5[a]	2.5[a]	2.0	Brugger, 1937
41.8[a]	38.9[a]	2.9	A. H. Leighton et al., 1963
9.0[a]	6.0[a]	3.0	Brugger, 1933
14.0[a]	9.6[a]	4.4	Gillis et al., 1965

Rate for Females Higher (%)

Male	Female	d	Author(s)
1.89[a]	1.91[a]	0.02	Rosanoff, 1917
3.0[a]	3.1[a]	0.1	Tsuwaga et al., 1942
1.5[a]	2.0[a]	0.5	Lemkau et al., 1942
2.0[a]	2.7[a]	0.7	Eaton & Weil,[b] 1955
1.6[a]	3.3[a]	1.7	Dube, 1968
22.1	24.0	1.9	Bellin & Hardt, 1958
12.3	14.9	2.6	Essen–Möller, 1956
27.2	30.0	2.8	Helgason, 1964
20.6	26.0	5.4	Bremer, 1951
10.0[a]	16.2[a]	6.2	Primrose, 1962
6.0	12.3	6.3	Pasamanick et al., 1959
11.3	20.4	9.1	Hagnell, 1966a
22.6	32.2	9.6	Phillips, 1966
8.6[a]	20.1[a]	11.5	Strotzka et al., 1966
12.9[a]	27.5[a]	14.6	Hare & Shaw, 1965
47.0	65.0	18.0	D. C. Leighton et al.,[c] 1963
22.0	43.0	21.0	Taylor & Chave,[d] 1964
51.8[a]	75.2[a]	23.4	Llewellyn–Thomas, 1960

[a] Calculated by B. S. Dohrenwend.

[b] Rates for both sexes are higher than the overall rate in Table 2-1 because the overall rate is for prevalence in the summer of 1951, whereas sex rates had to be calculated from data on lifetime morbidity.

[c] Results reported in A. H. Leighton et al. (1963, p. 149).

[d] Based on survey data without supplementary physicians' reports included in total rate.

Table 2-4. Rates of Psychological Disorder Reported for Whites and Negroes

Rate for Whites Higher (%)				Rate for Negroes Higher (%)			
White	Negro	d	Author(s)	White	Negro	d	Author(s)
1.9[a]	1.2[a]	0.7	Lemkau et al., 1942	2.2[a]	2.8[a]	0.6	Cohen et al., 1939
7.1	5.0	2.1	Rowntree et al., 1945	1.8[a]	7.0[a]	5.2	Rosanoff, 1917
7.8	4.2	3.6	Roth & Luton, 1943	11.1[a]	37.2	26.1	Hyde & Chisholm, 1944
11.2	4.6	6.6	Pasamanick et al., 1959	. . .	. . .	. . .	D. C. Leighton et al.,[b] 1963

[a] Calculated by B. S. Dohrenwend.
[b] Results reported in ridits rather than percentages.

rates for whites and Negroes. Of the 8 studies in Table 2-4, 4 reported higher rates for whites and 4 for Negroes.

Against this background of inconsistent results, it is almost startling to find, as Table 2-5 shows, that 20 of the 25 studies that presented data on the relationship with social class yielded the highest rate of judged psychopathology in the lowest economic stratum. Of the remaining five, two of the early studies by Brugger (1933, 1937), Llewellyn-Thomas' (1960) Canadian village study, and the study by Strotzka and his colleagues (1966) gave the highest rate in a middle stratum. The index of social class is somewhat problematical in the first three of these studies, however, since it is based on our grouping of the occupations reported by the authors, which may not reflect accurately the stratifications in these rural areas. Only one study reported the highest rate in the highest income group.

Although Table 2-5 shows that the rate of psychological disorder is consistently highest in the lowest social class, it does not indicate whether or not this excess of cases reflects a sharp contrast between the lowest class and all other classes. Table 2-6 is designed to determine whether there is evidence of such a contrast. This is done by determining whether, in studies in which the lowest social stratum was found to yield the highest rate, the difference in rates between the lowest stratum and the stratum with the next highest rate is greater than expected on the assumption

Table 2-5. Minimum and Maximum Rates of Psychological Disorder Reported According to Socioeconomic Status

| | Percentage | | | |
	Minimum	Maximum	d	Author(s)
	Minimum in Highest Stratum			
Maximum in	0.8	0.9	0.1	Hagnell,[a,b] 1966a
lowest stratum	2.7	4.0	1.3	Dube,[c] 1968
	1.4[d]	3.2[e]	1.8	Akimoto et al.,[e] 1942
	0.7	3.7	3.0 ⎫	Cohen et al.,[f] 1939
	1.1	6.6	5.5 ⎭	
	14.3[d]	20.5[d]	6.2	Hare & Shaw,[g] 1965
	19.5	27.0	7.5	Bremer,[b] 1951
	30.0	37.8	7.8	Taylor & Chave,[h] 1964
	7.3	16.6	9.3	Hyde & Kingsley, 1944
	17.4[d]	29.4[d]	12.0	Bellin & Hardt,[b] 1958
	5.0	17.0	12.0	Gillis et al., 1965
	1.6	15.1	13.5 ⎫	Gnat et al.,[i] 1964
	6.0	25.4	19.4 ⎭	
	18.0	32.2	14.2	Phillips, 1966
	12.5	47.3	34.8	Srole et al., 1962
	. . .	. . .	. . .	Cole et al.,[j] 1957
	. . .	. . .	. . .	D. C. Leighton et al.,[k] 1963
	Minimum in a Middle Stratum			
	2.3[d]	2.9[d]	0.6	Tsuwaga et al.,[e] 1942
	0.8	1.9	1.1	Lin, 1953
	1.2[d]	2.5[d]	1.3	Brugger,[l] 1931
	23.9[d]	30.6[a]	6.7	Helgason, 1964
	10.3	29.7	19.4	Primrose, 1962
	Minimum in Lowest Stratum			
Maximum in a	3.4[d]	5.3[d]	1.9	Brugger,[l] 1937
middle stratum	45.0	54.1[d]	9.1	Llewellyn-Thomas,[m] 1960
	7.4[d]	25.7[d]	18.3	Brugger,[l] 1933
	0.0	22.7[d]	22.7	Strotzka et al., 1966
	Minimum in a Middle Stratum			
Maximum in	6.2	13.6	7.4	Pasamanick et al., 1959
highest stratum				

[a] Annual incidence rates.

[b] Subjects divided into only two strata.

[c] These figures are for adults of two educational levels. Dube reported that family income was not related to rate of disorder, but this finding is confused by the fact that the study population included both single and extended family units, and the rate of psychological disorder was higher in the latter, implying that per person income might be inversely related to rate of disorder.

of a linear relation between social class levels and rates of disorder. Plus signs in the fifth column of Table 2-6 indicate that this gap is larger than would be expected on the assumption of a linear relationship; minus signs, that it is not. The fact that 9 of the 15 studies showed a gap larger than that expected between the rate in the lowest social stratum and that in the stratum with the next highest rate suggests a discontinuity between the lowest stratum and higher strata. In addition, the fact that 10 of the 15 studies yielded minimum rates in the highest stratum suggests that the relationship may be inverse rather than curvilinear.

Although, in the face of other inconsistencies in the studies here reviewed, the apparent inverse relation must command attention, its interpretation presents two problems. First, as noted in Chapter 1, a number of investigators have pointed out that the relationship between social class and psychological symptoms can be explained as social selection, with pre-existing psychological disorder leading to low social status (e.g., Ødegaard, 1956), or, equally plausibly, as social causation, with environmental factors in the lower class producing psychopathology (e.g.,

---

Table 2-5. (Continued)

d Calculated by B. S. Dohrenwend.

e Distribution of population in socioeconomic strata was reported only by number of families; since Japanese census reports do not include information on family size by SES, rates were calculated on the assumption of equal family size in all four strata. Rates for socioeconomic strata are below total rate for Tsuwaga because of reduction by 12 of number of cases reported according to SES.

f Data for whites only, reported for two wards separately.

g Males and married females only.

h Based on survey data without supplementary physicians' reports included in total rate.

i Rates for two cities reported separately.

j Cole et al. do not report rates but state: "Four-fifths of the families in the lower social strata contained at least one mentally ill member, while less than one-half of the upper-stratum families were thus affected" (p. 395).

k Results reported in ridits rather than percentages.

l Occupations grouped by B. S. Dohrenwend into three strata: high (self-employed merchants, manufacturers, and farmers, and middle-level civil servants); middle (merchants, manufacturers, and farmers employed by others, and low-level civil servants); and low (workers and servants).

m Occupations grouped by B. S. Dohrenwend into three strata: high (independent business and salaried workers); middle (fishermen and farmers); and low (laborers). The maximum rate in these strata is below the overall rate because of the exclusion of two categories of persons with high rates, grouped separately by Llewellyn-Thomas: housewives, with a rate of 76%, and miscellaneous, with a rate of 65%.

Table 2-6. Comparison of Expected and Observed Differences in Rates of Psychological Disorder between Lowest Social Stratum and Stratum with Next to Highest Rate in Studies Yielding Highest Rates in Lowest Stratum and Reporting on More than Two Strata*

Difference between Highest and Lowest Rate (d_t)	Difference between Highest and Next to Highest Rate (d_a)	Observed d_a/d_t	Expected† d_a/d_t	Sign of Observed d_a/d_t minus Expected d_a/d_t	Author(s)
		Minimum in Highest Stratum			
1.8	0.4	0.22	0.33	−	Akimoto et al., 1942
3.0	2.2	0.73	0.50	+ ⎫	Cohen et al., 1939
5.5	3.4	0.62	0.50	+ ⎭	Hare & Shaw, 1965
6.2	0.5	0.08	0.50	−	Taylor & Chave, 1964
7.8	4.2	0.54	0.33	+	Hyde & Kingsley, 1944
9.3	3.9	0.42	0.20	+	Gillis et al., 1965
12.0	4.0	0.33	0.50	−	Gnat et al., 1964
13.5	6.5	0.48	0.20	+ ⎫	
19.4	5.5	0.28	0.20	+ ⎭	Phillips, 1966
14.0	0.0	0.0	0.20	−	
		Minimum in Middle Stratum			
0.6	0.1	0.17	0.50	−	Tsuwaga et al., 1942
1.1	0.6	0.55	0.50	+	Lin, 1953
1.3	0.6	0.46	0.50	−	Brugger, 1931
6.7	5.1	0.76	0.50	+	Helgason, 1964
19.4	9.1	0.47	0.25	+	Primrose, 1962

* For notes concerning special characteristics of studies see Table 2-5.

† Calculated on the assumption that differences in rates between strata are equal parts of the full range of rates in each study; for example, in a study including four social strata each difference between adjacent rates is expected to be one third of the full range.

Dunham, 1961). The former explanation is compatible with the position that genetic factors are important in the etiology of psychological disorder. The direction of the relationship between social class and rate of psychological disorder, therefore, requires investigation before the relationship itself can provide persuasive support for either the hereditary or the social environmental etiological hypothesis.

The second problem raised by this relationship is whether it applies equally to all types of disorder. The overall rates include disorders ranging in severity from psychoses to mild neuroses, and manifested in behaviors as disparate as grossly antisocial acts and mild complaints of subjective distress. Perhaps, however, only some types of disorder contribute to the excess of cases in the lowest social stratum.

It is also possible that the lack of a relation between psychological disorder and other status factors may conceal contrasting relationships with different types of disorder. Analysis of social statuses in relation to subtypes of disorder may, therefore, yield further leads with respect to the etiological issue.

Different Types of Psychological Disorder

Since the field studies differ in the categories of disorder that they reported in relation to status variables, the main foci of this analysis will be limited to three broad types: psychosis, neurosis, and personality disorder. Because of the importance of schizophrenia and manic-depressive psychosis, we will also analyze data on these two subtypes, despite the scantiness of the information available. When disorders with a known organic basis, for example, senile psychoses, were reported separately, they will be excluded from the overall category of psychosis.

The data available permit us to study three status factors: age, sex, and social class. The small number of studies of race differences does not provide a basis for investigating relations with subtypes of disorder.

Relationships with Age. The results for subtypes of disorder, like the results for overall rates of disorder, show little relation to age. Table 2-7 indicates that the minimum rate of psychosis, usually zero, is associated with the youngest group in 11 of the 16 studies, but is also found at varied periods in the middle and later years. The maximum rate appears, in all but one study, either before age 40 or after age 50. Since the maximum is in age groups over 70 in 6 of the 9 studies in the latter group, these high rates are probably based primarily on senile psychoses. To find the highest rates of nonsenile psychoses, therefore, we also determined maximum rates for ages under 60 and found them reported for all ages from 20 to 60.

Table 2-7. Minimum and Maximum Rates of Psychosis Reported
According to Age

Minimum		Maximum under 60		d	Maximum for All Ages		Author(s)
Age	%	Age	%		Age	%	
5–9[a] 70–79[b]	0.00	20–29	1.70[c]	1.70	20–29	1.70[c]	Akimoto et al.,[d,e] 1942
40–59	1.09[c]	–39	2.02[c]	0.93	–39	2.02[c]	A. H. Leighton et al.,[f,g] 1963
10–19[a] 60+	0.00	30–39	1.52[c]	1.52	30–39	1.52[c]	Bremer,[d] 1951
40–49	0.46[c]	30–39	1.83[c]	1.37	70+	2.33[c]	D. C. Leighton et al.,[g] 1963
41–60 71+ –10	0.00	31–40	0.70[c]	0.70	31–40	0.70[c]	Brugger,[d] 1937
21–30 61+	0.00	31–40	1.33[c]	1.33	31–40	1.33[c]	Tsuwaga et al.,[d] 1942
–9	0.00	35–44	1.12	1.12	65+	2.16	Lemkau et al., 1942
5–14[a]	0.02[c]	35–54	0.91[c]	0.89	35–54	0.91	Dube, 1968
–15	0.00	35–64	0.58	0.58	65+	2.78	Pasamanick et al., 1959
–15 80+	0.00	36–40	0.627[c]	0.63	71–75	0.634[c]	Brugger,[d] 1931
25–45 60–65	0.00	45–50	2.63[c]	2.63	75+	12.16[c]	Primrose, 1962
15–24[a] –39	0.29[c]	45–54	1.38[c]	1.09	75+	2.09[c]	Cohen & Fairbank, 1938
–9	0.00	50–59	2.40[c]	2.40	50–59	2.40[c]	Essen-Möller, 1956
–9 70+ –20	0.00	50–59	0.98[c]	0.98	50–59	0.98[c]	Lin,[d] 1953
61–70 81+	0.00	51–60	1.74[c]	1.74	51–60	1.74[c]	Brugger,[d] 1933
35–49 60–69	0.00	55–59	5.55[c]	5.55	70+	8.50[c]	Gillis et al.,[g] 1965

[a] Minimum age reported.

[b] Maximum age reported.

[c] Calculated by B. S. Dohrenwend.

[d] Functional psychoses only.

[e] Inconsistencies in age and sex distribution of sample reconciled by making smallest possible number of changes in order to correct what appear to be printer's errors.

[f] Villages only; no psychoses reported in city sample.

[g] Figures are given for "symptom patterns" which may or may not be "cases."

Table 2-8. Minimum and Maximum Rates of Neurosis Reported According to Age

	Minimum Age	Minimum %	Maximum Age	Maximum %	d	Author(s)
Maximum under 40 years	16–24	5	25–34	9	4	Hare & Shaw, 1965
	5–19[a] 60–79[b]	0.00	30–39	1.00[c]	1.00	Akimoto et al.,[d] 1942
	10–19[a] –9	2.14[c]	30–39	10.10[c]	7.96	Bremer, 1951
	15–19 80+	0.00	30–39	2.70[c]	2.70	Essen-Möller, 1956
	–4 –10	1.00[c]	30–39	7.92[c]	6.92	Hagnell, 1959
	16–20 61+	0.00	31–40	0.58[c]	0.58	Brugger, 1933
	–15 71+	0.00	36–40	0.42[c]	0.42	Brugger, 1931
Maximum between 40 and 60 years	0–14[a]	0.06[c]	35–54	3.02[c]	2.96	Dube, 1968
	60+	66.20[c]	40–59	77.12[c]	10.92	A. H. Leighton et al.,[e] 1963
	–30	40.88[c]	40–59	60.83[c]	19.95	D. C. Leighton et al.,[e] 1963
	65–70 –19	7.23[c]	50–55	24.53[c]	17.30	Primrose, 1962
	60+	0.00	50–59	0.36[c]	0.36	Lin, 1953
	20–24	14.71[c]	55–59	38.88[c]	24.17	Gillis et al.,[e] 1965
Maximum over 60 years	–15	0.83	65+	7.08	6.25	Pasamanick et al., 1959
	–10 31–50	0.00	70+	2.63[c]	2.63	Tsuwaga et al., 1942

[a] Minimum age reported.
[b] Maximum age reported.
[c] Calculated by B. S. Dohrenwend.
[d] Inconsistencies in age and sex distribution reconciled by making smallest possible number of changes in order to correct what appear to be printer's errors.
[e] Figures are given for "symptom patterns" which may or may not be "cases."

In Table 2-8 we see even less indication of a relation between age and rate of neurosis. Minimum rates were found in age groups ranging from the youngest to the oldest, and maximum rates were reported at all ages except the years of childhood and adolescence.

Similarly, age shows no consistent relation with rates of personality disorder. Table 2-9 indicates that the minimum rates range widely, and maximum rates were found in all but the youngest groups.

Table 2-9. Minimum and Maximum Rates of Personality Disorder Reported According to Age

	Minimum		Maximum			
	Age	%	Age	%	d	Author(s)
Maximum under 40 years	40+	0.00	25–29	7.14[a]	7.14	Gillis et al.,[b] 1965
	51–60	0.00	31–40	1.17[a]	1.17	Brugger, 1937
Maximum between 40 and 60 years	5–9⌐ 70–79[d]	0.00	40–49	0.81[a]	0.81	Akimoto et al.,[e] 1942
	–30	8.76[a]	40–49	22.58[a]	13.82	D. C. Leighton et al.,[b,f] 1963
	–9	0.00	40–49	0.28[a]	0.28	Lin, 1953
	–15 71+	0.00	41–50	0.95[a]	0.95	Brugger, 1933
	–4	0.00	50–59	10.40[a]	10.40	Essen-Möller, 1956
	40–45	1.09[a]	55–60	3.94[a]	2.85	Primrose, 1962
Maximum over 60 years	–39	6.06[a]	60+	11.27[a]	5.21	A. H. Leighton et al.,[b,g] 1963
	70+	0.00	60–69	17.07[a]	17.07	Bremer, 1951
	70+	0.00	61–70	3.09[a]	3.09	Tsuwaga et al., 1942

[a] Calculated by B. S. Dohrenwend.

[b] Figures are given for "symptom patterns" which may or may not be "cases."

[c] Minimum age reported.

[d] Maximum age reported.

[e] Inconsistencies in age and sex distribution reconciled by making smallest possible number of changes in order to correct what appear to be printer's errors.

[f] Personality disorder and sociopathic behavior combined; although these categories are not mutually exclusive, of 128 cases in the two categories, only 10 are classified in both.

[g] Personality disorder and sociopathic behavior combined, although not mutually exclusive, on the basis of the small overlap found in D. C. Leighton et al., which provided the procedural base for this study.

The failure to find any age group that consistently shows the highest rate for any of the types of psychological disorder analyzed may be due to the heterogeneity of even these more refined categories. The obvious association between senile psychosis and age, for example, is lost in overall figures for psychosis. It does appear, however, that age is not a variable that has provided consistent empirical relationships on which to base etiological studies.

Relationships with Sex. Table 2-10 indicates no sex differences in rates of psychosis. Of the 21 studies, 10 yielded the higher rate for males and 11 for females, and the differences between the rates for the two sexes cover approximately the same range no matter which sex is higher. Moreover, there is no clear difference according to sex for schizophrenia and manic-depressive psychosis. Four studies (Akimoto, Simazaki, Okada & Hanasiro, 1942; Brugger, 1933; Dube, 1968; Tsuwaga, Okada, Hanasiro, Asai, Takuma, Morimura, & Tsubei, 1942), reported higher rates of schizophrenia for males and three (Bremer, 1951; Brugger 1931; Helgason, 1964) for females. Four studies (Akimoto et al., 1942; Bremer, 1951; Helgason, 1964; Tsuwaga et al., 1942) reported higher rates of manic-depressive psychosis for males, and three (Brugger, 1931; Brugger, 1933; Dube, 1968) for females.

By contrast, Table 2-11 indicates a consistent relationship between rate of neurosis and sex, since 17 of 21 studies reported higher rates for females than for males. Personality disorder is like neurosis in showing a consistent pattern in relation to sex, but the relationship is reversed, as Table 2-12 indicates. In 13 of 17 studies higher rates were reported for males than for females.

Although the sex differences found for both neurosis and personality disorder could be explained in terms of heredity, explanation in terms of social factors seems, on the surface, at least as plausible. However, since males show an excess of personality disorder whereas females have relatively high rates of neurosis, and neither shows an overall higher rate of psychological disorder, these sex differences do not suggest a greater magnitude of social stress impinging on one or the other sex. Rather, they imply that each sex tends to learn a different style with which it reacts to whatever factors produce psychological disorder.

Relationships with Social Class. We find no consistent relation between overall rates of psychosis and social class. As Table 2-13 shows, the highest rate of psychosis was reported about equally often in the lowest social stratum and in some stratum other than the lowest. However, analysis of the few studies that provided the relevant data suggests that these overall rates may mask varied relations between class and subtypes of psychosis. Thus, of the seven studies that reported rates of schizophrenia

Table 2-10. Minimum and Maximum Rates of Psychosis Reported According to Sex

Rate for Males Higher (%)				Rate for Females Higher (%)				Rate for Males and Females Equal (%)			
Male	Female	d	Author(s)	Male	Female	d	Author(s)	Male	Female	d	Author(s)
0.252[a]	0.247[a]	0.005	Brugger,[b] 1937	0.90[a]	0.91[a]	0.01	Cohen & Fairbank, 1938	1.60	1.60	0.00	Gillis et al.,[e] 1965
0.45[a]	0.40[a]	0.05	Brugger,[b] 1933	0.34[a]	0.35[a]	0.01	Dube, 1968				
0.70	0.63	0.07	Lemkau et al., 1942	0.44[a]	0.46[a]	0.02	Kaila, Study I,[b] 1942				
0.57[a]	0.44[a]	0.13	Akimoto et al.,[b,c] 1942	0.23[a]	0.27[a]	0.04	Brugger,[b] 1931				
0.51[a]	0.22[a]	0.29	Tsuwaga et al.,[b] 1942	0.53[a]	0.70[a]	0.17	Eaton & Weil,[g] 1955				
0.60	0.30	0.30	Pasamanick et al., 1959	1.7	1.9	0.2	Hare & Shaw (New Adam), 1965				
0.91[a]	0.57[a]	0.34	Bremer,[b] 1951	0.85[a]	1.48[a]	0.63	Primrose, 1962				
2	1	1	A. H. Leighton et al.,[d,e] 1963	0.23[a]	0.97[a]	0.74	Essen-Möller, 1956				
4.6	3.0	1.6	Hare & Shaw (Old Bute), 1965	1	2	1	D. C. Leighton et al.,[e] 1963				
...	...	...	Gnat et al.,[f] 1964	1.84[a]	3.63[a]	1.79	Fremming,[b,g] 1951				
				3.99[a]	6.15[a]	2.16	Helgason,[b,g] 1964				

[a] Calculated by B. S. Dohrenwend.

[b] Functional psychoses only.

[c] Inconsistencies in age and sex distribution of sample reconciled by making smallest possible number of changes in order to correct what appear to be printer's errors.

[d] Villages only; no psychoses reported in city sample.

[e] Figures are given for "symptom patterns," which may or may not be "cases."

[f] Rates by sex are not given, but text states, "The incidence of mental disorders is greater among women than among men. This applies to all psychiatric disturbances with the exception of psychosis . . ." (p. 6).

[g] Rates for lifetime morbidity.

Table 2-11. Minimum and Maximum Rates of Neurosis Reported According to Sex

Rate for Males Higher (%)				Rate for Females Higher (%)			
Male	Female	d	Author(s)	Male	Female	d	Author(s)
0.14[a]	0.11[a]	0.03	Brugger, 1931	0.22[a]	0.26[a]	0.04	Brugger, 1933
0.36[a]	0.15[a]	0.21	Akimoto et al.,[b] 1942	0.20	0.42	0.22	Lemkau et al., 1942
				0.00	0.37[a]	0.37	Tsuwaga et al., 1942
81	69	12	A. H. Leighton et al. (city),[c] 1963	1.07[a]	1.86[a]	0.79	Essen-Möller, 1956
				1.46[a]	2.34[a]	0.88	Fremming,[d] 1951
76	64	12	A. H. Leighton et al. (villages),[c] 1963	0.30[a]	1.31[a]	1.01	Eaton & Weil,[d] 1955
				0.40[a]	2.28[a]	1.88	Dube, 1968
				3.56	6.80	3.24	Pasamanick et al., 1959
				3.2	6.9	3.7	Hagnell, 1959
				3.6	8.0	4.4	Hare & Shaw (New Adam), 1965
				5.6	10.5	4.9	Hare & Shaw (Old Bute), 1965
				2.91	8.30	5.39	Bremer, 1951
				24.40[a]	36.80[a]	12.40	Gillis et al.,[c] 1965
				6.85[a]	13.95[a]	7.10	Helgason,[d] 1964
				4.4	13.6	9.2	Primrose, 1962
				44	64	20	D. C. Leighton et al.,[c] 1963
				...	...	...	Gnat et al.,[e] 1964

[a] Calculated by B. S. Dohrenwend.

[b] Inconsistencies in age and sex distribution of sample reconciled by making smallest possible number of changes in order to correct what appear to be printer's errors.

[c] Figures are given for "symptom patterns" which may or may not be "cases."

[d] Rates for lifetime morbidity.

[e] Rates by sex are not given, but text states, "The incidence of mental disorders is greater among women than among men. This applies to all psychiatric disturbances with the exception of psychosis, alcoholism and mental disorders following brain injury" (p. 6).

Table 2-12. Minimum and Maximum Rates of Personality Disorder Reported According to Sex

Rate for Males Higher (%)				Rate for Females Higher (%)			
Male	Female	d	Author(s)	Male	Female	d	Author(s)
0.11[a]	0.01[a]	0.10	Brugger, 1931	0.046[a]	0.047[a]	0.001	Eaton & Weil,[c] 1955
0.40[a]	0.11[a]	0.29	Akimoto et al.,[b] 1942	9.27	9.43	0.16	Bremer, 1951
0.63[a]	0.12[a]	0.51	Brugger, 1937	0.73[a]	0.97[a]	0.24	Tsuwaga et al., 1942
10.0	9.3	0.7	Hare & Shaw (Old Bute), 1965	4.5	6.5	2.0	Hare & Shaw (New Adam), 1965
1.08[a]	0.18[a]	0.90	Brugger, 1933				
5.02[a]	4.09[a]	0.93	Helgason,[c] 1964				
5.85[a]	2.94[a]	2.91	Fremming,[c] 1951				
4.73[a]	1.14[a]	3.59	Primrose, 1962				
5.20[a]	0.00	5.20	Gillis et al.,[d,f] 1965				
18[a]	11[a]	7	D. C. Leighton et al.,[d,e] 1963				
9.15[a]	1.62[a]	7.53	Essen-Möller, 1956				
13[a]	5[a]	8	A. H. Leighton et al.,[d,f] 1963				
...	...	...	Gnat et al.[g] 1964				

[a] Calculated by B. S. Dohrenwend.

[b] Inconsistencies in age and sex distribution reconciled by making smallest possible number of changes in order to correct what appear to be printer's errors.

[c] Rates for lifetime morbidity.

[d] Figures are given for "symptom patterns" which may or may not be "cases."

[e] Personality disorder and sociopathic behavior combined; although these categories are not mutually exclusive, of 128 cases in the two categories, only 10 are classified in both; also, rate for males is higher than for females in each category.

[f] Personality disorder and sociopathic behavior combined, although not mutually exclusive, on the basis of the small overlap in D. C. Leighton et al., which provided the procedural base for this study; also, rate for males is higher than for females in each category. Figures are given for "symptom patterns" which may or may not be "cases."

[g] No figures were given, but text stated that males exceeded females on alcoholism while females exceeded males on behavior disorders. Since 29 cases of the former and 3 of the latter were given, the presumption is that males exceed females in the two categories combined.

Table 2-13. Minimum and Maximum Rates of Psychosis Reported According to Social Class

| | Percentage | | | |
	Minimum	Maximum	d	Author(s)
Maximum in	0.16	0.45	0.29	Hyde & Kingsley, 1944
lowest	0.18[a]	0.51[a]	0.33	Lin,[b] 1953
class	0.56[a]	0.92[a]	0.36	Bremer,[b] 1951
	4.10[a]	5.78[a]	1.68	Helgason,[b,c] 1964
	0	4	4	Gillis et al.,[d] 1965
	3.6	13.1	9.5	Langner & Michael, 1963
Maximum in	1.35[a]	1.48[a]	0.13	Brugger,[b,c,e] 1933
other than	0.42[a]	0.72[a]	0.30	Brugger,[b,c,e] 1931
lowest	0.21[a]	0.60[a]	0.39	Tsuwaga et al.,[b] 1942
class	0.00	0.47	0.47	Primrose, 1962
	0.08	0.87	0.79	Pasamanick et al., 1959
	0.25[a]	1.30[a]	1.05	Akimoto et al.,[b] 1942
	. . .	. . .	. . .	D. C. Leighton et al.,[d,f] 1963

[a] Calculated by B. S. Dohrenwend.

[b] Functional psychoses only.

[c] Rates for lifetime morbidity.

[d] Figures are given for "symptom patterns" which may or may not be "cases."

[e] These rates are higher than the overall rates, apparently because more information about symptoms was available on the subgroup for whom occupation was known.

[f] It is estimated in D. C. Leighton et al. (1963, p. 291) that the rate in the lowest employed occupational stratum is either equal to or slightly lower than the two middle strata; estimates are not presented here because, with rates in the range of 1 or 2 per cent, error in estimation would be unduly large. Stratum 5 was not considered in this comparison because it is composed largely of retired people, thereby confounding age with social class.

by class, five (Bremer, 1951; Brugger, 1931; Brugger, 1933; Helgason, 1964; Lin, 1953) yielded the highest rate in the lowest class, whereas only two (Akimoto et al., 1942; Tsuwaga et al., 1942) showed the highest rate in another stratum. All seven of these studies reported the highest rate of manic-depressive psychosis in other than the lowest class.

Since the rates for schizophrenia and manic-depressive psychosis are based on a small number of studies, these relationships would be strengthened if investigations of treated cases were found to yield the same results. Comparison of our results with those previously reported for treated cases suggests, however, that the evidence for a direct relationship between class and rate of manic-depressive psychosis is not consistent. Although Tietze, Lemkau, and Cooper (1941) found some support for this relationship in three studies they reviewed, neither Faris and Dunham (1939) nor Wechsler (1961, p. 15) detected any such relationship in their studies of treated cases. Furthermore, Mintz and Schwartz (1964, p. 102) concluded from their reanalysis of Faris and Dunham's data that this study actually provided evidence of an inverse relation between social class and rates of manic-depressive psychosis.

By contrast, our finding that schizophrenia tended to show the highest rate in the lowest class is consistent with the results of most studies of incidence of treated cases (Mishler & Scotch, 1965, p. 268), though not all (Kohn, 1968). This generally consistent inverse relationship raises for schizophrenia, therefore, the question described with respect to overall rates: Does the highest rate in the lowest social stratum result from social

Table 2-14. Minimum and Maximum Rates of Neurosis Reported According to Social Class

| | Percentage | | | |
	Minimum	Maximum	d	Author(s)
Maximum in	0.11[a]	0.28[a]	0.17	Brugger, 1931
lowest	0.00	0.33[a]	0.33	Akimoto et al., 1942
class	1.34	8.01	6.67	Pasamanick et al., 1959
	29	47	18	Gillis et al.,[b] 1965
	50[c]	70[c]	20	D. C. Leighton et al.,[b] 1963
	. . .	. . .	. . .	Cole et al.,[d] 1957
Maximum in	0.09[a]	0.29[a]	0.20	Lin, 1953
other than	0.00	0.32[a]	0.32	Tsuwaga et al., 1942
lowest	0.00	0.46[a]	0.46	Brugger, 1933
class	2.9	4.7	1.8	Hyde & Kingsley, 1944
	4.40	6.74	2.34	Bremer, 1951
	9.43[a]	12.43[a]	3.00	Helgason, 1964
	7.16	15.47	8.31	Primrose, 1962
	30.00[a]	49.30[a]	19.30	Langner & Michael, 1963

[a] Calculated by B. S. Dohrenwend.

[b] Figures are given for "symptom patterns" which may or may not be "cases."

[c] Approximations estimated from Figure 15 in D. C. Leighton et al. (1963, p. 289).

[d] Without giving actual figures, Cole et al. reported that neuroses were found to be about twice as frequent in lower-level families as in upper-level families.

selection of the genetically handicapped or from the social stress in the lower-class environment?

For neurosis, Table 2-14 shows that the maximum rate was reported about equally often in the lowest social class and in some class other than the lowest. As Table 2-15 indicates, personality disorder, unlike neurosis, shows a consistent relationship with social class. Of 13 studies, 10 yielded the highest rate of personality disorder in the lowest social class.

The fact that maximum rates of personality disorder were found among males and in the lower class raises the question of whether it is lower-class males who generally show the highest rate of this type of disorder. This

Table 2-15. Minimum and Maximum Rates of Personality Disorder Reported According to Social Class

	Percentage			
	Minimum	Maximum	*d*	Author(s)
Maximum in lowest class	0.07[a]	0.19[a]	0.12	Lin, 1953
	0.19[a]	0.46[a]	0.27	Brugger, 1931
	0.00	0.59[a]	0.59	Akimoto et al., 1942
	3.02[a]	5.71[a]	2.69	Helgason, 1964
	7.49[a]	11.17[a]	3.68	Bremer, 1951
	3.4[b]	9.7[b]	6.3	Hyde & Kingsley, 1944
	0	7	7	Gillis et al.,[c] 1965
	4.5	14.9	10.4	Langner & Michael, 1963
	0.99	15.20	14.21	Primrose, 1962
	. . .	. . .	. . .	Cole et al.,[d] 1957
Maximum in other than lowest class	0.43[a]	0.96[a]	0.53	Tsuwaga et al., 1942
	1.90[a]	3.31[a]	1.41	Brugger, 1933
	13.23[e]	15.69[e]	2.46	D. C. Leighton et al.,[c] 1963

[a] Calculated by B. S. Dohrenwend.

[b] Calculated by B. S. Dohrenwend by addition of rates given by Hyde and Kingsley to one decimal place.

[c] Figures are given for "symptom patterns" which may or may not be "cases."

[d] Cole et al. do not give actual figures but report that " 'acting-out' types of aberrations [tend to be more frequent] in the lower [levels]" (p. 395).

[e] Calculated by B. S. Dohrenwend from combination of estimates for personality disorders and sociopathic behavior made from Figure 16, in D. C. Leighton et al. (1963, p. 290); these categories were combined despite not being mutually exclusive because, of 128 cases in the two categories, only 10 are in both.

question cannot be answered with much confidence from published materials, however, since only four studies reported the joint distribution according to class and sex of personality disorder. In three (Helgason, 1964; D. C. Leighton, Harding, Macklin, Macmillan, & A. H. Leighton, 1963; Primrose, 1962) of these for the maximum rate was reported for lower-class males, and in one (Bremer, 1951) it was reported for lower-class females.

In general, then, we conclude that personlity disorder, like schizophrenia, contributes to the higher rate of overall disorder in the lowest social stratum. This finding again poses the problem of whether the excess of cases in the lowest class is due to downward social selection of individuals with the disorder or to causation of the disorder by the social environment of the lowest class.

SUMMARY

Examination of rates of certain types of psychological disorder, as well as overall rates of disorder in different age, sex ethnic, and socioeconomic groups, suggests that relations involving socio-economic status provide the most promising leads for etiological research. With the exception of an absence of maximum rates in the very youngest groups, age shows no consistent relation to any of these rates. Although there is evidence of a difference between the sexes in type of disorder, no indication has been found that one sex is more generally prone to psychological disorder. Nor is there evidence of a difference between whites and Negroes in rates of disorder.

By contrast, low socioeconomic status within a community is consistently found to be associated with relatively high overall rates of disorder and with high rates of both schizophrenia and personality disorder. Although these consistent relationships demand explanation, they do not in and of themselves clearly imply either environmental or hereditary etiology.

CHAPTER 3

Etiological Leads From Genetically Oriented Studies of Psychological Disorder

Most investigators interested primarily in testing genetic hypotheses have focused their research on the relation between degree of genetic similarity and concordance in rates of psychological disorder. In these studies the general procedure is to select a set of index cases of a type of psychological disorder, usually from hospital records, and then trace the geneology of these cases to determine what proportion of certain classes of relatives also suffered from psychological disorder. The hypothesis of genetic etiology predicts that persons more closely related to the index cases, and thereby genetically more similar, will have higher rates of disorder than persons more distantly related.

GENEOLOGICAL STUDIES

Studies of this type have most frequently started with schizophrenic index cases and have shown that relatives with genetic endowment more similar to the index cases have higher rates of schizophrenia than relatives with less similar endowment. For example, in Kallmann's (1938) landmark study of 1087 schizophrenic index cases, he found that the concordance rate for children of these cases was 14 per cent whereas the rate for grandchildren was only 3 per cent.

Although such findings have been interpreted by Kallmann and others as implying a genetic factor in the determination of schizophrenia, they are inherently ambiguous, since relatives with greater genetic similarity also ordinarily share more social experience with the index cases. Thus the higher rate of schizophrenia among children of schizophrenic index cases than among grandchildren could be due either to the direct influence of the index cases on their children or to the common exposure of parent and child to a schizophrenogenic environment. In either case, it is not necessary to invoke a genetic factor to explain the difference in concordance between children and grandchildren of schizophrenic index cases. On the other hand, the plausibility of the environmental explanations does not disprove the genetic hypothesis.

TWIN STUDIES

To avoid this confounding of social and genetic factors in geneological studies, many investigators have taken advantage of an experiment provided by nature in monozygotic twins, who have identical genetic endowment. The trick is to locate index cases who are members of monozygotic twin pairs. The rate of disorder among the twins of these index cases is then usually compared with the rate among twins of dizygotic index cases, whose genetic similarity is no greater than that of any two siblings, but who, like the monozygotic twins, have grown up under similar social influences. The genetic hypothesis predicts that the rate of disorder among twins of monozygotic index cases will be higher than the rate among twins of dizygotic index cases.

Almost all twin studies have involved schizophrenic index cases. Table 3-1 summarizes the comparisons from these studies of concordances for monozygotic twins and dizygotic twins of the same sex. This summary shows that until recently the monozygotic concordances yielded by these studies were high and remarkably uniform. It should be noted, however, that these figures are not as high as Kallmann's (1946) frequently cited value of 86 per cent concordance between schizophrenic index cases and their monozygotic twins. Kallmann's rate was calculated by using Weinberg's short method of correcting for age, which increases the concordance over the actually observed rate. This correction assumes that half of the discordant twins who are between 15 and 44 years old and have not yet developed schizophrenia will do so at a later date. However, since Kallmann (1946) found that over 70 per cent of his concordant twins became ill within 4 years of each other, it seems likely that application of the Weinberg correction to the twin data produced a misleadingly high rate.

The fact that recent studies have not yielded uncorrected concordance rates of the same order as those obtained in earlier research poses a problem of explanation. It has been pointed out, for example, that Kallmann's results might be explained by the severity of his index cases, since he drew heavily, though not exclusively, on the chronic hospital population in his search for twin index cases. By contrast, some investigators who

Table 3-1. Concordance Rates of Monozygotic versus Dizygotic Twins for Schizophrenia

(Rates uncorrected for age except as noted)

Monozygotics		Dizygotics				
Number of Pairs	Concord-ance	Number of Pairs	Concord-ance	Author(s)	Date	Study Site
17	59	33	0	Luxenburger	1928	Germany
a	52	a	10	Luxenburger	1936	Germany
41	68	53	19	Rosanoff et al.	1934	U.S.
7	71	24	17	Essen-Möller	1941	Sweden
174	69	296	18[b]	Kallmann	1946	U.S.
41	68	61	18	Slater & Shields	1953	England
55	60	17	12	Inouye	1961	Japan
16	6[c]	20	5	Tienari	1963	Finland
8	25	. . .	. . .	Kringlen	1964	Norway
55	38	90	10	Kringlen	1967	Norway
24	42	33	9	Gottesman & Shields	1966	England

[a] Total number of twin pairs equals 118, but number of each type could not be found.

[b] Age, corrected life expectancy; uncorrected data were not presented by Kallmann for same-sex dizygotic twins.

[c] Although Tienari initially reported a concordance of zero for monozygotic twins, one cotwin subsequently became schizophrenic (Tienari, 1968).

obtained lower rates, such as Kringlen (1967) and Gottesman and Shields (1966), selected their samples so as to secure a greater number of less severe index cases. This explanation is supported by the finding of Gottesman and Shields (1966) that, when they divided their monozygotic twin index cases into mild and severe, the concordance for mild cases was only 17 per cent, whereas that for severe cases was 75 per cent, and by a similar though smaller difference reported by Kringlen among concordance rates for index cases at three levels of impairment (Kringlen, 1967, p. 76). Although this factor probably does explain some of the variation in rates, unfortunately it leaves the problem of Tienari's (1963) low concordance unsolved since his index cases were relatively severe.

Although no single explanation of the differences in rates has been found, the fact that recent studies have generally been based on more representative samples of twins than earlier studies suggests that their relatively low concordances cannot be dismissed and probably represent a correction of earlier overestimates. However, except in Tienari's study, the concordance for monozygotic twins, no matter how low, is significantly higher than the rate for dizygotic twins (cf. Kringlen, 1967, pp. 80–93).

Before accepting this difference as indicating a genetic factor in the etiology of schizophrenia, however, let us consider how well the problem of confounded social and genetic influences is solved in twin studies. One very powerful solution would be comparison of monozygotic twins who had been separated at birth and raised in contrasting environments. Unfortunately, coincidence of schizophrenia, monozygosity, and separation of twins into contrasting environments has proved too rare to permit such a crucial test of the issue.

In practice, therefore, comparisons are made between concordance rates for monozygotic and dizygotic same-sexed twins. Underlying these comparisons is an assumption that the extent of common social experience is the same for both types of twins. In fact, studies of the habitual activities of monozygotic and dizygotic twin pairs indicate greater similarity of experience for the former (Kety, 1965), particularly for female pairs (Smith, 1965). Some of the observed similarities, such as eating habits (*ibid.*, pp. 53–56) may, however, actually reflect a likeness in hereditary predisposition. Moreover, the discrepancy between environmental similarity scores for the two types of twins does not seem large enough to account for the difference in concordance rates (Kety, 1965).

The results of twin studies seem to point, therefore, to the conclusion that schizophrenia is induced by a combination of genetic and environmental factors. Although the concordance rates for monozygotic twins are difficult to explain without assuming a genetic factor in the etiology, even the highest rates do not suggest that the true concordance might be 100 per cent, and recent rates without the misleading Weinberg correction are generally below 50 per cent. Thus, the implication is that environmental influences must act to precipitate the schizophrenic disorder in individuals who are vulnerable because of genetic endowment.

The evidence concerning other types of disorder is much less extensive than that for schizophrenia. However, investigators have presented findings suggesting a genetic factor in other types of psychoses (e.g., Kallmann, 1953; Kringlen, 1967; Rosanoff, Handy, & Plesset, 1935), in neuroses (e.g., Shields, 1954; Slater & Shields, 1953; Taylor & Chave, 1964, p. 169), and in personality disorder (e.g., Lange, 1931; A. J. Rosanoff, Handy, & I. A. Rosanoff, 1934). These results have been summarized in an excellent review by Essen-Möller (1965), which demonstrates convincingly that the etiological issue is not limited to schizophrenia.

INTERACTION OF HEREDITY AND SOCIAL ENVIRONMENT

The results of twin studies seem, then, to imply that both environmental and genetic factors are involved in the etiology of many major types of psychological disorder. A number of influential authors have argued that this interaction is well enough established so that, at least for schizophrenia, the dispute about heredity versus environment should be closed (e.g., Böök, 1960, p. 31; Dobzhansky, 1962, p. 121). At the same time, as Meehl has pointed out (1962, p. 827), many investigators in the United States question whether, even in the case of schizophrenia, there is a genetic factor in the etiology (see e.g., American Psychiatric Association, Committee on Nomenclature and Statistics, 1952, p. 5). Jackson (1960), for example, in a thorough, critical review of genetic studies of schizophrenia, concluded:

"Although the statistics that have been gathered in twin studies are impressive, there are . . . reasons to suppose that they have been inadequately controlled for nongenetic factors. Possible environmental causes and particularly psychic identification have been ignored in favor of possible genetic causes" (pp. 80–81).

This seems, however, to be a minority view. For most investigators, questions about environment versus heredity in either-or terms appear to have been settled in favor of the view that the two factors interact in producing at least some types of psychological disorder. That is, as Dobzhansky (1962) described the situation with respect to schizophrenia, ". . . certain genotypes give rise to the hazard of schizophrenic breakdown, and this breakdown may or may not occur depending on environmental good or bad luck" (p. 121).

DIFFERENT VIEWS OF THE NATURE-NURTURE ISSUE

Such closure of the nature-nurture debate can be bought, however, only at the price of consigning social factors or, alternatively, genetic factors to the never-never land of good and bad luck. When this is not done, the problem appears to be far from settled. To clarify the issue, let us look more closely at how various investigators interpret the interaction of heredity and environment.

The geneticists' view of this interaction is expressed in statements about the penetrance of the gene for a disorder, that is, the probability that a person carrying the gene will develop the disorder. Estimates have been made mostly for schizophrenia and show considerable variation. For example, Kallmann (1938) concluded from his early work that ". . . the genotype of schizophrenia is a single-recessive trait, penetrating only with probable manifestation of approximately 70 per cent" (p. 163). And Böök (1953) estimated from his study of a northern Swedish community that ". . . the type of schizophrenia prevalent in the investigation area is primarily due to a major simple dominant gene with a heterozygous penetrance of about 20 per cent and a homozygous penetrance of about 100 per cent" (p. 91). Slater, however, reanalyzing Böök's data, suggested that they better fitted a recessive gene model, with 26 per cent penetrance in heterozygotes and only rare occurrence in homozygotes (1958).

With the exception of Böök's nearly 100 per cent penetrance of homozygotes, all of these estimates imply that factors in addition to the gene for schizophrenia determine whether the disorder actually develops in a given case. These other factors are not limited to the social environment, however, since the geneticist's conception of nongenetic determinants of a phenotype includes pre- and perinatal factors (Stern, 1960, p. 300). Thus, for example, one group of investigators found, in a study of sets of identical twins discordant for schizophrenia, that the schizophrenic individuals were more poorly developed at birth than their normal twins (Pollin, Stabenau, & Tupin, 1965), while other investigators reported that children in a psychiatric hospital were more likely to have been born prematurely than were normal controls (Zitrin, Ferber, & Cohen, 1964).

Although such findings do not rule out the possibility of social factors being involved as well (e.g., Pollin et al., 1965), they indicate what, from the genetic point of view, may constitute environmental bad luck. That is, the geneticist's estimate that penetrance of the gene for schizophrenia is less than 100 per cent does not necessarily imply commitment to social factors as partial determinants of the disorder. Such a commitment could be explicitly indicated by the geneticist's hypothesizing varied penetrances under different social conditions (Stern, 1960, p. 305). For example, an estimate of higher penetrance in the lower class than in the middle class would attribute a role to social stratum in the etiology of schizophrenia. By contrast, estimates of penetrance that ignore social class at least imply the hypothesis that this status is not a factor in the etiology of schizophrenia.

By contrast, investigators such as the Leightons (D. C. Leighton, Harding, Macklin, Macmillan, & A. H. Leighton, 1963) emphasize the importance of social conditions as determinants of whether or not individuals will suffer psychological disorder:

"If our environmental hypothesis is correct, a high prevalence and incidence of psychiatric disorder should be a regular finding in . . . disintegrated communities. It should, moreover, be reversible in situations where disintegration is reversed as the responses to change become stabilized" (pp. 391–392).

Even though the possibility of genetic factors in the etiology of psychological disorder is recognized by these authors (p. 391), this reversal in prevalence rate is not premised on a substantial change in the genetic pool of the community, implying that genetic endowment is believed to play a relatively minor part in producing psychological disorder.

It appears, therefore, that the nature-nurture issue persists. Even though most investigators appear to agree, largely on the basis of results of twin studies, that heredity and environment probably interact to produce psychological disorder, the relative importance of heredity and the nature of the environmental factors remain in dispute.

SUMMARY

A number of studies using the twin design to minimize confounding of social and genetic factors point to the existence of a genetic factor in the etiology of schizophrenia. Although the data on other types of disorder are much less extensive, they at least raise the possibility that a genetic factor is also involved in the etiology of a variety of other disorders. However, the relationship between genetic factors and psychological disorder, even in the case of schizophrenia, is not so strong as to rule out a role for environmental factors. It is plausible to conclude from the twin studies, therefore, that heredity and environment interact in the etiology of at least some major types of disorder.

The assumption of nature-nurture interaction does not, however, resolve the etiological issue. Examination of how this interaction is conceived by genetically oriented investigators in comparison to socially oriented investigators indicates that the relative importance of hereditary and social environmental factors is still in dispute.

CHAPTER 4

Studies Aimed at Determining the Relative Importance of Heredity and Social Environment

We have seen that there are important differences in the research strategies used by investigators concerned primarily with social environmental factors and investigators concerned primarily with genetic factors in the etiology of psychological disorder. The social environmentalists have looked for correlations between social statuses and a wide variety of different types of psychological disorder through cross-sectional surveys of patient or community populations. By contrast, investigators who have focused on genetics have examined concordance rates for relatives of persons treated for particular types of psychological disorder, usually schizophrenia. The consequence of these differences has been that, in most of their work, the investigators with these contrasting orientations have not confronted each other's ideas directly.

STUDIES OF ADOPTED CHILDREN

One partial exception to this rule is represented by two ingeniously designed studies of adopted children. In one, Heston (1966) followed up 47 subjects, who ranged in age from about 20 to 50 and who had been permanently separated from their schizophrenic mothers at birth. They were compared with a control group of children from the same foundling homes matched for sex, length of time in a child care institution, and type of placement after leaving the institution. In view of this matching of early environment, Heston's finding that 5 of the children of schizophrenic mothers were schizophrenic, but none of the children in the control group was, led him to infer a genetic factor in the etiology of schizophrenia.

Rates of mental deficiency, sociopathic personality, and neurotic personality disorder were also higher among the children of schizophrenic mothers than among controls, a pattern of results reported in other geneological studies. Furthermore, about half of the schizophrenic mother group showed "major psycho-social disability," whereas only 18 per cent of the control group was thus classified. On the other hand, 21 children of schizophrenic mothers showed no psychosocial impairment and ". . . were not only successful adults but in comparison to the control group were more spontaneous when interviewed and had more colourful life histories. They held the more creative jobs . . ." (Heston, 1966, p. 824). Thus the interesting implication of Heston's findings is that there is a genetic factor underlying schizophrenia which may produce either pathological or nonpathological, even desirable, phenotypes.

Another set of studies of foster children. (Rosenthal & Kety, 1968) used as index cases schizophrenics raised as adopted children, and included control groups raised by their natural parents. Comparison of the natural and adoptive parents permitted prediction of alternative outcomes from the genetic and social causation hypotheses: the genetic hypothesis predicts that a higher rate of schizophrenia should be found among the natural than among the adoptive parents, whereas the social causation hypothesis predicts the opposite. The findings in three separate studies that used this design and two parallel designs indicate higher rates among natural than among adoptive parents of schizophrenics and therefore strongly support the hypothesis of genetic etiology (Rosenthal & Kety, 1968).

Although the results of these studies seem clear, their generalizability is limited on two counts. First, they apply only to schizophrenia. Second, they apply only to the special social circumstances associated with being an adopted child, which may include a period of institutionalization followed by adoption into a home presumably selected to provide a favorable environment. Except in cases of extended and poor institutional care, therefore, the design does not test the effects of exposure to unfavorable social conditions.

STUDIES OF GEOGRAPHIC MOBILITY

One type of study that attempts to assess the effect of unfavorable environmental circumstances as against genetic endowment on rates of disorder involves the comparison of migrants and nonmigrants. An early and outstanding example of this type of research is Ødegaard's (1932) study of Norwegian migrants to Minnesota. His explanation of the higher rate of hospitalized cases of schizophrenia among these migrants, compared to the native Norwegian population, emphasized genetic etiology:

"In the etiology of schizophrenia constitutional factors are generally considered more important than the life situation of the individual, and this was found to be true also of the schizophrenic immigrants. There was no indication that the hardships of immigrant life had played any part at all in the development of the disease" (p. 194).

The results of this pioneering study have not been supported by later investigators on two counts. First, in some studies migrant groups have been found to have lower rather than higher rates of treated psychological disorder when compared to nonmigrant populations (Murphy, 1965). Second, the higher rate of disorder among migrants, when it is found, can be explained just as plausibly by the "hardships of immigrant life" as by selective migration of the genetically handicapped (Braatoy, 1937; Malzberg, 1940). For these reasons, studies of the relation of migration to rates of psychological disorder have not resolved the question of whether social environmental factors or hereditary factors are more important in the etiology of psychological disorder.

STUDIES OF SOCIAL MOBILITY

The most widely used strategy for attempting to resolve the etiological issue is based on the results reviewed in Chapter 2, which showed that the highest rates of certain types of disorder are found in the lowest social stratum. The empirical question that this strategy poses is whether the lower-class cases of psychological disorder are downwardly mobile or whether they originated in the lower class. The argument is that the social pressures and deprivations usually considered likely to be pathogenic are most characteristic of the lower class. If these environmental conditions associated with low class position are major determinants of psychological disorder, lower-class persons with such disorder should be found to have originated in families of the same social type, that is, their parents should also usually be from the lower class. However, if the disorder is to be attributed to the lower-class social rather than biological environment, it must be established that the cases of psychological disorder are not systematically associated with unfavorable pre- or perinatal factors or with an unusually unfavorable biological environment during the developmental years. Moreover, the most unambiguous outcome would require also that the parents' lower-class status be attributable to factors such as recent migration or stage of ethnic assimilation, rather than to a family history of psychological disorder, to rule out conclusively the possibility of hereditary disability.

If, by contrast, downward social selection of the genetically handicapped is the important factor in accounting for the high rates of psychological disorder in the lower class, the most unambiguous finding would show little difference between the class origins of lower-class persons with psychological disorder and the class origins of the general population. In other words, persons with psychological disorder would be shown frequently to be downwardly mobile relative to the higher class status of their parents. Moreover, there should be some evidence of psychological disorder in the family history.

Thus unambiguous outcomes with respect to hereditary versus social environmental etiology from mobility studies of lower-class cases of psychological disorder depend on certain combinations of three factors in relation to those cases. These factors are:

1. Mobility history.
2. History with respect to biological deprivation.
3. Family history with respect to psychological disorder.

If we dichotomize these factors and assume that the problem of biological deprivation is not pervasive in classes other than the lowest, we have the five ideal-typical combinations shown in Table 4-1. Only two of these

Table 4-1. Implications, with Respect to Etiology of Lower-Class Cases of Psychological Disorder, of Combinations of Family Class Background, Biological Environmental History, and Family History of Psychological Disorder

Family History of Psycho-logical Disorder	Family Class Background	
	Other than Lowest	Lowest
Present	I. Social selection implying genetic etiology	Unusually deprived biological environmental history present or absent III. Vicious circle of social and/or biological environmental deprivation, implying genetic and/or environmental etiology
Absent	II. Environmental accident	Unusually deprived biological environmental history <table><tr><td>Present</td><td>Absent</td></tr><tr><td>IV. Biological and/or social environmental causation</td><td>V. Social environmental causation</td></tr></table>

combinations, those shown in cells I and V, would provide clear evidence concerning the issue of the relative importance of heredity and social environmental factors in accounting for the high rate of psychological disorder in the lowest social class.

In cell II the lack of a family history of disorder brings into question the genetic explanation for the observed downward mobility of the cases. On the other hand, for stable lower-class cases in the combination of conditions described in cell III, environmental and genetic factors are so entangled that there is no basis for determining their relative etiological importance. In cell IV, environmental causation is clearly implicated, but the effects of social environmental factors cannot be separately evaluated from those of biological factors. In the light of this conception of the evidence required to resolve the issue, let us see, then, what studies of the social mobility of lower-class cases of psychological disorder have shown.

Results for An Overall Measure of Psychological Disorder

In a rare instance of investigation of social mobility in relation to an overall measure of psychological disorder, Srole and Langner, in the Midtown Study (Srole, Langner, Michael, Opler, & Rennie, 1962, pp. 212–213, pp. 228–229), attempted to choose between the social selection and social causation alternatives by investigating the class positions of the parents of their adult subjects. Finding a significant inverse relation between their subjects' impairing symptomatology and the socioeconomic status of the subjects' parents, the investigators suggested that environmental deprivation in childhood is a causal factor in psychological disorder. However, they also found that the relation between parental socioeconomic status and impairing symptoms was weaker than the relation of the subjects' own socioeconomic status to impairing symptoms. Moreover, subjects rated impaired were most likely to be found among people who were downwardly mobile in comparison to their parents, and least likely to be found among those who were upwardly mobile. Accordingly, the Midtown researchers suggested that perhaps both social causation, in the form of childhood deprivation, and social selection, in the form of intergeneration mobility, contribute to the strong inverse relation between rates of impairment and subjects' own socioeconomic status.

There are problems, however, in addition to lack of parsimony, with this explanation of their results. As Michael, one of the Midtown researchers, implied (Srole et al., 1962, p. 329), genetic predisposition could be substituted for childhood deprivation with equal plausibility. Without data on family history of disorder, it is impossible to tell. Thus this research cannot be classified into any of the outcomes diagramed in Table 4-1, and it does not provide a basis for assessing the extent to which class position is cause and the extent to which class position is consequence of psychological disorder.

Results for Personality Disorder

The high rate of personality disorder in the lowest social class has led some investigators to consider the issue of whether this relationship can be attributed equally plausibly to social selection and to social causation. For this type of disorder, however, doubts about the plausibility of the social selection explanation are raised by the fact that, of all psychological disorders, it is most likely to be identified in terms of variable social definitions of acceptable behavior, as opposed to more general psychiatric criteria. For example, one study in the southern United States reported that cases were identified on evidence such as miscegenation and unacceptable use of tobacco (Roth & Luton, 1943), thus clearly reflecting local norms of propriety. Similarly, a change in reported rate of psychopathic personality from 13 to 5.2 per 10,000 of population in the Eastern Health District of Baltimore between 1933 and 1936 was explained by ". . . the fact that early in the depression years there was a tendency for the sources on which the survey was dependent to interpret the inability to earn a satisfactory living as an evidence of psychopathic personality. By 1936, the seriousness of the world financial depression had been more clearly recognized, familiarity with unemployment had made it less a mark of defective character" (Lemkau, 1949, p. 408). A category of disorder defined by behavioral criteria which vary thus with time and place would seem difficult to trace to a particular genetic endowment.

Nevertheless, insofar as the amorphous category of personality disorder includes persons who show "a gross, repetitive failure to conform to societal norms in many areas of life, in the absence of a thought disturbance suggesting psychosis," Robins (1966) provided evidence that social selection might be a factor of major importance in the class relationship. Her study, which includes a combination of design features unique in social psychiatric research, was a follow-up 30 years later of 524 children who had been referred in the 1930's to a municipal child guidance clinic in St. Louis, Missouri, and 100 controls ingeniously selected from school records to have a similar distribution as to residence, sex, ethnicity, and year of birth. The focus was on children of white, Protestant, American-born parents, mainly of lower-class circumstances.

Robins and her colleagues found that children diagnosed as sociopathic personalities as adults, like their fathers before them, tended to be found in the lower class. In contrast, members of the control group tended to have risen to higher class positions. Moreover, the finding that a record of sociopathic behavior on the part of the father, together with amount of childhood sociopathy, constituted the strongest predictor of adult sociopathy, with class showing no independent effect, suggests that low class status was in large part a consequence of pre-existing sociopathy.

These results fit quite neatly into the type III combination described in Table 4-1, a combination of factors that is ambiguous with respect to the etiological issue. Robins correctly concluded that it is not clear whether the father's sociopathy is transferred to the child through social learning or through genetic endowment (pp. 301–302). Nor is it certain whether the results just described would hold for other areas in the United States or for other ethnic groups, given the variability in the definition of this disorder. Accordingly, the available evidence does not definitely eliminate either social causation or social selection of the genetically handicapped as a possible explanation for the strong inverse relation between social class and personality disorder.

Results for Schizophrenia

The largest number of studies utilizing the phenomenon of social mobility to test alternative genetic and social environmental etiological hypotheses have been based on treated cases of schizophrenia, a type of disorder that also shows a strong inverse relation to social class. Some of these studies have been interpreted as supporting the social causation alternative (e.g., Hollingshead and Redlich, 1958, pp. 246–247; Tietze, Lemkau and Cooper, 1941) insofar as they showed that schizophrenics tended to be in the same class as their parents, but such an interpretation requires the assumption, unfounded in the absence of diagnostic data, that the family histories were relatively free of schizophrenia. Without these diagnostic data, these studies cannot be classified into any of the outcomes shown in Table 4-1.

In sharp contrast, moreover, are results obtained in two United States towns by Dunham (1965) and in England by Goldberg and Morrison (1963); both studies reported that schizophrenics displayed downward mobility from father's occupations, which did not differ significantly from those of the general population. Between these extremes are studies such as that of Turner and Wagenfeld (1967), who, like Dunham and like Goldberg and Morrison, found evidence of downward intergenerational mobility on the part of schizophrenics, but also obtained results showing that the fathers of the schizophrenics tended disproportionately to have had lower-class occupations. Thus, not only do these studies fail to provide the crucial data on family history, but also their results concerning the direction of the relationship between low social class and psychological disorder seem to be inconsistent.

Methodological Problems in Social Mobility Studies

This inconsistency appears, however, to be a spurious consequence of the use of an inappropriate index of social class in some of the studies (Turner, 1968). Specifically, the problem focuses on the use of occupation as against education in the measure of class position. While the distribution of occupations at different prestige levels has changed somewhat over succeeding generations (Blau and Duncan, 1967), educational opportunities as well as the educational requirements of higher-prestige occupations have changed drastically. Thus, for example, when Hollingshead and Redlich (1958) used an index that included educational level and place of residence as well as occupational level to measure class, they found that schizophrenics were stable in relation to the social class of their fathers. By contrast, Goldberg and Morrison (1963), finding that schizophrenics were downwardly mobile, observed that inclusion of educational level and place of residence along with occupation in their index of class would have obscured the picture of downward drift by their schizophrenic subjects.

The use of education in the index of class in intergeneration mobility studies of schizophrenics has confused results not only because of changes in educational opportunities and requirements over time, but also because of the difference in the pattern of educational and occupational achievement in schizophrenic cases. This pattern is indicated by the results of a study by Dunham, Phillips, and Srinivasan (1966), who calculated for schizophrenics, their fathers, and several other control groups the discrepancy for each individual between his educational and occupational levels. They found that this discrepancy score indicated low occupational attainment, relative to their education, for schizophrenic patients in comparison to their fathers, whereas the same was not true for nonschizophrenic patients relative to their fathers, or for an undescribed group of nonpatient controls.

Therefore, it appears that occupation is the appropriate index of class position for studies of intergeneration mobility of schizophrenics, both because of its relative stability of meaning over time and because of its sensitivity to the deficit in the performance of schizophrenics. When studies that used education in their index of class are eliminated, the results of social mobility studies of schizophrenics become consistent (Turner, 1968); that is, studies that employed occupation alone to indicate class have quite consistently found downward intergenerational social mobility.

However, some studies that demonstrated the existence of downward mobility among the mentally ill in general or among schizophrenics in particular also found a considerable number of cases who were born into the lower class rather than having drifted into it from a higher social status. Recall, for example, some of the Midtown Study results. These investigators found on the one hand that subjects rated impaired were more likely to be downwardly mobile than to be upwardly mobile or stable in relation to their fathers; they also found, however, a significant inverse correlation between number of impairing symptoms and parental social class. This finding that nonmobile lower-class persons tended to have a relatively high level of symptoms was interpreted by the authors as pointing to deprived childhood social environment as a factor in the etiology of psychological disorder.

Turner and Wagenfeld (1967) obtained similar results in a study of schizophrenics based on a complete roster of diagnosed patients in Monroe County, New York. Comparing their male patients to the overall population of Monroe County, they found that three times as many patients as expected, 15 per cent, were at the lowest occupational level, and over twice as many fathers of patients as expected, 12 per cent, had usually worked at this same level. Furthermore, comparison of their schizophrenic sample with a national sample for whom data were available on sons' and fathers' occupations revealed that ". . . the broad trend is one of relatively less upward movement and more downward movement within the schizophrenic population" (p. 109). Turner and Wagenfeld argued that these results point to social selection as the explanation of the high rate of schizophrenia in the lowest social class.

Note, however, that their interpretation, in contrast to that of Srole and Langner, assumed that "less upward movement," that is, a disproportionate number of nonmobile lower-class cases, can be taken as evidence of social selection. There seems, however, to be room for either the social selection or the social causation interpretation unless further information is available about the family histories of psychological disorder of both the nonmobile lower-class cases and their controls. Furthermore, if family histories of the nonmobile lower-class cases were found to contain a relatively high rate of psychological disorder, the results would remain ambiguous, as in Robins' (1966) study of personality disorder, and as indicated in cell III of Table 4-1.

Further clarification of the meaning of the higher rate of nonmobile persons of lower-class origins among patients, compared to the general population, would also depend on ascertaining whether the ethnic composition of the two groups was the same. This was done in Robins' well-controlled study of personality disorder by limiting the investigation to a generally homogeneous group of white, Protestant subjects. In most mobility studies, however, no evidence is available on this issue. Give the fact that objective social barriers to upward mobility are higher for some ethnic groups than for others (Blau & Duncan, 1967), one could be misled by comparisons between patients from relatively disadvantaged ethnic groups and controls from more advantaged groups. The patients' higher rate of failure to rise might actually be due to their disadvantaged ethnic status.

On balance, then, it appears that social mobility studies have not yet resolved the issue of the extent to which the excess of cases in the lower class is due to social selection and the extent to which social causation is responsible, even for schizophrenia, on which most of the studies have been done. In some instances, the means of assessing social mobility have led to confusing results, and by and large the studies have failed to provide the needed data on family history of disorder.

SUMMARY

Three types of studies have aimed at determining the relative importance of heredity and social environment in the etiology of psychological disorder. The first type, studies of foster children who either are schizophrenic themselves or had schizophrenic mothers, has yielded results that favor genetic etiology but have limited generality. The second type of study, comparing migrants and nonmigrants, has produced inconsistent and inconclusive results.

The most commonly used design involves investigation of the social mobility history of lower-class cases of psychological disorder, usually schizophrenia. These studies, however, have encountered problems in the measurement of mobility and have failed, for the most part, to provide information about family history with respect to psychological disorder. Their results remain inconclusive, therefore, with respect to the etiological issue.

CHAPTER 5

A Design for a Crucial Test of the Etiological Issue

We have seen that limitations and difficulties are inherent in various designs that have been employed in efforts to resolve the issue of the relative importance of heredity and social environment in the etiology of psychological disorder. Alternative approaches to a crucial test also appear to present difficulties. We might, for example, design experiments involving the manipulation of hypothesized pathogenic factors to determine their effects, but would hardly care to execute such investigations if we really thought the manipulations would succeed in producing psychopathology. Or we might initiate a massive prospective study of the relation between social mobility and psychological disorder over several generations, necessarily leaving it to succeeding generations of researchers to carry to completion. Short of these unlikely possibilities, is there any key to a solution? We will argue that, potentially, at least one such key does exist, in the form of a quasi experiment fortuitously provided by the process of ethnic assimilation in relatively open-class societies.

SOME SOCIAL HISTORY

As an example, the history of New York City has been marked by great successive waves of new immigrant groups: the Irish and Germans in the 1840's, the Jews and Italians starting in the 1880's, the Negroes after World War I, and the Puerto Ricans after World War II. With the possible exception of non-Jewish Germans, the initial conditions of these new groups in the city have been those of poverty, slums, and working-class jobs. The Jews, the Irish, and, to a lesser extent, the Italians have moved up over succeeding generations into relatively affluent and largely middle-class circumstances. In this process of assimilation, these three ethnic groups have achieved a substantial share in the wealth and power of the city.

49

In sharp contrast to these now relatively advantaged ethnic groups are the Negroes and Puerto Ricans, who are concentrated geographically in the city's slums and occupationally in its low-paying unskilled and semi-skilled jobs. Glazer and Moynihan (1963) summarize the economic picture in the city as follows:

". . . the economy of New York . . . is dominated at its peak (the banks, insurance companies, utilities, big corporation offices) by white Protestants, with Irish Catholics and Jews playing somewhat smaller roles. In wholesale and retail commerce, Jews predominate. White collar workers are largely Irish and Italian if they work for big organizations, and Jewish if they work for smaller ones. The city's working class is, on its upper levels, Irish, Italian, and Jewish; on its lower levels, Negro and Puerto Rican" (p. 5).

It would thus be consistent with the earlier reports of an inverse relation between social class and psychological disorder to expect relatively high rates of disorder among New York Negroes and Puerto Ricans. Indeed, Srole (Srole, Langner, Michael, Opler, & Rennie, 1962, p. 365) made this prediction from Midtown Study results concerning differences among white, non-Puerto Rican groups.

If such an expected finding were confirmed by the facts, consider for a moment how it would be explained in social selection terms. One would have to argue that high rates of prior psychological disorder, probably genetically produced, were causing the low status of Negroes and Puerto Ricans in New York City. Against the background of the history and contemporary circumstances of ethnic groups in the city, however, such an explanation would strain credulity. This brings us face to face with a consideration of major importance: in the context of the history of the assimilation of ethnic groups in New York City, social selection makes sense only as an explanation of high rates of disorder among the lower-class members of ethnic groups that, on the whole, have become relatively advantaged. Herein lies our possibility for a crucial test of the etiological issue. Let us spell it out.

SOME ASSUMPTIONS

Our society has been described as one ". . . which places a high premium on economic affluence and social ascent for all its members" (Merton, 1957, p. 146). And a basic conclusion from studies of social mobility in societies such as ours has been that ". . . the desire to rise in status is intrinsic in all persons of lower status, and individuals and groups will attempt to improve their status (and self-evaluation) whenever they have a chance to do so" (Lipset & Zetterberg, 1959, p. 73).

It has been argued, however, that lower-class groups are not motivated by this success goal (e.g., Miller, 1958; Porter, 1968). Also, evidence has been presented that shows the occupational level of aspiration to be lower in lower- than in higher-class groups (e.g., Hyman, 1953, p. 435). Thus the generality of the success norm in our society appears to have been called into question on empirical grounds. Yet the issue is not so clear-cut.

Consider that an individual's occupational level of aspiration must be a joint function of how desirable the goal of economic advancement appears to him on the one hand, and how he assesses his chances of achieving it on the other (e.g., Child & Whiting, 1949). Given the facts of inequality of opportunity in our society, there is every reason to expect a difference between the lower-class person's and the middle-class person's assessment of his probability of reaching a high-level occupation. Thus it is not surprising that investigators have found greater discrepancies between occupational aspirations and occupational expectations in high school students of lower-class background than in their counterparts of higher-class background (Caro & Pihlblad, 1965). Furthermore, the relation between social class background and occupational aspiration changes radically when the aspiration is measured in relation to father's occupation rather than in absolute terms: although, among high school students, the absolute measure is positively correlated with class background, the relative measure yields a significant negative correlation (Empey, 1956). Thus the goal of upward mobility does not appear to be limited to the middle class.

Additional evidence on this point is the finding that large majorities of both Negro and white mothers at all class levels have been shown to desire high status occupations for their children (Bloom, Whiteman, & Deutsch, 1965). Moreover, historical evidence indicates that the relative occupational pessimism in the lower class with respect to absolute expectations has not led to abandonment of the goal of economic success, since over the generations each new immigrant group has risen on the economic and occupational prestige scale.

Our first assumption, then, is that most people in our urban society, regardless of class and ethnic background, place a high valuation on economic and other forms of personal, prestige-securing achievement and social ascent, though they may differ in their assessment of their chances of achieving such goals. Exceptions to this generalization about our urban society would be limited, we believe, to small groups of drop-outs and opt-outs such as hippies and members of monastic orders.

Given a widespread conception that upward mobility is desirable, let us make the further assumption that the probability of success for a particular individual is a function of two factors. One is his own capability. Since serious psychological disorder is likely to lower this capability, we can predict that the disordered individual will be less likely than others to improve a low class position or maintain a high one.

The other factor affecting the probability of upward mobility is opportunity, which in turn depends both on the state of the economy and on the degree of help or hindrance provided by those already occupying positions at and above the level to which the individual aspires. On both of these counts, it appears that the probability of upward mobility varies for members of different ethnic groups in New York City. Specifically, Glazer and Moynihan (1963) concluded from their investigation that the economic situation faced today by Negro and Puerto Rican New Yorkers is different from that encountered by Jews, Irish, and Italians at the start of their climb. At the same time as the supply of Negro and Puerto Rican labor has increased, relative industrial wages have been decreasing. Furthermore, reactions of established groups to differences in skin color and culture in the new immigrant groups have led to their being hindered more often than helped by those already occupying higher positions. Since the social obstacles to achievement now facing Negroes and Puerto Ricans either were never encountered or have been removed for Anglo-Saxon, Jewish, Irish, and Italian New Yorkers, Negro and Puerto Rican immigrants face greater downward social pressure than do their class counterparts in these more advantaged ethnic groups.

Such considerations have led Glazer and Moynihan (1963) to the following pessimistic observation: "To a degree that cannot fail to startle anyone who encounters the reality for the first time, the overwhelming portion of both groups constitutes a submerged, exploited, and very possibly permanent proleteriat" (p. 299). One does not have to share the pessimism of these investigators to see the essential point: there is greater downward social pressure on Negroes and Puerto Ricans than on members of other, more advantaged ethnic groups.

Moreover, to the extent that this pressure is associated with the assimilation status of the ethnic groups as wholes, it should operate independently of the class positions of individuals. Thus, the downward social pressure should be greater on middle-class Negroes and Puerto Ricans than on middle-class members of more advantaged ethnic groups, just as it should be greater on lower-class Negroes and Puerto Ricans than on their class counterparts in more advantaged ethnic groups.

In summary, then, we are making three assumptions:

1. There is an almost universally shared norm in our society that upward social mobility is desirable.

2. Serious psychological disorder involves disability that decreases the probability of upward social mobility and increases the probability of downward social mobility.

3. There is greater downward social pressure on Negro and Puerto Rican New Yorkers than on their class counterparts in more advantaged ethnic groups in New York City.

ALTERNATIVE PREDICTIONS

On the basis of these assumptions, let us consider what the social environmental and genetic hypotheses predict with respect to the relative rates of psychological disorder in different ethnic groups *within the same social class*.

The Social Environmental Prediction

If rate of psychological disorder in a particular social class is mainly a function of the strength of the social pressures experienced by members of this class, we should find higher rates of disorder among Negroes and Puerto Ricans than among their class counterparts in other ethnic groups. In other words, the greater social pressure exerted on these relatively disadvantaged groups would be expected to produce an increment in psychopathology over and above that produced by the lesser social pressure, at any particular class level, on members of more advantaged ethnic groups. Before accepting this prediction, however, let us see whether a higher rate of disorder among Negroes and Puerto Ricans could be explained as plausibly by differences in genetic endowment as by differences in amount of social pressure.

The alternative explanation is possible only if one is willing to assume that Negroes and Puerto Ricans are, at the same time, similar to each other genetically and different from the more advantaged Anglo-Saxon, Jewish, Irish, and Italian ethnic groups, who must in turn be assumed to be similar to each other.

Consider, however, that, if we turn back the historical clock, an assumption of genetic handicap could have been made to explain the low status of Jews or Irish or Italians when they were disadvantaged immigrant groups. The subsequent history of the assimilation of Jews, Irish, and Italians to more advantaged group positions, however, clearly disproves any hypothesis that they were genetically handicapped when they entered the slums several generations ago as new immigrants. Thus it would be counter to what is known about the history of the assimilation of past ethnic groups in our relatively open-class urban society to assume that immigrant members of the lower class are genetically handicapped.

Nevertheless, although no clear evidence, direct or indirect, supports the assumption that Negro and Puerto Rican New Yorkers are genetically handicapped in relation to previous new immigrant groups, there is no direct evidence that enables us unequivocally to reject this possibility. But the strategy we are advocating would not require that we accept even this degree of uncertainty about the implication of a finding of higher rates of psychological disorder among Negroes and Puerto Ricans than among their class counterparts. We could test the social environmental interpretation of these results by replicating the comparisons in other settings with other ethnic groups—comparing, perhaps, Mexican-Americans with more advantaged ethnic groups in the southwestern United States; Indians, Pakistanis, and West Indians with more advantaged groups in England; ex-untouchables with relatively advantaged caste groups in the Hindu population of India; southern Italians with northern Italians in northern Italian cities; and so on. The greater the racial heterogeneity, geographical dispersion, and variety of social histories of the groups on which these results were replicated, the greater the certainty with which we could reject the hypothesis that a common genetic defect accounted for their disadvantaged status.

Successful replication of results in a variety of other ethnic groups in other settings would also serve to reduce the plausibility of alternative etiological explanations in terms of such factors as unfavorable prenatal or perinatal conditions. Although members of one or another ethnic or racial group might suffer in this respect regardless of their class (e.g., Pasamanick, Knobloch, & Lilienfeld, 1956), it seems unlikely that this disability would be characteristic at all class levels of a wide range of disadvantaged ethnic groups.

The Genetic Prediction

Let us turn now to the alternative prediction. If psychological disorder is mainly an outcome of genetic endowment, we would expect the rate in a given class to be a function of social selection processes, whereby the able tend to rise or maintain high status and the disabled to drift down or fail to rise. Since the downward social pressure is greater on Negroes and Puerto Ricans, we would expect more of their healthier members to be kept in low status—thereby diluting the rates of disorder. By contrast, with less pressure, the low status members of more advantaged ethnic groups should tend to rise if they are healthy, leaving behind what Gruenberg (1961, p. 269) has termed a "residue" of ill—thereby inflating the rate of disorder. Thus social selection should function to produce a lower rate of disorder among Negroes and Puerto Ricans than among their class counterparts in more advantaged ethnic groups. Again, however, let us consider the plausibility of an alternative, environmental explanation for such an outcome.

Such an alternative seems in this case to be highly implausible, since it would require us to assume that the more advantaged groups were exposed to less favorable environmental influences. Thus, one would have to show that the advantaged Anglo-Saxon, Jewish, Irish, and Italian ethnic groups suffered some common social deprivation not encountered by Negroes or Puerto Ricans, and that this deprivation was associated with psychological disorder. In the absence of this seemingly unlikely finding, the case for interpreting higher rates of disorder among the advantaged ethnic groups in comparison to their Negro and Puerto Rican class counterparts as evidence of genetic etiology would be very strong.

Generalization of Alternative Predictions

1. The hypothesis that social environmental factors are primary in the etiology of psychological disorder would be supported by the finding that Negroes and Puerto Ricans in New York City have higher rates of psychological disorder than their class counterparts in more advantaged ethnic groups.

2. The hypothesis that genetic factors are primary in the etiology of psychological disorder would be supported by the finding that Negroes and Puerto Ricans in New York City have lower rates of psychological disorder than their class counterparts in more advantaged ethnic groups.

Moreover, further specification is possible in view of the evidence from previous field studies, which suggests that class shows a stronger relationship to rate of disorder than ethnic status (see Chapter 2). Table 5-1 shows the relative rates of psychological disorder for four ethnic-class status groups, as predicted from each of the hypotheses stated above. Although the present investigation is concerned with Negro and Puerto Rican as against other, more advantaged, ethnic groups in New York City, the same predictions can be made, as suggested earlier, for any situation in which ethnic stratification exists together with some degree of social class mobility. Furthermore, they can be tested for any type of psychological disorder that poses the issue of the relative importance of genetic endowment and of social pressures and deprivation as etiological factors.

SUMMARY

A strategy is proposed that appears to offer a crucial test of the etiological issue of heredity versus social environment. This strategy involves a comparison of relatively advantaged and disadvantaged ethnic groups in any society with some degree of social mobility. Alternative predictions from the genetic and social environmental hypotheses are made for relative rates of psychological disorder in the advantaged and the disadvantaged ethnic groups within a given social class.

Table 5-1. Hypothetical Support for Social Selection Hypothesis as against Social Causation Hypothesis in Relative Rates of Disorder According to Class and Ethnic Status
(1 = lowest rate of disorder; 4 = highest rate)

	Ethnic Group Status	
Class Status	Advantaged	Disadvantaged
	Support for	
	Social Selection Hypothesis	
Higher	2	1
Lower	4	3
	Support for	
	Social Causation Hypothesis	
Higher	1	2
Lower	3	4

CHAPTER 6

The State of the Evidence

If our analysis in Chapter 5 is correct, it would seem that we have something quite rare, a major substantive issue that could turn on a simple question of fact, namely, what are the rates of psychological disorder among Negroes and Puerto Ricans relative to the rates for their class counterparts in more advantaged ethnic groups? Let us see whether existing studies provide an answer to this question.

PREVIOUS STUDIES OF UNTREATED AS WELL AS TREATED CASES

Among the 44 community studies of untreated as well as treated cases of psychological disorder, 8 provided data from which rates comparing Negroes and whites could be obtained. In Chapter 2 these results were presented in Table 2-4, which showed that the 8 studies divided evenly, with 4 showing higher rates for Negroes and 4 showing higher rates for whites. Although the available data did not permit us to control social class, it is certain that the average social class of the Negroes in these comparisons was lower than that of the whites. Therefore, in view of the inverse relation between social class and rates of disorder, the rates for Negroes relative to whites may be overestimated. On the surface, therefore, these results, which suggest that Negroes are at least as healthy as their white class counterparts, tend to support the social selection explanation of the inverse relation between social class and psychiatric disorder.

It is necessary to question, however, whether these results can be taken at face value. In particular, let us consider possible implications of the fact that 3 of the 4 studies showing higher rates for whites were done in the South, whereas 3 of the 4 studies showing higher rates for Negroes were conducted in the northern United States or in Canada. Hyman (Hyman, Cobb, Feldman, Hart, & Stember, 1954) showed, with data collected in Tennessee, and J. A. Williams (1964), with data collected in North Carolina, that significantly different results were obtained from Negro respondents by white and by Negro interviewers. For example, Hyman reported that to the question "Do you think this country will win the [Second World] war?" 79 per cent of the Negro respondents interviewed by whites responded "Yes," whereas only 59 per cent of those interviewed by Negroes gave this positive answer (p. 160); Williams found that 24 per cent of Negro respondents interviewed by whites reported disapproval of sit-ins, whereas only 15 per cent of those interviewed by Negroes expressed disapproval (p. 346). Since the field studies of psychological disorder appear to be based on data collected by whites, it is necessary to pay attention to Hyman's and Williams' findings.

Consider these findings, for example, in relation to Pettigrew's (1964) explanation that Negroes in white America are always acting, transforming their behavior to conform to white prejudices and to avoid white punishment, and presenting a facade so convincing that ". . . many white Americans have long interpreted it as proof that Negroes are happy and contented with their lot" (p. 50). To the extent that these pressures on Negroes to act "happy and contented" are stronger in the South than in the North, the results in Table 2-4 may reflect the white-oriented role behaviors of Negroes in the South rather than their psychiatric condition, and the results from northern studies, which suggest that Negroes have considerably higher rates of disorder than whites, may present a more accurate picture. If this is so, and if we ignore for a moment the problem of controlling social class in these comparisons, the data from these field studies could be viewed as supporting not the social selection but rather the social causation explanation of class differences in rates of psychological disorder.

This result would be consistent with the findings of the Midtown Manhattan Study (Srole, Langner, Michael, Opler, & Rennie, 1962), the one previous investigation of untreated disorder that contains some data on Puerto Ricans. Although there were very few Puerto Ricans in the area of New York City studied by the Midtown researchers, 27 were included in the sample of about 1600 respondents. These Puerto Ricans were psychiatrically evaluated as having the largest proportion with impairing symptoms of all the subgroups in the study (pp. 290–292). Furthermore, when the researchers compared a subsample of 252 non-Puerto Rican respondents who had family incomes identical with those of 18 Puerto Ricans in the lowest income bracket, they found that only 31 per cent of the non-Puerto Ricans were rated as showing impairing symptoms, while 61 per cent of the low-income Puerto Ricans were judged to display these symptoms.

On balance, then, the results of previous studies of untreated as well as treated disorder seem to lend somewhat more support to the social causation than to the social selection explanation. However, the studies are not in most instances controlled for social class. Moreover, interpretation of the results rests on considerable speculation about possible methodological problems. Let us see, then, what results will be yielded by further investigation.

RESULTS FROM STUDIES IN WASHINGTON HEIGHTS, NEW YORK CITY

Two studies in Washington Heights, a section of Manhattan in New York City, provided more detailed data. The four largest ethnic groups in Washington Heights, in order of size, are Jewish, Negro, Irish, and Puerto Rican. There are also small representations from other ethnic groups such as Greek and Italian.

The Samples

Our subjects in the first study come from a large-scale collaborative endeavor, the "Master Sample Survey," that was conducted for various study groups in 1960–61 by the Community Population Laboratory of Columbia's School of Public Health and Administrative Medicine. A portion of this Master Sample consisted of 1713 respondents drawn on a probability basis to represent the adult population of Washington Heights. For most purposes, our focus is on the 1283 of these respondents whose ages ranged from 21 to 59, closely matching the 20 to 59 age limits in the Midtown Study (Srole et al., 1962).

Elinson and Loewenstein (1963) described the sampling procedure used for this survey and reported a highly satisfactory comparison with data from the 1960 census on demographic characteristics of the households from which our subjects were drawn. This close correspondence between census and sample estimates was obtained despite the fact that nonresponse in the survey was a substantial 27 per cent at the time that the main field work ended. In a special follow-up, interviews were obtained with about 60 per cent of a one-third sample of the harder-to-obtain cases. Elinson and Loewenstein noted (p. 130) that, if the assumption is made that these represent all the hard-to-obtain interviews, they could be triple-weighted and added to the 73 per cent previously obtained to provide an overall representation of about 90 per cent of those eligible for interview.

This possibility raised the question for us of whether or not to triple-weight these harder-to-obtain cases in our studies, giving us a total n of 1883 instead of 1713. An analysis by Loewenstein, Colombotos, and Elinson (1962) showed that triple-weighting the harder-to-obtain cases made no difference in the distribution of about 200 characteristics, including the symptom items in which we are most interested. Our own experience in a number of analyses that we have run both with and without the weighted cases is the same. Thus, although we have previously presented some findings employing the triple-weighted cases (B. P. Dohrenwend, 1966), our present procedure will be to dispense with added weights on the harder-to-obtain cases. Our reasoning is that analyses so far provide little reason to use them; moreover, their retention could be misleading if they turn up in cells with small numbers of actually interviewed respondents; and, finally, the weights artificially increase, albeit only slightly, the n's on which statistical tests are based, thereby artifically increasing the chance of an unimportant difference being statistically significant.

The second study in Washington Heights was done approximately 2 years after the first and used a small probability subsample of subjects from the first study. This subsample was selected on the basis of the ethnicity of the male head of the household. An equal number of households was designated from each of the four main ethnic groups, and within each of these groups proportional allocation according to the educational level of the male head was employed. In contrast with the first study, Negro and Puerto Rican respondents were interviewed by Negro and Puerto Rican interviewers. Husbands and wives were interviewed separately but simultaneously in different parts of their apartments by male and female interviewers, respectively. In all, 94 married couples and 26 single male household heads, 214 individuals in all, were to be interviewed. Interviews were completed with the designated respondents in 69 per cent of the households. An additional 12 per cent had to be removed from the sample because of inability to locate them and because of verified moves out of the state, death, etc. Respondents in 19 per cent of the households, disproportionately first-generation Irish (B. S. Dohrenwend & B. P. Dohrenwend, 1968), refused to be interviewed after repeated call-backs. In all, 71 per cent of the designated respondents were interviewed.

Socioeconomic Characteristics of the Ethnic Groups in Washington Heights

Let us start, then, with the data on family income from the larger sample of respondents aged 21 through 59. The total n in this and subsequent tables on this sample is usually less than the potential total of 1283 because of failure of some respondents to answer some questions.

Table 6-1 shows that Negroes and Puerto Ricans in Washington Heights have far lower incomes than members of other ethnic groups. The Bureau of Labor Statistics estimated at the time of the study that the annual cost of a "modest but adequate" level of living for a working-class family

Table 6-1. Family Income According to Ethnicity
(Values in per cent)

Family Income	Ethnicity				
	Puerto Rican	Negro	Jewish	Irish	Other
Under $3000	16.7	26.1	7.3	9.1	10.0
$3000–$4999	38.6	26.1	18.5	20.0	24.5
Under $5000	55.3	52.2	25.8	29.1	34.5
$5000–$7499	31.8	28.5	37.3	44.2	35.5
$7500 or more	12.9	19.2	36.9	26.7	30.0
$5000 & over	44.7	47.7	74.2	70.9	65.5
Total per cent	100.0	99.9	100.0	100.0	100.0
Number of respondents	132	291	260	165	310

Note: χ^2 = 97.44; df = 12; p < .001

in New York City was about $5200 excluding taxes (Miller, 1963). As Table 6-1 shows, over half the Negroes and Puerto Ricans had family incomes under $5000 a year before taxes as against a quarter to a third of the other ethnic groups. Outright poverty was most striking in the Negro groups, where fully a quarter had family incomes under $3000.

The clearest evidence of downward pressure by the larger society on Negroes and Puerto Ricans was found in the relation of education to income in these groups as compared with the more advantaged ethnic groups. Table 6-2 shows that, with the possible exceptions of minorities of respondents at the extremes of high education, that is, college graduates, and low education, that is, 7 years or less, income in the Negro and Puerto Rican groups was well below that of their educational counterparts in the other ethnic groups. Thus, although a person's education determines to a large degree what income he can potentially earn, a Negro or a Puerto Rican who has spent some time in high school or is a high school graduate is likely at the present time to have to settle for less than members of other ethnic groups with comparable education.

Measures of Psychological Disorder

Although most epidemiological investigations have not reported in detail the procedures whereby they collected data for the assessment of psychological disorder, a few recent studies have innovated in this respect (e.g., A. H. Leighton, Lambo, Hughes, D. L. Leighton, Murphy, & Macklin,

**Table 6-2. Per Cents with Family Incomes Under $5000 per Year
According to Ethnicity and Educational Level**
(Figures in parentheses are bases for per cents)

Years of Education	Ethnicity					Statistical Test (Puerto Rican and Negro Combined vs. All Others Combined)		
	Puerto Rican	Negro	Jewish	Irish	Other	χ^2	df	p
0–7	60.0 (40)	58.2 (43)	(3) (6)	58.4 (12)	51.4 (35)	0.51	1	< .50
8–11	60.4 (53)	60.0 (100)	31.0 (55)	32.8 (67)	40.2 (117)	21.94	1	< .001
12–15	42.8 (35)	51.2 (129)	22.5 (160)	23.0 (74)	23.2 (116)	36.54	1	< .001
16 and over	(2) (4)	5.6 (18)	26.4 (34)	18.2 (11)	31.6 (38)	1.85	1	< .20

1963; D. C. Leighton, Harding, Macklin, Macmillan, & A. H. Leighton, 1963; Srole et al., 1962). Moreover, in one of these, the Midtown Study (Srole et al., 1962), the reseachers found that, among the 120 symptom items in their interviews, which were done by lay interviewers, 22 could be scored to provide a close approximation of the evaluations made from records of the entire interview by the psychiatrists on the study. This score was adopted in our first study in Washington Heights as a measure of general psychological disorder, not only because it had been shown to discriminate statistically between psychiatric patients and a nonpatient group (Langner, 1962), but also because it had been used in a section of New York City that, although containing few Negroes and Puerto Ricans, is nevertheless close in the complexity of its class structure to our own research setting in Washington Heights.

The 22 Midtown items are listed in Table 6-3. As indicated there, many of these items have been used in a number of different studies, and 10 of the 22 can be traced back to the World War II Army Neuropsychiatric Screening Adjunct, which demonstrated a high statistical ability to discriminate between diagnosed psychoneurotic patients in Army hospitals and a sample of white enlisted men.

The Midtown researchers scored the response to each item either 0,

Table 6-3. 22 Symptom Items from Midtown Study Ordered in Terms of Magnitude of Per Cents in Washington Heights Sample Giving Symptomatic Responses
(The symptomatic response is underlined; base for per cent excludes "no answers")

Item	Per Cent of Symptomatic Responses	Base for Per Cent
1. Are you the worrying type—you know, a worrier? (<u>Yes</u>—No)	37.7	1680
2. You sometimes can't help wondering if anything is worthwhile anymore. (<u>Yes</u>—No)	15.6	1682
3. You have periods of such great restlessness that you cannot sit long in a chair. (<u>Yes</u>—No)	14.9	1684
4. Every so often you suddenly feel hot all over. (<u>Yes</u>—No)	14.9	1683
5. Do you feel somewhat apart or alone even among friends? (<u>Yes</u>—No)	13.9	1674
6. You have personal worries that get you down physically, that is, make you physically ill. (<u>Yes</u>—No)	13.1	1677
7.[a] You have had periods of days, weeks or months when you couldn't take care of things because you couldn't "get going." (<u>Yes</u>—No)	12.1	1681
8.[a,b,c] Do you ever have any trouble in getting to sleep or staying asleep? Would you say: <u>often, sometimes,</u> or never?	11.5	1673
9. Nothing ever turns out for you the way you want it to. (<u>Yes</u>—No)	11.5	1682
10.[a,b] Are you ever bothered by nervousness, that is, by being irritable, fidgety, or tense? Would you say: <u>often,</u> sometimes, or never?	11.4	1681
11. There seems to be a fullness or clogging in your head or nose much of the time. (<u>Yes</u>—No)	10.5	1682
12.[a,b,c] You are bothered by acid or sour stomach several times a week. (<u>Yes</u>—No)	9.8	1685
13. You feel weak all over much of the time. (<u>Yes</u>—No)	8.7	1684
14.[a,b,c] Are you ever troubled with headaches or pains in the head? Would you say: <u>often,</u> sometimes, or never?	6.8	1668

Table 6-3. (Continued)

Item	Per Cent of Symptomatic Responses	Base for Per Cent
15.[c] In general, would you say that most of the time you are in very good spirits, good spirits, low spirits, or very low spirits?	5.1	1671
16. Your memory seems to be all right (good). (Yes—No)	4.8	1676
17.[a,b] Would you say your appetite is poor, fair, good, or too good?	3.9	1686
18.[a,b] Have you ever been bothered by shortness of breath when you were not exercising or working hard? Would you say: often, sometimes, or never?	3.4	1684
19.[a,b] Have you ever been bothered by your heart beating hard? Would you say: often, sometimes, or never?	3.0	1686
20.[b,c] Have you ever been bothered by "cold sweats"? Would you say: often, sometimes, or never?	2.2	1674
21.[b] Have you ever had any fainting spells? Would you say: never, a few times, or more than a few times?	1.8	1666
22.[a,b,c] Do your hands ever tremble enough to bother you? Would you say: often, sometimes, or never?	1.6	1684

[a] Nationwide study (Gurin, Veroff, & Feld, 1960).

[b] Psychosomatic scale item from Army Neuropsychiatric Screening Adjunct (Star, 1950a) or close approximation to such item.

[c] Stirling County Study (D. C. Leighton et al., 1963) item or close approximation to such item.

indicating the absence of a symptom, or 1, indicating its presence. On most items, the response scored 1 is either "yes," where "yes" and "no" are alternative responses, or "often" where "often," "sometimes," and "never" are possible responses. Table 6-3 gives the per cent of symptomatic responses to each item in the entire sample of 1710 respondents.

Langner, one of the Midtown researchers, described a score of 4 or more symptomatic responses on these 22 items as useful ". . . since it identifies only one per cent of the psychiatically evaluated Wells, but . . . almost three quarters of the entire Impaired group" (1962, p. 275).

Table 6-4. Midtown 22-Item Symptom Score According to Family Income

(Values in per cent)

Symptom Score	Income Group			
	Less than $3000	$3000–$4999	$5000–$7499	$7500 and over
4 or more	27.0	26.1	17.3	19.5
Number of respondents	163	284	405	307

Note: χ^2 = 11.40; df = 3; p < .01.

On this basis, we used a score of 4 as the cutting point for identifying cases of probable psychological disorder.

The Midtown Study, like the great majority of other studies included in Table 2-5 in Chapter 2, found an inverse relation between social class and psychological disorder. This finding was based on the study psychiatrists' assessments of respondents' interview protocols; as we mentioned, these assessments were closely approximated by the 22-item scores. Therefore, our confidence that this score is measuring the same thing in the population we sampled as it did in the Midtown Study sample would be increased by finding an inverse relation between the score and social class in our sample. As Table 6-4 shows, there is an inverse relationship in our sample between these symptoms and family income. Table 6-5 indicates that the relationship is even stronger with educational level. Thus it appears reasonable to interpret the 22-item score as measuring much the same thing that the Midtown psychiatric evaluations measured.

Although the Midtown researchers reported that they attempted to in-

Table 6-5. Midtown 22-Item Symptom Score According to Educational Level

(Values in per cent)

Symptom Score	Years of Education			
	0–7	8–11	12–15	16 or more
4 or more	33.3	24.8	17.4	9.6
Number of respondents	147	427	552	115

Note: χ^2 = 30.51; df = 3; p < .001.

clude a sample of ". . . such symptoms as would demonstrably represent the most salient and *generalized* indicators of mental pathology" (Srole et al., 1962, p. 41) they also suggested that the full battery of items on which their psychiatric evaluation was based, and perhaps especially the derivative 22-item screening instrument, tended to miss certain types of disorder, such as alcoholism, sociopathic traits, and the early stages of paranoid schizophrenia (*ibid.*, pp. 65, 269). These possible omissions are particularly important for our purposes since, among the gross subtypes of disorder that we investigated in our review of epidemiological studies, the two for which we consistently found the highest rates in the lowest social class were schizophrenia and personality disorder, the latter subsuming alcoholism and sociopathic traits. For these types of disorders, therefore, the issue of social selection versus social causation is salient.

For the purpose of investigating this issue, in addition to the 22 Midtown items, items designed to provide clues to paranoid tendencies, sociopathic traits, and alcoholism were included in the second study in Washington Heights of a subsample of 151 Jewish, Irish, Negro, and Puerto Rican respondents. The additional items are shown in Table 6-6.

The items on paranoid tendencies and sociopathic traits were selected, on the basis of their face validity, from the Minnesota Multiphasic Personality Inventory. For each item, alternative wordings were constructed, with one choice keyed "true" and the other "false." The decision on which wording to use in the actual questionnaire was made on a random basis, so that each item had an equal chance of being keyed "true" or "false." The two items on alcoholism were suggested by Margaret Bailey and Paul Haberman, then of the National Council on Alcoholism.

The six items related to paranoid tendencies are listed in Table 6-6 in order from most to least likely to elicit the symptomatic response. The responses fall short of meeting the criteria for a Guttman scale, since Guttman's coefficient of reproducibility for the six items is .884, Menzel's coefficient of scalability is .418, and neither was brought to an acceptable level by dropping an item. For purposes of comparability with the Guttman scale of sociopathic traits described below, these paranoid items were nevertheless scored as if they formed a Guttman scale.

Responses to all but the first of the six items on sociopathic traits shown in Table 6-6 conform to the Guttman scale pattern, thus providing a cumulative scale score from 0 to 5. Guttman's coefficient of reproducibility for the five items that scaled is .905; Menzel's coefficient of scalability is .606. It is interesting to speculate about why the item on "lying to get ahead" did not scale. Possibly this item involves achievement orientation and hence focuses to a greater extent than the other five on a form of middle-class sociopathy. Some evidence that this is the case is provided

Table 6-6. Items Used as Possible Indicators of Paranoid Tendencies, Sociopathic Traits, and Alcoholism
(Subsample n = 151)

Type of Item	Item	Response Indicating Presence of Symptom	Per Cent of Symptomatic Responses	Base for Per Cent
Paranoid	I do not tend to be on my guard with people who are somewhat more friendly than I had expected.	False	31.9	144
	My way of doing things is apt to be misunderstood by others.	True	30.8	146
	Behind my back people say all kinds of things about me.	True	21.5	144
	I have no enemies who really wish to harm me.	False	15.3	144
	I feel it is safer to trust no-body.	True	13.0	146
	I do not believe I am being plotted against.	False	12.9	147
Sociopathic	I think most people would not lie to get ahead.	False	54.1	146
	It is all right to get around the law if you don't actually break it.	True	50.3	147
	I don't blame anyone for trying to grab everything he can get in this world.	True	42.1	145
	I think most people are honest more for other reasons than for fear of being caught.	False	21.2	146
	Most respectable people in my neighborhood would not object to the kind of people I've gone around with.	False	15.2	145
	I can easily make people afraid of me and sometimes do just for the fun of it.	True	6.8	147
Alcoholism	I have not had trouble with my health or my work because of drinking.	False	12.2	148
	I have had arguments with my family because of my drinking.	True	9.0	145

by the fact that, unlike the sociopathy scale as a whole, subscription to this item tends to vary positively with educational level, as fully 60 per cent of the college graduates believe that most people would lie to get ahead, by contrast with only 44 per cent of those with less than 8 years of formal education and about 54 per cent of the remaining respondents.

Group Differences in Symptom Scores

Let us see now what results these indicators of possible psychological disorder provided with respect to the crucial question about rates among Negroes and Puerto Ricans in contrast to their class counterparts in more advantaged ethnic groups. Recall that the social causation explanation of class differences led to the prediction of higher rates for *both* Negroes and Puerto Ricans. By contrast, the social selection hypothesis led to the prediction of lower rates for *both* Negroes and Puerto Ricans.

The results of comparisons among ethnic groups are shown for income in Table 6-7 and for education in Table 6-8. No attempt was made to combine income and education into a composite index of social class because of the fact, shown in Table 6-2, that education has different implications for income according to ethnicity.

Consider first the results for Puerto Ricans in comparison with their class counterparts in more advantaged ethnic groups. Table 6-7 shows that, using income as the index of class, the Puerto Ricans have larger proportions with four or more symptoms on the 22-item indicator of general psychological disorder, and Table 6-8 indicates that the results are much the same if education level is used as the index of class. Therefore the results of comparisons between Puerto Ricans and their class counterparts in the more advantaged groups support a social causation explanation of class differences in rates of psychological disorder. Yet, when we look at the Negroes in relation to the more advantaged ethnic groups, it is clear that they do not show higher rates of symptoms. Table 6-7 and 6-8 show that there is even a tendency for the Negroes, in sharp and unexpected contrast with the Puerto Ricans, to display lower rates of symptoms than their class counterparts in more advantaged ethnic groups. Thus the results for Negroes on the 22 Midtown items, unlike those for Puerto Ricans, appear more consistent with a social selection explanation of class differences in rates of disorder. Perhaps the picture will be more consistent for paranoid tendencies, sociopathic traits, and alcohol problems, three types of symptoms that the Midtown items may miss.

To investigate these latter symptoms, it is necessary to rely on our small subsample of about 150 Jewish, Irish, Negro, and Puerto Rican

Table 6-7. Per Cents with Four or More Symptoms on the Midtown 22 Items According to Family Income and Ethnicity

(Figures in parentheses indicate bases for per cents)

Yearly Family Income	Ethnicity					Statistical Test					
						Puerto Ricans vs. Jews, Irish, and Other Combined (excluding Negroes)			Negroes vs. Jews, Irish and Other Combined (excluding Puerto Ricans)		
	Puerto Rican	Negro	Jewish	Irish	Other	x^2	df	p	x^2	df	p
Less than $3000	36.4 (22)	26.3 (76)	10.5 (19)	26.7 (15)	32.3 (31)	1.14	1	<.30	0.05	1	<.50
$3000–$4999	37.3 (51)	14.5 (76)	29.2 (48)	21.2 (33)	30.3 (76)	1.55	1	<.30	−5.22	1	<.05
$5000–$7499	31.0 (42)	15.7 (83)	18.6 (97)	12.3 (73)	15.5 (110)	5.82	1	<.02	0.00	1	>.50
$7500 and more	41.2 (17)	21.4 (56)	15.6 (96)	11.4 (44)	22.6 (93)	5.69	1	<.02	0.37	1	>.50
Sum of directed x^2's						14.20	4	<.01	−4.80	4	<.50

Note: Negative x^2 indicates that disadvantaged group has fewer symptoms than advantaged groups.

Table 6-8. Per Cents with Four or More Symptoms on the Midtown 22 Items According to Ethnicity and Educational Level

(Figures in parentheses indicate bases for per cents)

Years of Education	Ethnicity					Statistical Test					
	Puerto Rican	Negro	Jewish	Irish	Other	Puerto Ricans vs. Jews, Irish and Other Combined (excluding Negroes)			Negroes vs. Jews, Irish and Other Combined (excluding Puerto Ricans)		
						χ^2	df	p	χ^2	df	p
0–7	34.1 (41)	25.0 (52)	(2)	33.3 (12)	45.7 (35)	−0.43	1	>.50	−2.97	1	<.10
8–11	43.1 (58)	19.1 (115)	21.1 (57)	17.9 (67)	27.1 (129)	9.37	1	<.01	−0.88	1	<.50
12–15	27.8 (36)	19.3 (140)	18.4 (174)	8.9 (79)	16.3 (123)	3.44	1	<.10	0.95	1	<.50
16 or more	(1) (3)	0.0 (20)	10.0 (40)	18.2 (11)	10.0 (40)	Too few Puerto Ricans			−2.42	1	<.20
	Sum of directed χ^2's					12.38	3	<.01	−5.32	4	<.30

Note: Negative χ^2 indicates that disadvantaged group has fewer symptoms than advantaged groups.

respondents, since only these individuals were asked the relevant items. This small subsample limits our ability to control indicators of social class since, as Table 6-9 shows, the Jews comprise almost all the college graduates, whereas those with 7 or fewer years of education are almost wholly concentrated among the Negroes and Puerto Ricans. With so small a sample, therefore, we cannot compare ethnic groups at the extremes of high and low educational level.

That this limitation creates a problem is evident when we look at the relationship of educational level to our index of possible paranoid tendency. As can be seen in Table 6-10, this index shows an inverse relation to educational level. Moreover, as shown in Table 6-11, our scale of possible sociopathic tendency is also inversely related to education. Our procedure, therefore, will be to present tables that examine ethnicity and educational level simultaneously, with categories of education limited to those in which all ethnic groups are represented: 8 to 11 years and 12 to 15 years.

The evidence of possible paranoid tendencies appears strongest, as Table 6-12 shows, among the less educated Negroes and Puerto Ricans. Moreover, among the better educated respondents, Negroes and Puerto Ricans also tend to have higher scores than the Jews and the Irish. Thus we have here results which, on the surface, appear more consistent with a social causation than with a social selection explanation.

Table 6-13 shows that the indications of possible sociopathic tendencies are also most pronounced among Negroes and Puerto Ricans of less education. And again there is a tendency for the Negroes and Puerto Ricans at higher educational levels to have higher scores than their educational

Table 6-9. Educational Level According to Ethnicity of
Subsample Respondents

(Values in per cent)

	Ethnicity			
Years of Education	Jewish	Irish	Negro	Puerto Rican
0–7	. . .	3.3	19.4	31.6
8–11	19.1	50.0	32.3	34.2
12–15	53.2	46.7	45.2	31.6
16 or more	27.7	. . .	3.2	2.6
Total per cent	100.0	100.0	100.1	100.0
Number of respondents	47	30	31	38

Table 6-10. Possible Indications of Paranoid Tendencies According to
Educational Level

(Values in per cent)

Number of "Paranoid" Responses (0–6)	Years of Education			
	0–7	8–11	12–15	16 or more
0	0.0	29.8	40.0	73.3
1	36.8	31.9	23.1	13.3
2	36.8	19.2	20.0	13.3
3	15.8	12.8	15.4	0.0
4	10.5	6.4	1.5	0.0
5	0.0	0.0	0.0	0.0
6	0.0	0.0	0.0	0.0
Total per cent	99.9	100.0	100.0	99.9
Number of respondents	19	47	65	15

Note: With paranoid scores 3 through 6 collapsed, $\chi^2 = 22.72$; df = 9; $p < .01$.

peers among the Jews and the Irish. These results, then, taken at their face value, also tend to support the social causation hypothesis.

Table 6-14 shows that, at higher educational levels, Negroes and Puerto Ricans were more likely than Jews and Irish to report drinking problems.

Table 6-11. Possible Indications of Sociopathy According to
Educational Level

(Values in per cent)

Number of "Socio-pathic" Responses (0–5)	Years of Education			
	0–7	8–11	12–15	16 or more
0	0.0	12.8	33.8	26.7
1	47.4	34.0	32.3	26.7
2	36.8	29.8	27.7	40.0
3	15.8	19.2	6.2	6.7
4	0.0	4.2	0.0	0.0
5	0.0	0.0	0.0	0.0
Total per cent	100.0	100.0	100.0	100.1
Number of respondents	19	47	65	15

Note: With sociopathy scores of 3 or more collapsed, $\chi^2 = 19.30$; df = 9; $p < .05$.

Table 6-12. Possible Indications of Paranoid Tendencies According to Ethnicity and Education
(Values in per cent)

Number of "Paranoid" Responses (0-6)	Years of Education							
	8-11[a]				12-15[b]			
	Jewish	Irish	Negro	Puerto Rican	Jewish	Irish	Negro	Puerto Rican
0	22.2	53.3	20.0	15.4	40.0	35.7	42.9	41.7
1	55.6	20.0	10.0	46.2	24.0	35.7	21.4	8.3
2	22.2	13.3	20.0	23.1	20.0	21.4	14.3	25.0
3	0.0	0.0	40.0	15.4	16.0	7.1	21.4	16.7
4	0.0	13.3	10.0	0.0	0.0	0.0	0.0	8.3
5-6	0.0	0.0	0.0	0.0	0.0	0.0	0.0	0.0
Total per cent	100.0	99.9	100.0	100.1	100.0	99.9	100.0	100.0
Number of respondents	9	15	10	13	25	14	14	12

[a] For Jews and Irish versus Negroes and Puerto Ricans with paranoid scores of 2 or more collapsed in order to avoid expected cell frequencies of less than 5, $\chi^2 = 4.69$; df $= 2$; $p < .10$.

[b] For Jews and Irish versus Negroes and Puerto Ricans with paranoid scores of 2 or more collapsed in order to avoid expected cell frequencies of less than 5, $\chi^2 = 1.50$; df $= 2$; $p < .50$.

Table 6-13. Possible Indications of Sociopathy According to Ethnicity and Education
(Values in per cent)

Number "Sociopathic" Responses (0-5)	Years of Education							
	8-11[a]				12-15[b]			
	Jewish	Irish	Negro	Puerto Rican	Jewish	Irish	Negro	Puerto Rican
0	0.0	26.7	0.0	15.4	36.0	42.9	35.7	25.0
1	33.3	46.7	10.0	38.5	28.0	50.0	14.3	33.3
2	44.4	26.7	40.0	15.4	32.0	0.0	42.9	33.3
3	22.2	0.0	40.0	23.1	4.0	7.1	7.1	8.3
4	0.0	0.0	10.0	7.7	0.0	0.0	0.0	0.0
5	0.0	0.0	0.0	0.0	0.0	0.0	0.0	0.0
Total per cent	99.9	100.1	100.0	100.1	100.0	100.0	100.0	99.9
Number of respondents	9	15	10	13	25	14	14	12

[a] For Jews and Irish versus Negroes and Puerto Ricans with sociopathic scores of 0 and 1, and 3 or more, collapsed in order to avoid expected cell frequencies of less than 5, $\chi^2 = 6.37$; df = 2; $p < .05$.

[b] For Jews and Irish versus Negroes and Puerto Ricans with sociopathic scores of 2 or more collapsed in order to avoid expected cell frequencies of less than 5, $\chi^2 = 3.03$; df = 2; $p < .30$.

Table 6-14. Possible Indications of Alcoholism According to Ethnicity and Education
(Values in per cent)

Problem with Drinking	Not High School Graduate[a]				High School Graduate or More[b]			
	Jewish	Irish	Negro	Puerto Rican	Jewish	Irish	Negro	Puerto Rican
Both:								
(a) Trouble with health and work								
(b) Arguments with family	0.0	0.0	0.0	8.0	0.0	0.0	0.0	7.7
Either (a) or (b)	11.1	18.8	18.8	20.0	5.3	14.3	26.7	38.5
Neither (a) nor (b)	88.9	81.2	81.2	72.0	94.7	85.7	73.3	53.8
Total per cent	100.0	100.0	100.0	100.0	100.0	100.0	100.0	100.0
Number of respondents	9	16	16	25	38	14	15	13

[a] For Jewish and Irish versus Negro and Puerto Rican, with "both" and "either" drinking problem collapsed: $\chi^2 = 0.65$; df $= 1$; $p < .50$.
[b] For Jewish and Irish versus Negro and Puerto Rican, with "both" and "either" drinking problem collapsed: $\chi^2 = 9.90$; df $= 1$; $p < .01$.

But the similarity of the proportions reporting these problems among the advantaged and the disadvantaged ethnic groups at lower educational levels, and the tendency of less educated Negroes and Puerto Ricans to report fewer drinking problems than their better educated ethnic counterparts, are puzzling from either the social causation or the social selection point of view.

SUBSTANTIVE PROBLEMS IN INTERPRETING THE SYMPTOM SCORES

Despite some differences between the ethnic groups which seem to support the social causation explanation of high rates of disorder in the lowest social class, it hardly seems, given the number of inconsistencies in the findings, that we can draw a firm conclusion about the etiological issue. The results with the Midtown Study's 22-item indicator of general psychological disorder seem especially difficult to explain in either social selection or social causation terms. Although it is possible, for example, that Puerto Ricans are constitutionally more predisposed to psychological disorder than Negroes, this explanation is not plausible. Nor is it plausible to think that the social pressure on Puerto Ricans in New York City is greater than that on Negroes. If anything, the opposite seems more likely because, in contrast to skin color, language and other learned aspects of culture can be changed. Thus Puerto Ricans have ways of escaping social pressure not open to Negroes. The problem becomes, then, to see whether there is some other way that we can account for the differences in the results for Negroes and Puerto Ricans.

METHODOLOGICAL PROBLEMS IN INTERPRETING THE SYMPTOM SCORES

In view of our results, two related questions can be formulated: Are Negroes spuriously low or are Puerto Ricans spuriously high on the 22-item Midtown measure of psychological disorder? Why are Puerto Rican and Negro results more similar on other measures than they are on the 22-item measure of disorder? Let us see how these questions are answered in terms of factors such as interviewer effects, acquiescence, social desirability of responses, and subcultural differences in symptoms used to express psychological distress, any of which may distort interview responses.

The Problem of Interviewer Effects

We referred earlier to Hyman's and Williams' reports that Negroes in the South responded differently to white and to Negro interviewers. Since two thirds of the Negroes in our Washington Heights study were born in the South, and almost all of the interviewers in our first study were white, it is possible that the Negro respondents were presenting a facade that concealed their true psychiatric condition. Evidence to support this supposition was provided by a separate analysis of interviewer-biasing effects on the 22 items, which indicated that in answering certain white interviewers Negro respondents did tend to underreport symptoms (B. S. Dohrenwend, Colombotos, & B. P. Dohrenwend, 1968). In an attempt to eliminate this distortion of responses, a probability subsample of 30 Negro respondents was reinterviewed on the 22 symptom items by a staff of 6 Negro interviewers in the second Washington Heights study described above. However, we found little difference in either the average number of symptoms reported, 2.07 the second time versus 2.40 on the first survey, or in the proportion showing four symptoms or more, 20 per cent both times. If therefore the Negroes in our Washington Heights studies were presenting a facade, it was not simply a response to the interviewers' race. The facade may, however, have been differently motivated. An indirect clue to the possible motivation is provided by some results of research reported by Manis, Brawer, Hunt, and Kercher (1963).

These researchers attempted to cross-validate the 22 Midtown items, using samples from patient and nonpatient populations. Finding that a group of predischarge ward patients had an average symptom score lower than the scores of two nonpatient groups consisting of college students and a cross section of a community, Manis and his colleagues argued that the result indicated a failure of the test, since "there is little or no reason to believe that the mental health of these predischarge patients is equal to or better than the nonhospitalized populations" (p. 111). It seems likely, however, that the predischarge ward patients, in the interest of "getting out," were less willing than the nonpatients to admit to having symptoms.

Note that the epidemiological studies shown in Table 2-4 of Chapter 2 were all done before the 1954 Supreme Court decision on school desegregation. At that time, the studies done in the North tended to show high rates of disorder for Negroes relative to whites. Is it possible that in the early 1960's, when our studies were conducted in Washington Heights, Negroes who originally came to New York to improve their lot also felt on the verge of "getting out" as movements for Negro civil rights and increased educational and occupational opportunity appeared to be gathering momentum? Like the predischarge ward patients, might these Negroes not have shown conscious or unconscious resistance to admitting characteristics they judged to be undesirable? Such an interpretation would be consistent with findings from recent studies that northern Negroes tend more than whites to underreport hospitalization for a variety of illnesses (U.S. National Health Survey, 1961, p. 10; U.S. National

Health Survey, 1963, p. 20) and are likely to state somewhat higher educational and occupational aspirations for their children than whites (e.g., Bloom, Whiteman, & Deutsch, 1965). Whether this interpretation is correct, and if so to what extent, is, however, uncertain. As our further results will show, it probably implies less chaos and more order in aspirations and attitudes than exist for northern Negroes under current conditions.

The Problem of Acquiescent Response Style

It was shown above that both Negroes and Puerto Ricans, in contrast to their scores on the 22-item Midtown measure, tended to score high relative to their class counterparts in the other ethnic groups on our measures of possible sociopathic and paranoid tendencies. This seemed to be especially true of the less educated Negroes and Puerto Ricans and appeared to support the social causation alternative.

Again, however, questions must be raised about accepting these group differences at face value. Recall that the possibly paranoid items did not scale and that on a random basis three of the six items were keyed "true" and the other three "false." It is necessary to inquire whether tendencies to yeasay or naysay, regardless of item content, may have constituted a competing dimension that both generated scale errors and distorted the substantive results (e.g., Couch & Keniston, 1960).

To investigate this problem of acquiescent response style, separate scores ranging from 0 to 3 were constructed for the "true"- and the "false"-keyed paranoid items, respectively. To the extent that respondents answered in terms of item content we would expect a positive correlation between the two indices, and to the extent that yeasaying or naysaying occurred, a negative correlation.

As Table 6-15 shows, we found a positive correlation of .33 for the

Table 6-15. Correlations between Possible Paranoid Items Keyed "True" and Items Keyed "False" According to Ethnicity and Education (Spearman rank-order correlation coefficients corrected for ties)

Ethnicity	Not High School Graduate	High School Graduate or More
Jewish	− .10	.42
Irish	.41	.22
Negro	− .32	.42
Puerto Rican	− .02	.39
All ethnic groups	− .03	.33

better educated respondents, but a zero-order correlation for the less educated respondents as a whole. And for the less educated Negro group, there is indeed a pronounced negative correlation, indicating the presence of an acquiescent response set.

Table 6-16 shows that we would have to make different interpretations from the results for the paranoid items depending on whether the index used was made up of the "false"-keyed or the "true"-keyed items, largely because the responses of the less educated Negroes depended to such a marked extent on how the items were keyed. For these respondents there appears to be a tendency toward yeasaying that we cannot afford to ignore.

At the same time, acquiescent response style appears to have played little or no part in the results obtained with the sociopathy scale. Since three of the items on this scale are keyed "true" and two are keyed "false," only roughly comparable indices can be constructed for still further checking. Nevertheless, the direction of relationships seems similar for an index built of the three "true"-keyed items versus one built of the two "false"-keyed items according to ethnicity and education.

Moreover, a check on the distribution of scale errors in the sociopathy scale according to ethnicity and educational level indicates that such error was not due in any important way to yeasaying or naysaying in specific ethno-educational groups. There is a tendency, not statistically significant, for the less educated Puerto Ricans to have fewer respondents who are scale types than the other poorly educated respondents. With this possible exception, error is not appreciably more frequent in any one of the eight ethno-educational groups than in any others. Overall, 62 per cent of the respondents were scale types; the range is from 44 per cent among the lower educated Puerto Ricans to 69 per cent among the lower-educated Negroes. The fact that these five items scaled thus appears to mean that yeasaying or naysaying response styles were not dominant in their case.

Given findings which suggest that for some, though probably not all, types of psychological symptoms a yeasaying tendency among less educated Negroes may lead to inaccurate measurement, can we conclude that control of this acquiescent response bias would result in adequate measures of psychological disorder? Additional considerations make it seem doubtful.

The Problem of Social Undesirability of Symptomatic Responses

If a tendency on the part of less educated Negroes to agree to items regardless of their content is the whole explanation of their higher scores on our measure of possible paranoid tendency, why did such a response style not produce similar high scores on the 22 Midtown items? For 11

Table 6-16. Comparisons of "True"- and "False"-Keyed Indices of Possible Paranoid Tendencies According to Ethnicity and Education

(Values in per cent)

Number of "True"- vs. "False"-Keyed "Paranoid" Responses	Not High School Graduate				High School Graduate or More			
	Jewish	Irish	Negro	Puerto Rican	Jewish	Irish	Negro	Puerto Rican
"True"-Keyed (0-3)								
0	55.6	68.8	25.0	44.0	52.6	71.4	60.0	61.5
1	44.4	25.0	31.3	32.0	36.8	14.3	26.7	30.8
2	0.0	6.3	18.8	24.0	10.5	14.3	13.3	7.7
3	0.0	0.0	25.0	0.0	0.0	0.0	0.0	0.0
Total per cent	100.0	100.1	100.1	100.0	99.9	100.0	100.0	100.0
Total respondents	9	16	16	25	38	14	15	13
"False"-Keyed (0-3)								
0	44.4	62.5	56.3	32.0	76.3	42.9	60.0	53.8
1	55.6	18.8	31.3	44.0	15.8	57.1	33.3	23.1
2	0.0	12.5	12.5	20.0	7.9	0.0	0.0	7.7
3	0.0	6.3	0.0	4.0	0.0	0.0	6.7	15.4
Total per cent	100.0	100.0	100.1	100.0	100.0	100.0	100.0	100.0
Total respondents	9	16	16	25	38	14	15	13

of these 22 items, a "yes" response was scored as indicating pathology. The response alternatives for most of the others were "often," "sometimes," or "never" and might also be influenced by yeasaying or naysaying tendencies. Yet, as Table 6-8 showed, less educated Negroes did not score high on this index, on which it is the Puerto Ricans at all class levels whose scores are high compared to those of the other groups. Again, however, we think that there are methodological problems, this time affecting the interpretation of these high scores by Puerto Rican respondents.

The entire Midtown sample reported an average of 2.8 of the 22 symptoms, and a score of 4 or more was found to identify the large majority of those judged impaired in the Midtown Study (Langner, 1962). When Langner (1965) administered the 22 items in questionnaire interviews to a sample of 297 Mexican-born residents of Mexico City, he found their mean score to be 5.4 symptoms. Is the *average resident* of Mexico City, then, a psychiatric case in the sense of the Midtown Study evaluations? Or is it possible that the difference between the respondents in Mexico City and those in Midtown stems from a difference in normative orientation toward these symptoms? Were Puerto Ricans in Washington Heights, with language and some other aspects of culture in common with Mexicans, showing similar differences, not in amount of disorder, but rather in culturally patterned mode of expressing distress or culturally patterned willingness to express distress?

Social Desirability Ratings of the 22 Midtown Symptom Items. Consider the actual Midtown items, which are shown in Table 6-3. As might be expected, people generally see the characteristics described by these items as socially undesirable. To check that this view was held by members of the ethnic groups we were studying, judgments of social desirability of the items were obtained from a subsample of 27 Jewish, Irish, Negro, and Puerto Rican respondents in Washington Heights; from a special supplementary sample of Negro males with fourth-grade education or below and, if they were married, from their wives, 22 respondents in all; and from 19 Puerto Rican residents of a tenement in a section of the Bronx adjacent to Washington Heights.* Altogether, it is possible to compare ratings made by 18 Jewish and Irish respondents with a mean education of 11.2 years, ratings by 26 Negroes with a mean education of 6.6 years, and ratings by 24 Puerto Ricans with a mean education of 8.7 years. All ratings were self-administered after the instructions developed by Edwards (1957, p. 4) were explained by interviewers who were Negro, Puerto Rican, or white non-Puerto Rican according to the

---

* We are indebted to Mrs. Aida Rosa, who worked as both a secretary and an interviewer on the study, for securing the last group of ratings.

ethnicity of the judges. Ratings were made on a scale with 1 representing extremely undesirable, 5 representing the neutral point, and 9 representing extremely desirable. Scale values were obtained by the method of equal appearing intervals, a procedure commonly employed by Edwards (1957) in his work on the social desirability variable.

As a point of contrast with the ratings by community respondents, social desirability ratings of the same items were also secured from 25 psychiatrists. All of these were students in classes conducted in the Division of Community and Social Psychiatry at Columbia University and at the William Alanson White Institute.

Table 6-17 contains the scale values secured from each group of raters

Table 6-17. Mean Social Desirability Ratings of 22 Midtown Symptom Items by Community Respondents and by Psychiatrists
(Single underline indicates lowest rating; double underline indicates highest rating for each item)

	Respondent Group				
Symptom Item	Psy-chia-trists	Jew-ish Irish		Negro	Puerto Rican
To often be bothered by one's heart beating hard	2.5	2.9	=	2.9	3.9
To often be bothered by shortness of breath when *not* exercising or working hard	2.2	2.9	>	2.8	3.9
To often be bothered by nervousness, that is, by being irritable, fidgety, or tense	2.4	3.4	>	3.2	4.0
To often have trouble in getting to sleep or staying asleep	2.5	3.7	>	3.4	4.3
To often be bothered by "cold sweats"	2.5	3.1	<	3.2	3.8
To often have one's hands tremble enough to be bothered by it	2.5	3.1	>	2.6	3.6
To often be troubled with headaches or pains in the head	2.4	3.2	>	2.3	3.7
To have had fainting spells more than a few times	2.1	2.9	>	2.3	3.4
To have a poor appetite	3.3	3.4	<	3.6	4.4
To be in low spirits most of the time	2.2	3.1	<	3.2	3.6
To feel weak all over much of the time	2.3	2.6	<	2.8	2.5

Table 6-17. (Continued)

Symptom Item	Respondent Group			
	Psychiatrists	Jewish Irish	Negro	Puerto Rican
To have had periods of days, weeks or months when one couldn't take care of things because of being unable to "get going"	1.7	2.1 <	2.6	2.7
To suddenly feel hot all over every so often	3.0	3.1 >	3.0	3.4
To have periods of such great restlessness that one cannot sit long in a chair	2.2	3.3 <	3.7	3.7
To be bothered by acid or sour stomach several times a week	2.6	3.2 >	2.9	2.9
To have one's memory not seem all right	1.9	2.4 <	2.7	2.5
To seem to have a fullness or clogging in one's head or nose much of the time	2.8	3.2 >	3.0	2.8
To have personal worries that get one down physically, that is, make a person physically ill	2.0	2.0 =	2.0	2.2
To have nothing ever turn out the way one wants it to	1.8	2.8 >	2.7	3.4
To sometimes wonder whether anything is worthwhile any more	2.1	2.5 <	2.7	5.4
To feel somewhat apart or alone even among friends	2.1	2.8 <	3.0	4.1
To be the worrying type—a worrier	2.7	3.0 =	3.0	3.3

Note: One-tailed Sign tests: Psychiatrists vs. community respondents, $N = 22$; $m = 0$; $p < .001$. Puerto Ricans vs. Jewish and Irish, $N = 22$; $m = 3$; $p < .002$. Negroes vs. Jewish and Irish, $N = 19$; $m = 9$; $p = .26$.

for the 22 symptom items of the Midtown Study screening instrument. It is not surprising to find that only one item placed as high as the neutral point, 5 on the scale, for any of these groups. However, less expected is the finding that, within this apparent agreement that the symptoms are undesirable, there is *consistent* disagreement about how undesirable they are.

As the underlined figures in Table 6-17 show, the psychiatrists' scale value is lower than that of any community group on all but four items. On one of these four the scale value obtained from Negro respondents is lower; on the other three, one or more community groups produced the same low scale value as the psychiatrists.

At the opposite extreme from the very undesirable judgments of the psychiatrists are the Puerto Ricans' judgments, which were less undesirable than those of any other group on 18 of the 22 items. Finally, although the differences between the Negro judges on the one hand, and the combined Jewish and Irish judges on the other, is slight, the tendency was for the Negroes to give slightly more undesirable ratings, exceeding the Jews and Irish on 10 of the 22 items and tying them on 3 more.

The Negroes, by contrast with the Puerto Ricans, then, are close in their judgments of social desirability to the norms of the more assimilated Jewish and Irish groups and to the psychiatrists' professional judgments. With a sensitivity to such norms developd under long-standing conditions of oppression and heightened, perhaps, at this time of increased striving toward greater equality within the value framework of the wider society (cf. Pettigrew, 1964, pp. 27–34), the Negroes may be more likely than the Jews or the Irish to deny symptoms they judge socially undesirable. If so, their actual rate of disorder may be much higher than the symptom measure suggests.

The Puerto Ricans, in turn, regard the characteristics described in the 22-item measure as less undesirable than do members of the other ethnic groups. It seems possible that they would also be more willing than the other groups, therefore, to admit such characteristics. If so, they may actually have a much lower rate of disorder than their rate of reported symptoms would suggest. On the other hand, the reason why Puerto Ricans see these symtpoms as less undesirable may be that they are actually more common among this ethnic group. If this is so, then higher rates of reported symptoms among Puerto Ricans and their lower tendency to see these symptoms as strongly undesirable may both indicate the same thing: higher actual rates of disorder (cf. Heilbrun, 1964).

Frequencies of 22 Midtown Items among Patients from DifferenEthnic Groups. Whether the higher rates of reported symptoms among Puerto Ricans indicate higher actual rates of disorder can be tested indirectly by comparing groups of Jewish, Irish, Negro, and Puerto Rican patients. Since all are independently defined as ill by their patient status, their levels of symptoms should not differ. To this end, we asked psychiatrists at three outpatient services in or adjacent to Washington Heights to select patients for us to study. In order to ensure rough comparability in the distribution of different types of disorder in each ethnic group, we used a quota system to secure patients of 6 different behavior types.

Psychiatrists at each service were asked to sort their current patients in terms of the descriptions of behavior most and least like the patients. In this way, we hoped to avoid problems of unreliability in diagnosis while still ensuring a diversity of patient types (e.g., Scott, 1958; Zubin, 1967). These "behavior types" are shortened adaptations of case descriptions of fictitious individuals developed by Shirley Star (1955) with psychiatric consultation for her study of public attitudes toward mental illness. As originally set forth, they were meant to illustrate paranoid schizophrenia, simple schizophrenia, anxiety neurosis, alcoholism, compulsive phobic behavior, and juvenile character disorder. The original descriptions have been used in a number of attitude studies since (see Chapter 10).

Table 6-18 shows the mean number of symptoms on the 22-item Midtown measure related to each behavior type among the 114 patients obtained for this study. The uneven n's in the various ethnic groups and among the different behavior types are due to scarcity of some of the desired types of patient at the facilities to which we had access. Nevertheless, our quota system provided a roughly similar distribution of 5 of the 6 behavior types in each of the 4 ethnic groups. Thus, if similar degrees and types of disorder are expressed in similar ways by all ethnic groups, we should find no ethnic differences among these patients in rates of symptoms. Table 6-18 shows, however, that, as in our nonpatient cross sections in Washington Heights, there was among the patients a generally higher rate of symptoms for the Puerto Ricans.

It would seem, then, that we must question high rates of such symptoms per se as indicators of high rates of psychological disorder in the Puerto Rican nonpatient cross sections. This would be true regardless of whether the high rates were due to greater willingness among the Puerto Ricans to admit such symptoms when they are present, or to Puerto Ricans' developing a greater number of symptoms to express a given degree of underlying disorder (cf. Kadushin, 1964). There is further evidence to suggest not only that one or both of these factors may be operating, but also that they selectively interact with the types of symptoms used by individuals in different groups to express distress.

Social Desirability Ratings of Paranoid, Sociopathic, and Drinking Items. The respondents who judged the social desirability of the 22 Midtown items also rated the items on alcoholism and on sociopathic and paranoid tendencies. Like the Midtown items, these items generally fell on the undesirable side of the scale. As Table 6-19 shows, the psychiatrists again tended to see the symptoms as more undesirable than the community groups. Among the ethnic groups in the community, however, the picture is changed somewhat from what it was for the 22 Midtown items. The Negroes tended to see the symptoms as less undesirable

Table 6-18. Mean Number of Symptoms on the 22-Item Screening Instrument among Jewish, Irish, Negro, and Puerto Rican Psychiatric Out-Patients According to Behavior Type
(Figures in parentheses indicate number of patients)

Behavior Type	Mean Number of Symptoms				
	Jewish	Irish	Negro	Puerto Rican	All Groups
One person is very suspicious; doesn't trust anybody; and is sure that everybody is against this person.	11.0 (3)	8.0 (3)	9.8 (8)	14.0 (3)	10.4 (17)
A second person is very quiet; doesn't talk much to anyone; acts afraid of people; stays alone and daydreams all the time; and shows no interest in anything or anybody.	6.7 (3)	5.7 (3)	10.1 (8)	14.3 (3)	9.5 (17)
A third person worries a lot about little things, seems to be moody and unhappy all the time; and can't sleep nights, brooding about the past, and worrying about things that *might* go wrong.	7.9 (10)	5.4 (7)	8.4 (12)	11.9 (10)	8.6 (39)
A fourth person drinks too much; goes on a spree when there is money in the pocket. This person promises to stop drinking, but always goes off again.	3.0 (1)	6.3 (3)	5.2 (8)	5.0 (1)	5.3 (13)
A fifth person just can't leave the house without going back to see whether the gas stove was left lit or not; always goes back again just to make sure the door is locked; and is afraid to ride up and down in elevators.	5.7 (6)	8.2 (4)	6.0 (9)	13.0 (7)	8.2 (26)
A sixth person has been telling lies for a long time now, and stealing things. Others are very upset about these acts, but the person pays no attention to others.	. . . (. . .)	. . . (. . .)	7.0 (2)	. . . (. . .)	7.0 (2)
Total	7.4 (23)	6.6 (20)	7.9 (47)	12.5[a] (24)	8.5 (114)

[a] Differs significantly at the 0.05 level or better (two-tailed t-tests) from Jewish mean, Irish mean, and Negro mean.

than did the combined Jewish and Irish raters. Thus, compared to the Jewish and Irish raters, the Negroes considered 4 of the 5 sociopathic items and 4 of the 6 paranoid items as less socially undesirable. The differences between the combined Irish and Jews and the Puerto Ricans are more pronounced, particularly because the latter tended to see the sociopathic items as even less undesirable than the Negroes.

It appears, then, that differences in appraisal of social desirability may account in part at least for our symptom results; that is, Negroes and Puerto Ricans may simply be more willing than the Jews and the Irish to admit problems involving possible paranoid or sociopathic beliefs and behaviors because they judge these things to be less undesirable. Similarly, Puerto Ricans may admit to more of the 22 Midtown symptoms because their judgment of the social undesirability of these symptoms is not so severe as that of the other ethnic groups. At the same time, it is possible that these "less undesirable" ratings are a function of the greater prevalence of such symptomatic beliefs and behavior in the Negro and Puerto Rican groups. In other words, the differences in results obtained on the

Table 6-19. Mean Social Desirability Ratings for Paranoid, Sociopathic, and Drinking Items by Community Respondents and by Psychiatrists (Single underline indicates lowest rating; double underline indicates highest rating for each item)

	Respondent Group			
Type of Item	Psychia-trists	Jewish Irish	Negro	Puerto Rican
Paranoid				
To tend to be on guard with people who are somewhat more friendly than one had expected	3.3	4.0 <	4.7	5.4
To think that one's way of doing things is apt to be misunderstood by others	2.7	3.5 <	3.9	4.7
To believe that behind one's back people say all kinds of things about one	1.0	3.0 >	2.7	2.4
To think one has enemies who really wish to do harm	2.0	2.4 <	2.7	2.7
To feel it is safer to trust nobody	1.1	2.8 >	2.7	4.9
To believe one is being plotted against	1.0	2.1 <	2.6	2.3

Table 6-19. (Continued)

Type of Item	Respondent Group			
	Psychia-trists	Jewish Irish	Negro	Puerto Rican
Sociopathic				
To get around the law without actually breaking it	2.9	3.2 <	4.0	4.7
To not blame anyone for trying to grab everything he can get in this world	3.7	4.5 >	3.4	4.9
To think that most people are honest chiefly through fear of being caught	3.4	3.2 <	4.7	5.3
To think that most respectable people in the neighborhood would object to the kind of people one has gone around with	3.4	4.0 <	4.2	4.6
To be able easily to make people afraid and sometimes to do so just for the fun of it	2.2	2.5 <	2.8	2.3
Drinking				
To have had trouble with health or work because of drinking	1.2	1.8 <	2.2	1.8
To have had arguments with one's family because of one's drinking	2.5	2.2 >	2.1	2.6

Note: One-tailed sign tests: Psychiatrists vs. community residents, $N = 13$; $m = 0$; $p < .001$. Puerto Rican vs. Jewish and Irish, $N = 12$; $m = 2$; $p < .02$. Negroes vs. Jewish and Irish, $N = 13$; $m = 4$; $p < .15$.

various symptom indices may be a function of cultural differences in the types of symptom used to express distress as well as or instead of cultural differences in willingness to admit symptoms when they are present.

The Problem of Subcultural Differences in the Types of Symptom Used to Express Psychological Distress

There are a number of vivid illustrations in the literature of possible cultural, including class subcultural, patterning of symptomatology and perhaps even of type of disorder (e.g., Blumenthal, 1967; Henry & Short,

1954; Opler & Singer, 1956; Field, 1960; Eaton & Weil, 1955; Hollingshead & Redlich, 1958; Langner & Michael, 1963). As we have suggested, it seems possible that the tendencies of the Negroes and Puerto Ricans to score higher on the sociopathic and paranoid items are due in large part to such cultural patterns.

To demonstrate conclusively the existence of subcultural patterning of the types of symptoms used to express distress, however, we need group differences that cannot be explained by differences in the social desirability ratings of the symptoms involved. Differences in social desirability ratings that correspond to differences in symptom scores may signify differences in the willingness to admit symptoms when they are present rather than in the actual rates of the symptoms themselves.

Four subscales developed by Crandell and B. P. Dohrenwend (1967) from the Midtown Study's 22-item screening instrument provide an opportunity to investigate whether there are group differences that cannot be accounted for in terms of differences in the social desirability ratings of the symptoms. Let us summarize how these subscales were developed and then investigate how the different ethnic groups compare on social desirability ratings and actual scores on the subscales.

Development of Four Subscales from the 22-Item Midtown Screening Instrument. In describing the 22-item screening instrument from the Midtown Study earlier, we noted that almost half of the items came from the Army's Neuropsychiatric Screening Adjunct of World War II. More specifically, these items were taken from what was termed, on the basis of the physiological content of several of them, the "Psychosomatic Scale" from the NSA.

Crandell (Crandell & B. P. Dohrenwend, 1967) noted that such items might have very different relations to physical illness in a young, relatively healthy male population and in the general population. Accordingly, as part of a larger investigation of relationships between physical illness and psychiatric symptoms, Crandell sent out a questionnaire to samples of 50 internists and 50 psychiatrists at the Columbia Presbyterian Medical Center asking them two questions about each of the 22 Midtown items:

"Would you consider this symptom as 'more psychological' or 'more physiological'?"

"In your opinion is this symptom associated with organic disease rarely or frequently?"

On the basis of the responses of 33 psychiatrists and 27 internists, supplemented by additional judgments from three board-certified psychiatrists about the relation of the items to descriptions of psychophysiological symptoms in the *Diagnostic and Statistical Manual* of the American Psychiatric Association Committee on Nomenclature and Statistics (1952), it was possible to group the 22 items into the following four subscales (Crandell & B. P. Dohrenwend, 1967):

Psychophysiological Symptom Index consisting of items (*a*) on which there was clear modal agreement by the samples of psychiatrists and internists that the symptoms were rarely organic and more psychological and (*b*) which were also judged psychophysiological by at least two of the three additional psychiatrists using the APA *Manual.*

Psychological Symptom Index consisting of the remaining items judged rarely organic and more psychological according to a clear modal concensus between the samples of psychiatrists and internists.

Physiological Symptom Index consisting of symptoms on which there was clear modal agreement by the samples of psychiatrists and internists that they were frequently organic and more physiological.

Ambiguous Symptom Index consisting of items on which there was no clear modal agreement between the samples of psychiatrists and internists.

Comparisons of the Ethnic Groups. The items included in these four subscales, together with their social desirability ratings by our small samples from the different ethnic groups, are shown in Table 6-20. Since a number of observers have suggested that Puerto Ricans and other groups of Spanish origin are unusually likely to express psychological distress in somatic terms (e.g., Kole, 1966, p. 173; Fabrega, Rubel, & Wallace, in press), we might expect to find this type of symptom rated least undesirable by Puerto Ricans. As Table 6-20 shows, however, items in the Psychophysiological Symptom Index are not seen as less undesirable by the Puerto Ricans than the items in the other three indices. And, even more important, the differences in ratings between the Puerto Ricans and the other ethnic groups are no greater for the Psychophysiological Symptom Index than for the other three indices. Hence, if Puerto Ricans show more difference from the other ethnic groups on the Psychophysiological Symptom Index than on the other indices, such as emphasis on psychophysiological symptoms cannot be accounted for by differences in social desirability ratings.

As Table 6-21 shows, the Puerto Ricans do indeed differ most markedly from the other ethnic groups on the Psychophysiological Symptom Index. Crandell and B. P. Dohrenwend (1967) found, however, that there was a strong tendency for scores on this index to vary inversely with educational level. The Puerto Ricans have the lowest educational level of any of the ethnic groups in our study. Is the ethnic difference in symptoms shown in Table 6-21 due mainly, therefore, to this educational dis-

Table 6-20. Mean Social Desirability Ratings by Different Ethnic Groups of the 22 Midtown Items Grouped into Four Symptom Indices

| Symptom Index | Ethnic Group | | | | |
	Puerto Rican	Negro	Puerto Rican Minus Negro	Jewish and Irish	Puerto Rican Minus Jewish and Irish
Psychophysiological					
Personal worries that get one down physically	2.2	2.0	+0.2	2.0	+0.2
Feel weak, all over	2.5	2.8	−0.3	2.6	−0.1
Cold sweats	3.8	3.2	+0.6	3.1	+0.7
Hot all over	3.4	3.0	+0.4	3.1	+0.3
Headaches	3.7	2.3	+1.4	3.2	+0.5
Mean	3.12	2.66	+0.46	2.80	+0.32
Ambiguous					
Acid or sour stomach	2.9	2.9	0.0	3.2	−0.3
Shortness of breath	3.9	2.8	+1.1	2.9	+1.0
Heart beats hard	3.9	2.9	+1.0	2.9	+1.0
Hands tremble	3.6	2.6	+1.0	3.1	+0.5
Mean	3.58	2.80	+0.78	3.02	+0.55
Physical					
Fainting more than a few times	3.4	2.3	+1.1	2.9	+0.5
Clogging in nose	2.8	3.0	−0.2	3.2	−0.4
Appetite poor	4.4	3.6	+0.8	3.9	+0.5
Mean	3.53	2.97	+0.57	3.33	+0.20
Psychological					
Feel somewhat apart	4.1	3.0	+1.1	2.8	+1.3
Can't get going	2.7	2.6	+0.1	2.1	+0.6
Nothing turns out right	3.4	2.7	+0.7	2.8	+0.6
Wonder if anything worthwhile	5.4	2.7	+2.7	2.5	+2.9
Nervous	4.0	3.2	+0.8	3.4	+0.6
Worrying type	3.3	3.0	+0.3	3.0	+0.3
Restlessness	3.7	3.7	0.0	3.3	+0.4
Trouble getting to sleep	4.3	3.4	+0.9	3.7	+0.6
Low and very low spirits	3.6	3.2	+0.4	3.1	+0.5
Memory not all right	2.5	2.7	−0.2	2.4	+0.1
Mean	3.70	3.02	+0.68	2.91	+0.79

Table 6-21. Per Cents Scoring 1 or More on Each of Four Symptom
Indices According to Ethnicity

Symptom Index	Puerto Rican	Negro	Jewish	Irish	Other	χ^2 (Puerto Rican vs. all others)	df	p
		Ethnic Group				Statistical Test		
Psychological	69.5	49.7	58.3	50.6	60.1	10.55	1	<.01
Psychophysiological	47.5	24.8	27.6	19.4	29.0	28.67	1	<.001
Physiological	19.9	13.9	12.0	11.2	17.2	3.43	1	<.10
Ambiguous	22.7	10.9	11.3	10.0	12.4	14.74	1	<.001
Number of respondents	141	330	283	170	331			

crepancy? As Table 6-22 shows, it is not. The difference between the
Puerto Ricans and the other ethnic groups remains when educational level
is controlled.

When these results are placed alongside our earlier finding that Puerto
Rican patients as well as Puerto Rican nonpatients score higher on the
22-item measure, we have additional reason for questioning the evidence
for higher rates of actual disorder among this ethnic group. For we must
conclude not only that sheer number of these symptoms is inadequate
to measure degree of disorder, but also that the 22-item battery is more
sensitive to some subcultural modes of expressing psychological distress
than to others. Specifically, the inclusion of psychophysiological items
tends to ensure high scores by Puerto Ricans relative to other ethnic
groups whose tendencies to develop somatic symptoms to express psychological distress are less pronounced.

EVALUATION OF RESULTS

Our analysis suggests that the results of previous studies, as well as
our studies in Washington Heights, comparing advantages and disadvantaged ethnic groups can be explained better in methodological than in
substantive terms. Thus the etiological issue has not yet been resolved.

Since our problem in drawing clear-cut substantive interpretations from
the evidence that so far exists centers on the inadequacy of the measures
of psychological disorder that we used in the research in Washington
Heights, we must ask whether other researchers have solved these method-

Table 6-22. Psychophysiological Symptom Scores According to Ethnicity
and Educational Level

(Values in per cent)

Psychophysiological Symptom Score	Ethnicity				
	Puerto Rican	Negro	Jewish	Irish	Other
0–7 Years of Education					
0	41.5	69.2	(3)	50.0	57.1
1	34.1	17.3	(3)	41.7	25.7
2 or more	24.4	13.5	(1)	8.3	17.2
Total per cent	100.0	100.0		100.0	100.0
Number of respondents	41	52	7	12	35
Puerto Ricans vs. all others: $\chi^2 = 4.92$; df = 2; $p < .10$.					
8–11 Years of Education					
0	56.9	78.3	73.7	77.6	65.9
1	27.6	13.0	21.0	11.9	22.5
2 or more	15.5	8.7	5.3	10.5	11.6
Total per cent	100.0	100.0	100.0	100.0	100.0
Number of respondents	58	115	57	67	129
Puerto Ricans vs. all others: $\chi^2 = 6.38$; df = 2; $p < .05$.					
12–15 Years of Education					
0	55.6	74.3	72.4	88.6	75.6
1	25.0	16.4	17.8	7.6	19.5
2 or more	19.4	9.3	9.8	3.8	4.9
Total per cent	100.0	100.0	100.0	100.0	100.0
Number of respondents	36	140	174	79	123
Puerto Ricans vs. all others: $\chi^2 = 9.13$; df = 2; $p < .01$.					
16 or More Years of Education					
0	(3)	85.0	82.5	81.8	85.0
1	(0)	10.0	17.5	9.1	12.5
2 or more	(1)	5.0	0.0	9.1	2.5
Total per cent		100.0	100.0	100.0	100.0
Number of respondents	4	20	40	11	40

ological problems. Are there more valid measures of psychological disorder
available from the field studies than the ones we employed? If so, would
using them have led us to substantially different findings?

SUMMARY

On the basis of our analysis in Chapter 5 we have argued that a major
substantive issue could turn on the answer to a simple question of fact:

What are the rates of psychological disorder among Negroes and Puerto Ricans relative to their class counterparts in more advantaged ethnic groups? If the rates among Negroes and Puerto Ricans proved higher, we would interpret this result as evidence for the social causation explanation of the general findings of an inverse relation between social class and psychological disorder. If, on the other hand, the rates for Negroes and Puerto Ricans turned out to be lower than the rates for their class counterparts in more advantaged ethnic groups, we would interpret these results as support for the social selection explanation of the class relationship.

On the basis of our review of the evidence from other studies, and to an even greater extent from our own research in the Washington Heights section of New York City, it seems that the existing results, accepted at face value, tend to give more support to the social causation alternative. This is due mainly, however, to the strong and consistently higher rates of symptoms on all measures reported by Puerto Ricans relative to their class counterparts in more advantaged ethnic groups. A major problem arises, however, because the results for Negroes do not consistently yield the same kinds of differences shown by the Puerto Ricans on the various measures used. On the 22-item screening measure from the Midtown Study, we find, for example, that Negroes in Washington Heights tended to score lower than their class counterparts in more advantaged ethnic groups—a result more consistent with the social selection explanation of the inverse relation between social class and pscyhological disorder.

When we question the results on methodological grounds, moreover, the analysis gives us grounds for modifying our interpretation that the relatively high rates of symptoms among Puerto Ricans indicate relatively high rates of psychological disorder in this group. Thus the strongest evidence for social causation has to be called into question on methodological grounds. Our conclusion is, therefore, that because of measurement problems the results of our quasi experiment have not yet resolved the etiological issue.

CHAPTER 7

The Problem of Validity in Field Studies of Psychological Disorder

Our attempts to determine the rates of psychological disorder among Negroes and Puerto Ricans relative to the rates for their class counterparts in more advantaged ethnic groups have uncovered a thicket of measurement problems. Underlying all of them is the basic issue of validity—that is, what measures will provide us with the true rates of untreated as well as treated psychological disorder in community populations? Let us look more closely at the procedures used in the epidemiological studies reviewed in Chapter 2 to see what evidence they provide for the validity of the measures of disorder that were employed.

As Table 2-1 showed, the rates of psychological disorder reported in the field studies ranged from under 1 per cent to over 64 per cent. Some critics have argued that a number of methodological problems underlie this variation in rates (e.g., Blum, 1962; Pasamanick, 1962; Plunkett & Gordon, 1960). One problem suggested is the thoroughness of the data collection procedures. Investigators who collected data directly from subjects, rather than relying entirely or partially on indirect sources of information, might be expected to detect more cases, as has happened with physical illness (Cartwright, 1957). On the other hand, as implied in Chapter 6, still more thorough investigation through physical examinations might reveal organic bases of symptoms, thereby reducing rates below those reported when subjects' self-descriptions are the investigator's only source of information. Still another methodological factor that might affect rates is the conception of what constitutes a case. This conception may, as Szasz (1961) implied, have changed with time, expanding and becoming more inconclusive over the years.

The effects of these methodological factors are tested in Table 7-1 by classifying the studies according to thoroughness of data collection procedures and decade of publication. There is a general tendency for more

Table 7-1. Percentage of Psychological Disorder Reported According to Thoroughness of Data Collection Procedures and Decade of Publication of Study

Decade of Publication	Indirect Contact: Records and/or Informants	Partial Direct Contact: Records and/or Informants plus Interviews with Some Subjects	Direct Contact	
			Interviews with All Subjects	Interviews with All and Physical Examination of Some Subjects
1910–1919		*1.3 (Rosanoff, 1917)*	*3.6 (Rosanoff, 1917)*	
1920–1929				
1930–1939	2.3 (Cohen et al., 1939) 4.2[a] (Strömgren,[b] 1950)	1.3 (Brugger, 1931)	3.5[a] (Brugger, 1937) 7.5 (Brugger, 1933)	
1940–1949	1.1[a] (Kaila, Study II, 1942) 1.8[a] (Lemkau et al., 1942) 9.0 (Mayer-Gross, 1948)	0.8[a] (Uchimara et al., 1940) 1.2[a] (Kaila, Study I, 1942) *6.4 (Roth & Luton, 1943)*	2.7[a] (Akimoto et al., 1942) 3.0[a] (Tsuwaga et al., 1942) *12.4 (Roth & Luton, 1943)*	
1950–1959	*1.2 (Eaton & Weil, 1955)*	*2.3 (Eaton & Weil, 1955)* 11.9 (Fremming, 1951) *28.0[c] (Cole et al., 1957)* 28.6 (Helgason, 1964)	1.1 (Lin, 1953) *2.9[a] (Eaton & Weil, 1955)* 13.6[a] (Essen-Möller, 1956) *35.4[c] (Cole et al, 1957)*	10.9 (Pasamanick et al., 1959) 18.0 (Trussell et al., 1956) 23.2 (Bremer, 1951)
1960 and after	14.8[a] (Strotzka et al., 1966)		0.8[a] (Rin & Lin, Ami, 1962) 0.8[a] (Rin & Lin, Paiwan, 1962)	13.2 (Primrose, 1962) 14.0 (Piotrowski et al., 1966)

1.2[a] (Rin & Lin, Saisait, 1962)

1.9[a] (Rin & Lin, Atayal, 1962)

3.4 (Manis et al., 1964)

11.8 (Gillis et al., 1965)

15.6[a] (Gnat et al., 1964)

15.6[a] (Hagnell, 1966)

20.6 (Hare & Shaw, 1965)

23.4 (Srole et al., 1962)

27.5 (Phillips, 1966)

33.0 (Taylor & Chave, 1964)

41.0 (A. H. Leighton et al., 1963)

50.0+[d] (D. C. Leighton et al., 1963)

54.0 (Rin et al., in press)

64.0 (Llewellyn-Thomas, 1960)

[a] Calculated by B. S. Dohrenwend.

[b] Eleven of the small studies summarized in Strömgren's rate were published in the 1930's, seven in the 1920's.

[c] Rates for wives are calculated for direct contact and other family members for partial contact on the basis of the statement that wives were usually interviewed; the base for each rate is the number of families interviewed.

[d] " . . . our conclusion from all the available information is that at least half of the adults in Stirling County are *currently* suffering from some psychiatric disorder defined in the American Psychiatric Association *Diagnostic and Statistical Manual* (p. 356)."

97

direct contact with subjects to produce higher rates of disorder. The importance of direct contact is given further weight by the work of the authors
in italics in Table 7-1, that is, Cole, Branch, and Orla, 1957; Eaton
and Weil, 1955; Rosanoff, 1917; and Roth and Luton, 1943. In each
of these studies, rates found in the same population are higher among
subjects with whom more direct contact was made. There is, however,
no evidence that physical examination lowered the reported rates of psychological disorder. The rates yielded by the seven studies that included
physical examinations cover most of the range.

There is a clear tendency for rates to be higher in more recent studies.
Especially notable is the increase in the 1950's and 1960's. It could be
argued, of course, that, rather than observing the effects of changes in
the researchers' concepts, we are observing a consequence of the times
in which we live. However, in view of statements suggesting a shift from
exclusive concern with avoiding overestimation (e.g., Cohen, Fairbank, &
Greene, 1939, p. 113; Lemkau, Tietze, & Cooper, 1942, p. 635; Rosanoff,
1917, p. 137) to concern with complete enumeration (e.g., Bremer, 1951,
p. 12; D. C. Leighton, Harding, Macklin, Macmillan, and A. H. Leighton,
1963, p. 195), it seems premature to infer a true change in prevalence
between the 1940's and 1950's. Moreover, there is ample evidence from
studies in which both inclusive and relatively exclusive standards were
applied to the same populations that rates can be markedly affected by
these standards. Essen-Möller (1956, p. 95), for example, reported a
rate of 13.6 per cent for "diagnoses constituting the main subject of most
psychiatric population studies," but an average of 54.7 per cent (calcula-
tion by B. S. Dohrenwend) for whom pathology was not definitely absent.
A similar contrast is offered by the figures of 23.4 per cent in the "impaired" group and 81.5 per cent judged less than "well" in the Midtown
Study (Srole, Langner, Michael, Opler, & Rennie, 1962, p. 138). Another
comparison with the Midtown Study is provided by an investigation
(Manis, Brawer, Hunt, & Kercher, 1964) that used the 22 Midtown items.
Although obtaining a distribution of responses similar to that reported
by the Midtown researchers, Manis and his colleagues found that their
decision to include only severe psychological disorder resulted in a rate
of 3.4 per cent.

The continuing importance of methodological problems is emphasized
by the difficulty of comparing results even from studies carried out by
the same investigators. For example, the Leightons and their colleagues
(A. H. Leighton, Lambo, Hughes, D. C. Leighton, Murphy, & Macklin,
1963) concluded, concerning their own studies, that "the differences and
similarities between the Yoruba and Stirling figures are to an unknown
degree under the influence of differences in the procedures employed in
the two studies" (p. 124). To complicate the problem of comparison

further, various procedures used within one of these, the Stirling County Study, yielded different rates of psychopathology (D. C. Leighton et al., 1963, pp. 123, 127).

In view of the variability of both procedures and results in attempts to assess "true" prevalence, the salient question is which, if any, among these field studies has produced valid measures of psychological disorder. Despite their deficiencies, studies restricted to treated disorder have one clear advantage. Except in the relatively few cases of elective psycho-therapy for training or other purposes, the fact that a person is in treat-ment indicates that he cannot function unaided in his customary social environments. The clinician diagnosing a patient has a "presenting problem" with which to start, so that the question he must answer is not *whether* something is wrong, but rather *what* is wrong. The diagnostic result of this analysis, moreover, can be changed on the basis of repeated observa-tions and interviews over a course of treatment.

The investigator of untreated disorder must work without the aids to diagnosis inherent in the clinical setting. Evidence of the difficulties he faces are found in the results of the psychiatric screening attempts asso-ciated with Selective Service in the United States during World War II. The psychiatric judgments were extremely unreliable, rejection rates within the same region varying in a number of areas by a factor of 3 to 1 (Star, 1950b, pp. 552, 554). Moreover, there is no evidence that among the unreliable judgments one or another was more effective, since strictness of screening procedures bore little relation to subsequent rates of separation on psychiatric grounds (E. Ginzberg, Anderson, S. N. Gins-burg, & Herma, 1959b, Ch. 11).

Nevertheless, clinical judgment was the tool relied upon for case identi-fication in almost all studies that included untreated as well as treated psychological disorder. In most, psychiatric diagnoses were made and find-ing were presented in terms of categories such as those described in the *Diagnostic and Statistical Manual* of the American Psychiatric Association Committee on Nomenclature and Statistics (1952). Neither the informa-tion available to the judge nor the criteria on which the diagnoses were based are usually reported in detail in these investigations. The validity of the results is assumed to be implicit in the diagnostic process, a shaky assumption in light of the World War II experience with psychiatric screening.

A few investigators, recognizing the difficulty of placing untreated cases in diagnostic categories, have also made judgments in more general terms, such as probability of pathology (Essen-Möller, 1956; Rosanoff, 1917), likelihood of being psychiatric cases (A. H. Leighton et al., 1963; D. C. Leighton et al., 1963), or degree of severity ranging from "well" to "incapacitated" (Langner & Michael, 1963; Srole et al., 1962). Among these relatively sophisticated investigations, the Leightons' Stirling County and Nigeria studies and the Midtown Study by Srole and his colleagues stand out. Although they differ in several aspects of their assessment procedures, they share an important innovation: both used structured questionnaires, thereby providing a standard, explicit set of data for psychiatric assessment. In this respect, these studies represent the methodologically most advanced epidemiological investigations of untreated and treated psychological disorder, with the possible exception of a Polish study not yet completely reported (Gnat, Henisz, & Sarapata, 1964; Piotrowski, Henisz, & Gnat, 1966). The question is whether the procedures of the Midtown, Stirling County, and Nigeria studies have dealt adequately with the central methodological problem of validity.

CONTENT VALIDITY

Content validity involves a demonstration that the items used are a representative sample from a universe generally accepted as defining the variable to be measured (Cronbach & Meehl, 1955). In the Midtown Study, the universe from which items were drawn was defined by Srole et al. (1962) as "the most salient and *generalized* indicators of mental pathology" (p. 41), as discussed in Chapter 6. Behavioral scientists selected a group of items from the U.S. Army Neuropsychiatric Screening Adjunct (Star, 1950a) and the Minnesota Multiphasic Personality Inventory (Dahlstrom & Welsh, 1960) "consisting principally of the psychophysiologic manifestations and those tapping the anxiety, depression, and inadequacy dimensions" (Srole et al., 1962, p. 42). In addition, the psychiatrists independently contributed 40 items "bearing particularly on psychosomatic symptoms, phobic reactions, and mood" (p. 60). The final decision determining the 120 items actually included was made by the senior psychiatrist on the basis of "clinical experience" (p. 60). Thus, in the absence of systematic sampling of items, no argument can be made for the content validity of the Midtown measure of psychological disorder. The same is true of the Stirling and Yoruba studies, in which items were taken from the NSA and other test sources without explicit specification of the selection procedures (e.g., A. H. Leighton et al., 1963, p. 85; D. C. Leighton et al., 1963, pp. 202, 205).

It is doubtful whether content validity, in the strictest sense, can be achieved in the measurement of untreated psychological disorder, since there appears to be no universe of items that experts agree on as defining the variable. Four different sources have been cited in recent studies by the relatively few researchers who related their procedures to an established diagnostic system: the Sjöbring system used at Lund University, Sweden (Essen-Möller, 1956); the system used in the Department of

Psychiatry of the National Taiwan University Hospital, Taipeh, based on Henderson and Gillespie's *Textbook of Psychiatry* and on Bleuler's *Lehrbuch der Psychiatrie* (Lin, 1953; Rin & Lin, 1962); the World Health Organization *International Classification of Diseases* (Primrose, 1962); and the American Psychiatric Association *Diagnostic and Statistical Manual* (D. C. Leighton et al., 1963; Rin, Chu, & Lin, in press). As Clausen pointed out (1961, pp. 131–132), the last two sources differ markedly as a function of the greater emphasis placed by European psychiatrists on hypothetical constitutional determinants.

CRITERION-ORIENTED VALIDITY:
CONCURRENT AND PREDICTIVE

Of the two types of criterion-oriented validity, concurrent and predictive (Cronbach & Meehl, 1955), there is no evidence in the field studies for the latter. Typically conducted at one point in time, the studies have thus far not tested their assessments of disorder against criteria of future psychiatric condition, admission to treatment, or social functioning. What evidence, then, is provided for concurrent validity?

In the Midtown Study (Srole et al., 1962), the NSA and MMPI items proposed by the behavioral scientists were tested in a study involving 139 diagnosed neurotic and remitted psychotic patients and 72 persons judged well by a psychiatrist on the basis of a half-hour interview. The result was that "almost all the NSA and MMPI symptom questions emerged with validity confirmed" (p. 42). As we reported in Chapter 6, 22 of the items included in the final questionnaire discriminated between the patient and well groups at the .01 level of significance (Langner, 1962). The remainder of the items contributed by the behavioral scientists discriminated at the .05 level (Thomas S. Langner, personal communication, February 1964). Although the Midtown psychiatrists reported that, in rating cases well or not well, they gave special weight to 8 of the 22 items that discriminated at the .01 level, they also paid particular attention to 6 items that failed to discriminate at this level (p. 396). Thus in the Midtown Study, although the data from which the psychiatrists worked had been tested for concurrent validity in the manner described above, this test did not determine the use of these data by the psychiatrists in making their ratings of cases.

In the Stirling County Study, an attempt to identify valid items was made by administering NSA questions and items from other tests to untreated community samples and to patients diagnosed as neurotic. The selection of items included in the survey interviews, however, was not wholly determined by the results of this study (D. C. Leighton et al.,

1963, p. 205). As in the Midtown Study, the Stirling County psychiatrists did not make use of objective scores based on these items in their judgmental assessment of psychiatric disorder.

Before considering how the psychiatrists actually used the symptom items in the Midtown and Stirling County studies, questions must be raised about the concurrent validity of the items themselves. In attempts to validate these items, the patient criterion groups were either homogeneous with regard to type of disorder (e.g., all neurotics in a study by Macmillan in D. C. Leighton et al., 1963, Chapter VII) or unspecified as to diagnostic composition (e.g., Manis, Brawer, Hunt, & Kercher, 1963). Moreover, the stubborn problem of well controls was not met head on, much less solved. For example, in Langner's (1962) study identifying 22 items that discriminated at the .01 level between patient and well groups, the fact that the well group was identified by means of clinical judgment brings the problem back to its origin, since the items can be no more valid than the psychiatrist's judgments against which they were tested.

Nor does the solution appear to lie in avoiding clinical judgments by using an unselected sample of the nonpatient population as the healthy criterion group. Reports from the field studies themselves of community rates of psychological disorder ranging up to 64 per cent argue against such a procedure. An attempt by Manis et al. (1963) to cross-validate the 22 Midtown study items, using samples from patient and nonpatient populations as criterion groups, both illustrates this problem and raises another. As we reported in Chapter 6, these workers found that a group of predischarge ward patients had an average symptom score lower than the scores of a community cross section and of a group of college students, and argued that the result indicated a failure of the test since "there is little reason to believe that the mental health of these pre-discharge patients is equal to or better than the non-hospitalized populations" (p. 111). In the absence of independent evidence concerning the mental health of their nonpatient populations, however, it seems difficult to interpret this result. It is conceivable, though unlikely, that the predischarge ward patients were cured, whereas the nonpatients needed treatment.

It is also possible, and perhaps more plausible, that the predischarge ward patients in the interest of "getting out" were simply less willing than nonpatients to admit socially undesirable behavior. In other words it appears that, as we argued in Chapter 6, there is evidence of the impact of response style on these items. What are the implications of such influence for the psychiatric evaluations that have relied heavily on the "face validity" of the items?

The measure of disorder in the Midtown Study consisted of psychiatrists' ratings of the symptom data, which ranged respondents on a scale from "well" through five degrees of severity of symptomatology: "mild," "moderate," "marked," "severe," and "incapacitated." Almost a quarter (23.4 per cent) of the respondents were classified in the last three categories: "marked," "severe," and "incapacitated." These are referred to collectively as "impaired" and constitute the "cases" in the Midtown Study. Michael, one of the evaluating psychiatrists on the Midtown Study, described the classification this way:

"The individuals in the Impaired category of mental health . . . are represented as being analogous to patients in psychiatric therapy. . . . When it is urged that the mental ratings "Marked" and "Severe" are comparable to the clinical conditions of patients in ambulatory treatment, and the rating "Incapacitated" to the clinically hospitalized, the distinction is presented . . . as an attempt to anchor our conceptualizations in relation to known degrees of psychopathology" (Srole et al., 1962, p. 333).

There is evidence that this claim requires scrutiny. In the Midtown sample, 40 respondents reported being current outpatients in psychotherapy at the time of the interview; 182 reported that they were ex-patients. The evaluating psychiatrists had full knowledge of these facts when they made their judgments. Since ex-patients might be expected to have benefited from treatment, it is not remarkable to find that 54 per cent of the 182 ex-patients in the Midtown sample was judged unimpaired. However, if respondents placed in the "impaired" categories indeed resemble psychiatric patients, as the Midtown researchers claim, it is hard to understand why the study psychiatrists placed 48 per cent of the 40 *current* patients in the unimpaired categories (Srole et al., 1962, p. 147).

In the Stirling County Study, disorder was defined in terms of judged similarity to descriptions in the 1952 *Diagnostic and Statistical Manual* of the American Psychiatric Association, rather than judged similarity to actual patients with whom the psychiatrists had had experience. The main rating was a psychiatric evaluation of "caseness" based on written summaries of symptom data collected for the most part by lay inteviewers. It is described by D. C. Leighton et al. (1963) as "a rating of the probability that, at some time in his adult life, up to the time of the interview, the individual would qualify as a psychiatric case" (p. 53). The evidence for the validity of the conclusion "that at least half of the adults in Stirling County are *currently* suffering from some psychiatric disorder defined in the APA *Diagnostic and Statistical Manual*" (p. 356) rests largely on the study psychiatrists' blind evaluation of the likelihood that 47 former clinic patients, mostly neurotic, were cases. Of these 47, 81 per cent were rated "almost certainly psychiatric" and an additional 11 per cent "probably psychiatric" (p. 175). Their problems, moreover, were viewed mainly as present rather than past (pp. 178–179). Thus the Stirling evaluators saw more disorder in their ex-patients than the Midtown evaluators detected in their current patients.

These results of the application of Midtown and Stirling County study evaluation procedures to patients and ex-patients suggest a number of possible interpretations: that patients get and remain sicker in Stirling County than in Midtown Manhattan, or that treatment in Stirling is less effective than in Midtown, or that Stirling methods are less able to distinguish between past and current problems, or that the definitions of cases are vastly different in the two studies, or that some combination of these circumstances has operated simultaneously. In brief, there is considerable ambiguity about the relations between the Midtown and the Stirling judgmental ratings of untreated disorder.

In a subsequent study, the Leightons had several psychiatrists conduct clinical interviews and make "caseness" ratings based on these interviews for respondents the great majority of whom had previously been evaluated as either most or least likely to be psychiatric cases. The new ratings showed a high level of agreement with the psychiatric ratings previously made from the survey data collected by lay interviewers (A. H. Leighton, D. C. Leighton, & Danley, 1966). However, the decision to use predominantly respondents originally evaluated as either most likely to be ill or most likely to be well, thus grossly underrepresenting the majority who had been given intermediate ratings, seriously limited the test. Moreover, the procedure whereby each psychiatrist reconciled his rating with the original judgment before proceeding to the next case reduced the independence of the second set of ratings and may have artificially increased the agreement between the two sets.

There is, then, much to criticize and improve upon in these past attempts to investigate the criterion-oriented validity of both objective and judgmental measures of untreated disorder. There is, first of all, the absence of evidence of predictive validity, evidence that can be supplied only by prospective studies. Criterion-oriented attempts to establish both concurrent and predictive validity, however, face a common problem. Even with more attention, for example, to larger and diagnostically more heterogeneous patient criterion groups, independent criteria of "wellness," and problems of response style, strong reasons exist not to rely primarily on attempts to establish criterion-oriented validity. Foremost is the fact that there are at present no generally agreed upon criteria of psychological health or disorder (cf. A. H. Leighton et al., 1963, p. 264).

CONSTRUCT VALIDITY

Cronbach and Meehl (1955) have argued that, when no generally accepted criteria for the variable of interest are available and when no universe of content is fully agreed upon as defining the variable, we must become interested in construct validity. These are the circumstances of untreated psychological disorder.

In Cronbach and Meehl's formulation, "A necessary condition for a construct to be scientifically admissable is that it occur in a nomological net, at least *some* of whose laws involve observables" (p. 290). Furthermore, ". . . *unless the network makes contact with observations and exhibits explicit, public steps of inference, construct validation cannot be claimed*" (p. 291).

As noted above, the Midtown Study measure of mental health consisted of psychiatrists' ratings which ranged subjects on a scale from "well" through five degrees of severity of symptomatology ranging from "mild" to "incapacitated." The two rating psychiatrists (Srole et al., 1962) explained, "Throughout the volumes of this Study, the data must be evaluated as *a rating of mental health based on the rating psychiatrists' perceptions operating through a questionnaire instrument*" (p. 66). Although they reported that positive responses to any of the 14 specific items ordinarily precluded the classification of a subject as "well" and that positive responses to other items suggested various degrees of severity of symptomatology (pp. 396–397), the psychiatrists summarized their impression of the rating process as follows: "We used our clinical judgment to the best of our ability. It would be a mistake, however, to overlook the fact that there remain some aspects of the process which are not altogether in our awareness" (pp. 62–63). To the extent that this measurement of psychological disorder is private and hence not replicable, a claim for construct validity is precluded.

The same problem exists in the Leightons' Stirling County and Yoruba studies (1963). Although the problem of achieving public steps of inference in psychiatric evaluation concerned them, they did not attain this goal in either of these studies. Optimistically, they suggested that the development of the procedures to date ". . . brings within sight the possibility that the evaluations could be done by a computer. To achieve this the steps would have to be broken down into even more specific items, and the intuitive leaps that are still allowed would have to be dissected so that their components could be identified" (p. 267).

A computer program would certainly be a step toward construct validation of measures of psychological disorder. However, the construct validity of such a program could be evaluated only in relation to a nomological net. It is not clear in the work of the Leightons how such a net would be formulated. Although the Stirling County study was introduced with a theoretical volume (A. H. Leighton, 1959), the propositions in the theory are developed at a level of abstraction such that it does not make direct contact with observations. Instead, the guide for psychiatric evaluation in the study was the American Psychiatric Association *Diagnostic and Statistical Manual* (1952). Although this *Manual* often includes etiological propositions in its descriptions of nosological types, etiological inferences were avoided in the Stirling and Yoruba studies in the interest of inter-rater reliability. Thus the psychiatric evaluations were removed entirely from a nomological framework within which construct validity could be evaluated.

Where, then, can we look for propositions placing psychological disorder in a nomological net? Not, it appears, to clinical experience. Unlike tuberculosis and pellagra, which are commonly cited as subjects of successful epidemiological research, psychological disorder does not constitute an etiologically defined disease entity (Clausen, 1961; Gruenberg, 1955). Instead:

"With symptoms still our primary basis for classification, we are at the same stage of knowledge about mental disease that medicine occupied a century ago with reference to the 'fevers.' Typhoid, malaria, and a number of other diseases, all readily distinguishable now, were lumped together" (Clausen, 1961, pp. 131–132).

Recognition of this situation has led a number of investigators to avoid psychodynamic inferences and assumptions in attempting to identify untreated disorder (e.g., A. H. Leighton et al., 1963, p. 89; D. C. Leighton et al., 1963, p. 48; New York State Department of Mental Hygiene, 1959, p. 83; Srole et al., 1962, pp. 63, 134). In the absence of connections with individual psychodynamics, however, we must look elsewhere for leads to a nomological network that can be used to validate measures of psychological disorder.

A LEAD TOWARD CONSTRUCT VALIDATION
OF MEASURES OF PSYCHOLOGICAL DISORDER

For this purpose let us reconsider the nature of the etiological issue that we are attempting to resolve. We asked whether psychological disorder is determined predominantly by hereditary or by social environmental factors and, in particular, which of these sets of factors is primarily responsible for the high rates of disorder consistently found in the lowest social stratum.

On the hereditary side, concepts such as penetrance leave room for differences about whether psychological disorder will develop from a given genetic endowment, as we saw in Chapter 3. There appears, however, to be little room for disagreement about the outcome should the potential disorder become manifest. The symptoms are expected to show the quality of persistence and intransigence that clinicians emphasize as indicative of psychopathology.

This quality of psychopathology is described, for example, in the widely used 1952 *Diagnostic and Statistical Manual* of the American Psychiatric Association, where we read of the ". . . increase in severity of symptoms over long periods . . ." that is characteristic of the simple type of schizophrenic reaction (p. 26) and of the ". . . chronic and prolonged course . . ." of paranoia (p. 28). Lifelong studies of psychoneurotics are said to ". . . usually present evidence of periodic or constant maladjustment of varying degree from early life" (p. 31). In most instances of personality disorder, including sociopathy and alcoholism, ". . . the disorder is manifested by a lifelong pattern of action or behavior . . ." (p. 34). And the symptoms of the psychophysiological, autonomic, and visceral disorders are held to be ". . . due to a chronic and exaggerated state of the normal physiological expression of emotion . . ." (p. 29).

The assumption that impairing symptoms indicate a self-perpetuating defect in personality is made not only by geneticists but also by most social environmentalists. For instance, in the Stirling County Study, the distribution of cases according to age was interpreted as indicating that "these symptoms in nonpatients have the same quality of persistence that has long been recognized as an outstanding feature of psychoneurosis when seen in clinics and private practice" (D. C. Leighton et al., 1963, p. 358).

This inference was drawn, however, despite compelling evidence that some portion of the symptoms observed were transient. In comparing the psychiatrists' evaluations based on interview data collected in 1952 with a general practitioner's independent diagnoses of 39 respondents about 4 years later, the authors noted that, of the 14 disagreements, 4 were due to "transient episodes of disorder" (p. 196). A fifth may also have been transient since he "either had a better relationship to the general practitioner than to his predecessor or had actually improved, so that he changed from ill to not ill by 1958" (p. 197).

The implications of this kind of observation have been spelled out by Tyhurst (1957), who has suggested that in some circumstances the symptomatology reported in community epidemiological surveys may indicate something quite different from persistent psychopathology. From the vantage of his clinical observation and analysis of "transition states" (e.g., marriage, childbearing, promotion, retirement, migration, and physical disaster), Tyhurst wrote:

"Our tendency to regard the appearance of symptoms as invariable signs of illness, and therefore a need for psychiatric treatment, requires some revision. It would be probably more appropriate if we regarded the transition state and its accompanying disturbance as an opportunity for growth. When an impasse develops in the resolution of the 'hitch,' we may speak of illness. Signs of psychological distress—somatic, emotional or intellectual—are thus not necessarily equivalent with that person's being a case of mental illness. . . . Thus, for example, prevalence surveys of such sumptoms . . . can have little meaning for the incidence of mental illness unless the *contextual relevance and timing* of the symptoms is determined at the same time. If symptom incidence [*sic*] is not close to 100 per cent in such surveys, this is probably because the survey has been incomplete in some way or the memories of informants were faulty" (p. 161).

M. J. Field (1960) has made a closely related point that is particularly relevant to the results of our studies in Washington Heights. She emphasized that in Ghana, where nobody looks twice at a lorry announcing in big letters "Enemies all about me," or "Be afraid of people," the universality of the "normal" paranoid attitude makes it necessary to diagnose paranoid schizophrenia with great caution. She writes, "But just as, in our own society, we are able to recognize as abnormal the man from whom no reassurance can shift the groundless conviction that he has cancer, so we are able in rural Ghana to recognize the morbidly ineradicable paranoid conviction" (p. 296). The sign of the difference between normal and abnormal she refers to as the "peculiar recalcitrant obstinacy" of the distorted outlook (p. 296).

Consider Field's observations in Ghana in connection with some comments by R. M. Williams (1964) on the basis of his research on Negro and white relations in several urban communities in the United States:

"In the communities we studied, it was impossible to find a Negro person who had not at some time been hurt, rebuffed, insulted, or deprived by a white person in a manner clearly based on a categorical racial distinction. It would be strange indeed if such experiences did not produce at least an initial wariness and reserve in dealing with whites, even with those who appear to be unprejudiced and friendly. The defensive insulation so produced is not merely a kind of rational prudence. It is also a *potential* basis for a fundamental moral and political alienation from white society altogether" (p. 300).

As Williams pointed out, this defensive insulation is most pronounced in lower-class Negroes.

How, then, are we to interpret the responses of lower-class Negroes and Puerto Ricans in our Washington Heights research to the kinds of paranoid and sociopathic items we used? Is it not possible that these responses are not so much evidence of psychological disorder as of a normal reaction to social conditions marked by forced segregation and systematic discrimination?

There apppears, then, to be considerable room for disagreement about the nature of the symptomatology observed in the community studies of "true prevalence." The crucial question centers on whether these symptoms are persistent manifestations of personality defects like the symptoms characteristically observed in psychiatric patients, or whether they are potentially transient reactions to the contemporary situations in which the respondents find themselves.

As suggested earlier, it seems reasonable to assume that, insofar as genetic defects are the main basis of symptoms, the symptoms would prove persistent. The question at issue, therefore, is whether social environmental factors are more likely to produce situationally specific symptoms in general populations or, rather, symptoms that tend to persist regardless of situational context. Our aim in examining this problem will be to develop a network of relationships that can be used to validate the construct of "psychological disorder."

SUMMARY

Analysis of the measures of psychological disorder used in the community studies of "true prevalence" indicates that none of these investigations has provided convincing evidence of validity. After considering each of the major types of validity for which evidence could have been sought, our position is that, with no generally accepted criteria available and no universe of content agreed upon, construct validity takes on central importance.

It becomes necessary, therefore, to develop a nomological net involving psychological disorder in order to validate this construct. The issue that will be investigated for this purpose is the extent to which social environmental factors produce transient as against persistent psychological symptoms.

CHAPTER 8

Persistent Disorder Versus Situationally Specific Symptoms

Our review of the evidence concerning the relation between social environmental factors and psychological symptoms will be organized around two questions: What social conditions produce symptoms of psychological distress? Under what conditions do these symptoms persist?

EVIDENCE THAT STRESSFUL EVENTS INDUCE REVERSIBLE SYMPTOMS

Reid (1961) has reviewed the literature on the relation of immediate external events to the onset of mental disorders. He found that "the epidemiological or statistical evidence about the effect of such externals on mental disease is relatively scanty . . . much of it comes from studies done in the war" (p. 197).

During World War II the U.S. Army Research Branch developed a battery of test items labeled the Neuropsychiatric Screening Adjunct, with the aim of increasing the efficiency with which draftees were screened. The findings concerning this instrument are particularly interesting because, as we noted in previous chapters, recent field studies such as the Midtown and Stirling County research relied heavily on the Psychosomatic Scale of the Screening Adjunct for items on which psychiatrists based their identification of cases of untreated psychological disorder (Langner, 1962; D. C. Leighton, Harding, Macklin, Macmillan, & A. H. Leighton, 1963, pp. 440–441; Srole, Langner, Michael, Opler, & Rennie, 1962, pp. 388–389). When the Neuropsychiatric Screening Adjunct was administered to World War II soldiers who had recently been exposed to different degrees of combat it was found that

". . . . men who had undergone air raids or buzz bomb attacks in Europe were more often subject to psychosomatic symptoms than men who had no personal experience with enemy fire. Men who had been subjected to close range enemy fire—rifle fire, mortars, artillery—indicated a somewhat higher level of disturbance while men who had been in actual combat were . . . most likely to have these emotional reactions" (Star, 1949, pp. 447–448).

In a detailed and careful analysis, Star showed that these effects could not be explained by differences in background such as educational level. Clearly, the experience of combat was producing symptoms resembling those observed in psychiatric patients.

Further evidence that normal individuals respond to stressful events with symptoms like those found in psychiatric patients is provided by Hastings' (1944) World War II study of 150 men in the Eighth Air Force who had completed their 30-mission tour of duty without reporting sick. Since men who are predisposed to breakdown were found in another study generally to report sick before flying half this many missions (Reid, 1961, p. 202), Hastings' finding that 95 per cent of his subjects had developed symptoms of operational fatigue is particularly compelling. Hastings identified operational fatigue as a condition that, unlike flying fatigue, is not cured by a few days' rest but can often be cured by a week and a half of therapy. It is a form of psychopathology attributed in these cases to the wartime flying experience rather than to previous neurotic symptoms or to family history.

Observations were also made during World War II of the responses of civilian populations to bombing. In a review of these materials, Janis (1951) concluded that repeated reports in both England and Germany indicate

"Under conditions of severe bombing there is marked incidence of temporary emotional shock, presumably even among persons who were previously emotionally stable. Such reactions may take the form of excessive anxiety symptoms or of mild depression and apathy" (pp. 96–97).

Unfortunately, the investigators whom Janis reviewed had no direct information about the psychological condition before the bombing experience of the persons whose reactions they observed. Bremer's (1951) study of a northern Norwegian village does not suffer from this defect. As resident physician from January, 1939, to August, 1945, he surveyed the entire population of 1400. When the village suffered enemy occupation and air raids he found that 22 persons developed "war neurosis," that is, "acquired nervous states caused by the direct effects of war," in which

"the main syndrome was fear with its accompanying somatic conditions: starting, tremor, palpitation, precardial pains. Add hereto in the majority of cases: fatigue, insomnia, and uncharacteristic dedolations. In a few cases the depression is extremely predominant.

"In two of the women, the nervous reaction is more correctly characterized as psychotic: in the one the syndrome was one of religious-ecstatic exaltation of one or two weeks' standing; the other suffered from a depression marked by anxiety lasting 3–4 weeks" (p. 57).

There have also been some relevant studies of reactions to stressful events other than those produced by war. For example, Stierlin reported that about 25 per cent of persons involved in railway and mine accidents in Valparaiso, Chile, developed symptoms immediately (Murri, 1912, p. 537).

Lindemann (1944, pp. 146–147) followed up the survivors of the Cocoanut Grove fire in Boston. On the basis of his observations of these persons and of others who had lost a friend or relative, he emphasized the importance of the situation, and the irrelevance of personal factors as determinants of extreme grief reactions.

Nor are such reactions observed only in obviously disastrous situations. Fried (1963) found indications of grief and mourning, similar to those described by Lindemann, in the majority of a sample of 566 men and women who had been forced to relocate from a slum section of Boston to make way for urban renewal. Their reactions included

"the feelings of painful loss, the continued longing, the general depressive tone, frequent symptoms of psychological or social or somatic distress, the active work required in adapting to the altered situation, the sense of helplessness, the occasional expressions of both direct and displaced anger and tendencies to idealize the lost place" (p. 15).

Finally, in a study of reactions to President Kennedy's death (Sheatsley & Feldman, 1964), 89 per cent of a national sample reported that during the 4 days following the assassination they experienced 1 or more of 15 physical and emotional symptoms such as "Didn't feel like eating," "Had headaches," "Had an upset stomach," "Had trouble getting to sleep," and "Felt nervous and tense." Most of these 15 items are similar to ones from the Army Neuropsychiatric Screening Adjunct discussed previously.

Whether or not the symptomatic responses to these events persist might be expected to depend on whether, when the event is over, the individual is returned to the *status quo ante* or, alternatively, finds that his circumstances have changed for the worse. Thus war-related stressful events such as bombing, might be expected to produce reversible symptoms unless the individual suffered severe injury or loss. On the other hand, when heavy loss is sustained, as in the case of the survivors of the Cocoanut Grove fire, it is not so obvious that recovery from symptoms should automatically occur.

As expected, the finding is that persons who have suffered a stressful event that does not involve a permanent loss generally recover spontaneously from its effects. Thus Bremer (1951, p. 57), following the civilian cases of "war neurosis" that he found in the northern Norwegian village, reported: "In all cases the prognosis was good, the symptoms disappearing when the patients were removed from the danger zone. In those who once more experienced war actions, the symptoms generally recurred."

Ginzberg and his colleagues (1959a, p. 19) studied the postwar adjustment of 534 "ineffective soldiers" systematically sampled from the men inducted in the last 4 months of 1942. An ineffective soldier was defined as "any man whom the Army discharged prior to demobilization for reasons of psychoneurosis, psychosis, inaptitude, or traits of character which made him unsuitable for retention in military service."

Relying mainly on Army and Veterans Administration records, Ginzberg and his colleagues classified types of readjustment after discharge into three major patterns: early, delayed, and unsuccessful. Early readjustment meant at least adequate civilian performance within 2 years of discharge. Delayed adjustment took longer than 2 years. Unsuccessful readjustment was indicated by failure of performance during the last 2 years for which information was available for a given soldier. Men in the modal group, 44 per cent, were judged to have made an early readjustment. Only 11.1 per cent were in the delayed readjustment category and 19.3 per cent were judged to have made unsuccessful readjustments. For the remaining 25.6 per cent of the sample, no data were available concerning adjustment.

The findings for persons suffering a stressful event that may involve a permanent loss are similar. Thus, for example, on the basis of his observations of reactions to the severe and destructive earthquake in Messina in 1907, Gabbi suggested that the special term "earthquake neurosis" be used to describe the fact that ". . . the clinical syndrome was produced immediately, that in general its duration was brief, as in acute illnesses, and that the symptoms disappeared without leaving any trace" (quoted without reference in Murri, 1912, p. 537). Similar conclusions were reported by Stierlin concerning reactions to railway and mine accidents in Valparaiso, Chile. He found that, although about 25 per cent of persons involved in the accidents developed symptoms immediately after the disaster, these symptoms diminished except in a few cases (Murri, 1912, p. 537).

Lindemann (1944) reported, in a follow-up of 13 bereaved victims of the Cocoanut Grove fire, that all but 1 were judged, after a series of psychiatric interviews, to have made a satisfactory adaptation in 4 to 6 weeks. Similarly, among 27 relatives of deceased hospital patients who were interviewed soon after the death and again 2 to 4 months later, 22 felt better and had fewer symptoms at the time of the second interview, and 4 others felt better although their symptoms continued (Clayton, Desmarais, & Winokur, 1968).

Also, Fried (1963) found that only the minority, 26 per cent, of the women in his sample of persons relocated from a Boston slum reported that they still felt sad or depressed 2 years later, with another 20 per cent stating that symptoms lasted for periods of 6 months to 2 years. Slightly smaller percentages were found among the sample of 316 men.

In the study by Sheatsley and Feldman (1964) of reactions to President Kennedy's assassination, interviews were done 5 to 9 days after the day of the assassination. Although 89 per cent of the sample had reported experiencing physical and emotional symptoms during the first 4 days, only 50 per cent reported that they still had at least one symptom at the time of the interview.

It appears, then, that in the majority of cases psychological symptoms developed in response to a stressful event disappeared spontaneously within a limited time after the termination of the event, even when a serious loss had been suffered. There was, however, almost always a minority of whom this was not true. Some of these exceptions may be individuals whose symptoms predated the stressful event, since most investigators did not have data on their subjects' prior conditions. Others, however, appear to be individuals for whom the symptoms yielded some advantage or secondary gain.

THE PROBLEM OF SECONDARY GAIN AND LOSS

Probably the most striking evidence that apparently reversible symptoms become fixed if they are rewarded is provided by the experience of the U.S. Army in the early years of World War II. During this period psychiatric casualties were evacuated to hospitals far from the front and given therapy designed to bring out the inner conflicts precipitated by the combat experience (Glass, 1953). As a result "During the abreaction procedures patients pleaded or insisted that they not be sent back to combat" (p. 287). Furthermore, "As the therapist participated with his patient in the dramatic reliving of battle scenes, he almost invariably identified with the distress and needs of the patient and was therefore impelled to promise relief from future battle trauma" (p. 287). Thus the patient's symptoms became his means of escape from further combat, and, not surprisingly, few recovered to the point where they could be returned to the front.

In contrast, experience during World War I and the latter part of World War II with treatment at a forward evacuation hospital indicated that a large proportion of cases of combat psychiatric breakdown could be returned to their units. The difference appeared to be that for the soldier in this situation loyalty to the men in his combat unit remained a strong and meaningful motivation which, if properly supported, reduced or eliminated the gain to be made from maintaining disabling symptoms and thereby escaping further combat (Glass, 1953). Thus it was found that even for the more severe reactions, including the "pseudopsychotic" or "3-day" psychoses, psychiatrists should be instructed to permit ". . . no doubt to arise in the patient's mind that he will not return to full combat duty after a brief rest" (Noyes & Kolb, 1963, p. 456).

For the soldier whose symptoms did persist, a further complication was introduced at a later stage by the issue of compensation (Kardiner & Spiegal, 1947). The patient's reactions to this therapist were confused by the fact that the latter was supposed both to rid him of his symptoms and to determine whether his symptoms indicated that he deserved compensation. In this situation, Kardiner and Spiegal concluded, ". . . the most important of all [external factors] that tend to render the neurosis chronic is compensation for the resulting disability" (p. 392).

Not only may the symptoms persist because they are rewarded but also, as shown in illuminating sociological analyses of mental illness, they may in some circumstances be perpetuated by a system that punishes the individual for attempting to escape the status of mentally ill person once he has been so labeled (e.g., Sheff, 1966, p. 87). Thus, Wilde (1968) has shown that once an individual has been labeled mentally ill by his family or friends, the official decision to start commitment procedures depends more on the determination of the relative or friend who is the petitioner than on his description of the potential patient's behavior. Furthermore, Scheff (1966) has demonstrated that, once proceedings for involuntary commitment to a mental hospital have been started, the decision to commit is likely to be made by psychiatrist and judge regardless of how the potential patient behaves (pp. 130–155). Finally, Goffman (1961) has vividly described how, once the person is in the hospital, ". . . the setting and the house rules press home to the patient that he is, after all, a mental case . . ." (p. 151).

On the basis of his analysis, Sheff (1966) proposed that persistent psychological disorder be considered nothing but a social role in which the individual remains because of social sanctions (p. 25). We must emphasize, however, Sheff's caveat that for heuristic purposes he made his analysis one-sided. Thus, although granting the existence of symptomatic responses to stressful social events which persist only because of social sanctions, let us look at evidence that stressful events can produce symptoms which persist without social support.

EFFECTS OF EXTREME SITUATIONS

In a review of clinical observations about psychological disorder together with results from laboratory investigations of frustration, traumatic avoidance learning, and experimental neurosis, Wilson (1963) found common themes:

"On the one hand, the foundation for pathology is laid by a progressive state of emotional arousal that finally reaches disastrous proportions. . . . Secondly, the constant feature of the behavioral symptoms is their stereotypy and repetitiveness. Once established, the symptoms are remarkably intractable to control by external reward or punishment. . . . These . . . characteristics of behavior pathology, anchored as they are in careful experimental work, furnish substantial corroboration for . . . similar features noted . . . in the clinical literature" (pp. 143–144).

Experimental Studies

Investigators who have succeeded in producing persistent disorders in the laboratory have employed two types of procedures. In one, an animal is forced to respond to a situation in which cues are insufficient for a consistent discrimination. Thus Liddell (1953) used weak electric shock to condition animals to respond with leg flexion to a metronome, and then changed the situation by, for example, reducing the time interval between metronome and shock or altering the rate of the metronome, so that the animal was no longer able to respond consistently to the conditioned stimulus. Liddell pointed out that the animal could not escape the necessity of responding since the restraining harness, together with ". . . preparation for the conditioning session induces in the animal a steadily maintained state of general expectancy or vigilance" (p. 169). Liddell's procedures consistently produced chronic behavior disorders in his subjects.

Working with instrumental rather than Pavlovian conditioning, Maier (1956) has demonstrated a similar effect. In his procedure the animal is trained on the Lashley jumping stand to jump consistently either to a lighted or to a dark door rather than to the alternate door, which is locked. After this discrimination is well established, the apparatus is programed so that the door, lighted or dark, to which the animal has learned to jump is locked on random trials. Thus the animal is placed in a situation in which it cannot obtain a consistent outcome by responding to previously learned cues. At the same time, it is forced to respond by means of a shock administered through the floor of the jumping platform. After a series of insoluble trials, unless special preventive conditions have been introduced most animals develop a fixated response, usually a position habit, which is not altered when the problem is again made soluble even if the fixated response is punished.

In both of these procedures it is the inconsistency or inadequacy of the environmental cues that appears to produce the maladaptive behavior. What psychological processes underlie this effect has not been established (e.g., Feldman & Green, 1967; Maier, 1956), but it is clear that severe physical punishment is not a necessary condition (e.g., Feldman & Green, 1967, p. 262).

In contrast, punishment is central to the prodecure used by Solomon (1954) to induce a fixed, ineradicable response. In Solomon's procedure the conditioned stimulus is followed by an intense, just subtetanizing, electric shock. After a few escape responses, the animal learns to avoid the shock by responding to the conditioned stimulus before the shock begins. Once this avoidance is established, it does not extinguish even though the animal is never again shocked.

Analogies have been drawn between the behaviors observed in animals subjected to these experimental procedures and psychological disorders seen in man. The inference is made that these human psychological disorders are produced by exposure to environmental conditions like those used in the laboratory studies of animals. However, in view of the immensely superior ability of human beings to master their environment by means of symbolic manipulation, the validity of such an analogy cannot be assumed. The question is, then, whether we have any information about how human beings react to environmental conditions like those used in the laboratory to produce irreversible maladaptive responses in animals. As it happens, we have extensive information on this matter as an unhappy legacy of recent history.

Effects of Extreme Situations on Human Adults

The conditions in a "normal German concentration camp" have been described by a researcher who was himself a prisoner:

"The prisoner was exposed to the severest forms of mental and bodily ill-treatment by violent criminals and other anti-social individuals, who here had every opportunity of giving vent to their aggression towards the community. Every one of the 'capos,' 'Blokkältester,' and even more the uniformed guards could, with impunity, knock down, ill-treat and kill a prisoner, without even having to explain their actions. Apart from this, one was confronted with a world of new stimuli which had no connection with anything in one's life outside the camp, but to which one had to react in an adequate manner or risk terrible punishment. No one was instructed about this 'new scale of values,' which was so completely absurd that it was not possible to find any relationship at all to the values one was familiar with in a normal world" (Eitinger, 1964, p. 130).

Thus it appears that the camp situation combined Solomon's severe punishment with Liddell's and Maier's environmental capriciousness. The longterm effects on survivors of this experience have been studied most thoroughly by Leo Eitinger in his comparison of three groups of Norwegian and three groups of Israeli ex-prisoners (1964).

The six groups studied by Eitinger are described in Table 8-1. The disorders found in each group, classified according to probable etiology and diagnosis, are summarized in Table 8-2. We see that in 5 groups psychological disorders were attributed to concentration camp experiences, the proportions of disorder in this category ranging from 16 per cent in the Norwegian Team Group to 82 per cent in the Israeli Work Group. Note that these are not the proportions of disorders attributed to concen-

Table 8-1. Descriptions of Six Groups of Ex-prisoners
Studied by Eitinger

Eitinger's Designation of Group	n	Composition of Group
Norwegian Clinical	96	Patients hospitalized in University Psychiatric Clinic, Vinderen, Oslo, between June 1, 1945 and June 30, 1961
Norwegian Team	152	First 152 persons examined by "the Medical Board of 1957" for possible compensation by the Norwegian government for disabilities resulting from imprisonment
Norwegian Work	80	Norwegian ex-prisoners fully employed
Israeli Psychotic	104	Inmates of all Israeli mental hospitals on October 1, 1961 except one hospital for tuberculosis cases
Israeli Neurotic	92	Patients receiving psychiatric treatment but not hospitalized in institutions for psychotics
Israeli Work	66	Members of two *kibbutzim*

Table 8-2. Eitinger's Findings Concerning Etiology and Types of Psychological Symptoms in Six Groups Studied
(Values in per cent)

Etiology	Symptom Type	Group					
		Norwegian Clinical (n = 96)	Norwegian Team (n = 152)	Norwegian Work (n = 80)	Israeli Psychotic (n = 104)	Israeli Neurotic (n = 92)	Israeli Work (n = 66)
All organic disorders whether due to captivity experiences or not		25.0	79.6	...	8.7	19.6	3.0
Psychological disorders possibly due to precaptivity personality or current stress situation	Psychosis	14.6	2.0	...	40.4	...	...
	Neurosis	12.5	2.0	...	...	21.7	...
	Psychopathy	19.8	...	...	1.9	...	...
	Neurasthenia	1.0	...	...	...	...	...
	Unclassified	...	...	...	...	...	10.6
	All symptom types	47.9	3.9	...	42.3	21.7	10.6
Psychological disorders attributed to captivity experiences	Psychosis	5.2	2.0	...	47.1	...	1.5
	Neurosis	21.9	9.2	...	...	...	6.1
	Psychopathy	...	5.3	...	1.9	...	...
	Personality change with impairment	...	...	...	...	58.7	74.2
	All symptom types	27.1	16.5	...	49.0	58.7	81.8
Well		...	...	100.0	...	...	4.5

tration camp experiences by Eitinger, who differentiated between organic disorders based on physical injuries sustained in camp and those based on organic defects of other origin. We have not maintained this distinction, however, since it is not relevant to our purpose of determining whether unfavorable social environments produce persistent symptoms of psychological rather than organic injury.

In order to evaluate the results summarized in Table 8-2, let us consider what the ideal conditions would be for determining whether concentration camp experiences produced persistent psychological disorder. These conditions are as follows:

1. Data on life histories are available from sources other than the subjects to eliminate all cases in which precaptivity experiences or personality might account for present disorders.

2. Physical examinations are done to eliminate cases in which physical injuries or defects could account for present symptoms.

3. Current stress situations are ruled out as explanations for present symptoms.

4. Secondary gain is ruled out as an explanation of current disorders.

Table 8-3 summarizes the advantages and disadvantages of each of the six groups in terms of these criteria for research design. Although each of Eitinger's groups meets some of these conditions, none meets them all. We could, then, conclude that the existence of environmentally produced persistent psychological disorder in human beings is not proved

Table 8-3. Advantages and Disadvantages of Eitinger's Six Groups For Testing Hypothesis That Concentration Camp Experiences Caused Psychological Disorder

| Control Factors | Group | | | | | |
	Norwegian Clinical	Norwegian Team	Norwegian Work	Israeli Psychotic	Israeli Neurotic	Israeli Work
Life history data available from sources other than the subjects	Yes	Yes	No	For some cases	For some cases	No
Physical examinations done	Thorough in all cases	Thorough in all cases	Only in doubtful cases	Less thorough in all cases	Less thorough in all cases	None
Present stress situations ruled out or identified	Probably	Probably	Not specified	Probably	Probably	Yes
Secondary gain ruled out	No	No	No	No	No	Yes

by this study, but could also conclude that because of the nature of the problem it may never be better proved. Doubts are raised because, in each group in which Eitinger attributed some cases of persistent psychological disorder to concentration camp experiences, one can find at least one other possible explanation of the symptoms observed. However, the fact that the other explanations vary from group to group makes them in sum less persuasive. For example, although secondary gain is a possible explanation for the Norwegian Team Group, it will not hold for the Israeli Work Group, given the norms concerning work in their *kibbutzim* (Eitinger, 1964, p. 44). Conversely, while unavailability of life history data makes precaptivity personality a possible explanation of current symptoms in the Israeli Work Group, this explanation is fairly well ruled out for the Norwegian Clinical and Team Groups. Let us, therefore, tentatively reject etiological explanations specially tailored to fit the gap in information or control in each of the groups studied, and see what the implications are of accepting Eitinger's findings that five of the six groups contained cases of persistent psychological disorder attributable to concentration camp experiences.

One question to be considered is whether psychological disorders resulting from captivity experiences are like the usual psychological disorders seen by clinicians. The results in Table 8-2 show that Eitinger found in both the Israeli Neurotic Group and the Israeli Work Group that the majority of cases, those we have labeled "Personality change with impairment," did not fit into any conventional nosological category. Summarizing his findings, Eitinger concluded:

"The most predominant sequel to the concentration camp captivity seems to be the deep changes in personality, a mental disability which affects every side of the personality's psychic life, both the intellectual functions and, especially, emotional life and the life of the will, with the many facets of difficulties in adaptation and the complications which this leads to in the victim's life. Chronic anxiety states, often provoked by nightmares and/or sleeplessness at night, by disturbing thought associations and memories during the day, chronic depressions of a vital type, inability to enjoy anything, to laugh with others, to establish new, adequate, inter-personal contacts, the inability to work with pleasure, to fill a position—in short, the inability to live in a normal way—are among the most characteristic symptoms of this condition" (pp. 190–191).

If this conclusion is correct, the uniqueness of this psychological disability in concentration camp victims argues against generalizing from the concentration camp to other, more usual types of unfavorable environments. As Eitinger pointed out, however, the findings on this issue are controversial. On the one hand, some other investigators who found a unique psychological disorder in concentration camp victims may have been biased by the German government's decision that compensation for injury in a concentration camp could not be granted to any person diagnosed as neurotic (Eitinger, 1964, p. 160). Furthermore, there are investigators who, aside from this consideration, explicitly rejected the conclusion that concentration camp experiences produced a unique form of psychological disorder (e.g., Targowla, 1954). On the other hand, a study comparing patients who had been in concentration camps with a control group of patients suggested that it was difficult to diagnose this special condition, and that this difficulty led to many cases being erroneously placed in conventional diagnostic categories (Nathan, Eitinger, & Winnik, 1963). In sum, the evidence concerning the uniqueness of psychological disorders among concentration camp victims raises doubts but is too controversial to lead to the conclusion that concentration camp findings are not relevant to the effects of other, more usual unfavorable environments.

Assuming for the moment, then, that examination of the effects of concentration camps will help us to understand the effects of more usual unfavorable environments, let us consider the implications of the differences Eitinger found among the various groups he studied. His subjects are not, of course, a representative sample of either Norwegian or Jewish concentration camp inmates since the death rate from injury, disease, and the effects of malnutrition was high among all prisoners, even the relatively favored Danish (Helweg-Larsen, Hoffmeyer, Kieler, E. H. Thaysen, J. H. Thaysen, Thygesen, & Wulff, 1952). Nor are his subjects a representative sample of survivors. Therefore, the percentages in Table 8-2 can only be taken to indicate in the most general way the differential effects of the concentration camp experiences on the various groups.

Some differences are so large, however, that it hardly seems reasonable to dismiss them as due to sampling bias. This is particularly true of the difference between the two work groups. Subjects in both of these groups were selected according to the criterion that they were apparently meeting normal community demands, even, in the case of the Israeli Work Group, the relatively stringent demands of the *kibbutzim*. The finding that less than 5 per cent of the Israeli Work Group who were probably healthy before captivity remained well, whereas 100 per cent of the Norwegian Work Group were well, seems strong evidence, therefore, of a real difference in the effects on these groups of the experiences suffered in concentration camps. The implication, given the relatively favored treatment of Norwegian compared to Jewish concentration camp prisoners (Nansen, 1949), is, as other studies have suggested (e.g., Häfner, 1968), that the probability of symptoms enduring increases with the severity and duration of captivity. Let us consider, then, the experiences of the Norwegian Work Group to throw light on how much punishment the human being can absorb without permanent psychological injury.

The modal period of captivity for the Norwegian Work Group was 1 to 2 years: 36 per cent were in camp for less than 1 year, 44 per cent for 1 to 2 years, and 20 per cent for 2 years or more. Six per cent underwent "organized and systematic" torture, and 4 per cent suffered head injuries. Although none was reduced to a "living corpse," all suffered what Eitinger (1964) characterized as relatively reasonable loss of weight, adding, "More emphasis should be laid on 'relatively' than on 'reasonable'" (p. 59). At least one third suffered from somatic illnesses during captivity. Nine per cent reported that they had ". . . suffered very severe mental stress, such as fear of being shot, anxiety for other members of the family, and so on . . ." (p. 61).

Although it is not possible to pinpoint the differences between the experiences of the Norwegian Work Group and those of the other groups, except for duration of captivity, the Norwegian Work Group generally suffered less than the others (pp. 57–62). Nearly half of the Norwegian Team Group suffered torture and head injuries; about 20 to 40 per cent of all Israeli groups and of the Norwegian Team Group were "living corpses"; and at least half of the Israeli Neurotic and Work Groups and two thirds or more of the Norwegian Team Group suffered from somatic illnesses. All of the Israeli captives suffered realistically from fear of death and anxiety about their families.

Recall now that we are asking what environmental conditions, if any, produce irreversible psychological disorder in human beings and that our concern with this question is motivated by our attempt to explain the consistently high rates of disorder found in the lowest socioeconomic stratum in society. We should consider at this point, therefore, whether we would expect to find anything like concentration camp conditions in the stratum with which we are concerned.

It seems unreasonable to suggest that either single unfavorable events or even the cumulation of unfavorable events that might be experienced by a lower-class person would approximate the concentration camp experience, even though the lowest stratum in society has at some times and in some places suffered severely from deprivation and abuse (e.g., Booth, 1889). Moreover, the epidemiological studies reviewed in Table 2-5 were all done in societies in which lower-class living conditions were not at their worst. All were conducted in the twentieth century, and most were done in relatively prosperous and relatively egalitarian societies. Thus, although Eitinger's study indicates that prolonged exposure to an abusive, irrational environment can produce irreversible psychological disorder, his findings do not suggest an explanation of the high rates of psychological disorder reported for the lower class. Rather, these considerations strongly suggest that, insofar as symptoms in the lowest social stratum indicate persistent psychological disorder, they cannot be explained as due to the impact on adults of harsh lower-class social environmental conditions.

Such a conclusion would not, however, rule out the possibility that the lower-class environment produces irreversible psychological disorder by its impact on children rather than on adolescent or adults. Let us, therefore, consider what is known about how unfavorable environments affect early personality development.

Effects of Early Deprivation on Development

Both stimulus deprivation and maternal deprivation have been implicated by some investigations as sources of irreversible personality defects, but these findings have also aroused controversy and attempts at disproof. Let us see where the matter stands today, first with respect to stimulus deprivation, by reference to evaluative reviews of this extensive literature.

There can be no doubt that animals raised in an environment which minimizes stimulus variability show intellectual and emotional defects as a consequence. However, comparison across mammalian species up to the chimpanzee indicates that, when the environmental deficit is removed, the power of recuperation increases as one moves up the evolutionary scale (Bronfenbrenner, 1968, pp. 691–692). Consistent with this evolutionary trend are Dennis's findings that children in an institutional environment providing an extremely low level of stimulation from the time of birth showed early, deleterious effects but seemed intellectually normal when tested at 4½ to 6 years of age, after they had started kindergarten. Moreover, these children showed little evidence of emotional disturbance (Bronfenbrenner, 1968, pp. 721–724).

As a number of critics have pointed out (e.g., Casler, 1968), in most studies of maternal deprivation this variable has been confounded with stimulus deprivation. Bronfenbrenner's careful comparison of studies of different species done under varied conditions suggests, however, that the two factors have independent effects. His analysis shows that the immediate effects of maternal deprivation, independent of stimulus deprivation, become more severe as one moves up the evolutionary scale. The longer period of dependence and the greater role played by learning and secondary reinforcement in the development of higher species apparently produce this difference by strengthening the bond between the infant and the nurturing mother. Despite this characteristic vulnerability, however, absence of the mother, although manifesting itself in clear differences in the quality of social relationships, does not necessarily lead to defective personality development either in monkeys (Bronfenbrenner, 1968, p. 682) or in human beings (pp. 743–746), so long as social relationships with peers are possible. Moreover, studies of adolescents and adults who spent periods of their early childhood in institutions and thereby suffered varying combinations of stimulus and maternal deprivation provide no evidence of long-term effects from the experience (pp. 741–743).

From his review Bronfenbrenner concluded, therefore, that there is no evidence that children exposed to stimulus and maternal deprivation, even in combination, will not recover from the immediate effects after a period of exposure to a more favorable environment. Furthermore, O'Connor (1968) comes to the same conclusion on the basis of a review of theoretical and methodological problems in studies of human subjects (pp. 549–558). On the other hand, both reviewers assume that there is a limit to human recuperative ability (O'Connor, 1968, p. 564), and Bronfenbrenner (1968) spells out this limit quite precisely:

"Nor do these results signify that more extreme or long lasting forms of early deprivation would not have correspondingly severe and persistent effects. Specifically, the evidence from work with monkeys strongly suggests that permanent debility might result if human infants were deprived early in life of any contact with other people—peers as well as adults" (p. 743).

Again, however, we must draw the same conclusion that we did with respect to the conditions Eitinger found productive of irreversible psychological disorder in adults: that it would be absurd to suggest that such conditions distinguish the lower-class environment from the environments of more favored classes.

The implications of these findings for the social environmental view of etiology are startling. For they point to the possibility that the conditions of social deprivation and pressure experienced by children and adults in the lowest social stratum are not severe enough to produce self-perpetuating psychological disorder in otherwise normal human beings.

SPECIFICATION OF THE SOCIAL CAUSATION HYPOTHESIS

This analysis of the available evidence suggests some major modifications in the social causation hypothesis about the high rates of psychological disorder in the lowest social stratum. For the weight of the evidence appears to be that the high rate of symptoms is not due to environmentally produced personality defects. Rather, it points to the importance of contemporary situational factors in contributing to potentially transient symptomatology. Accordingly, let us restate the social causation hypothesis as follows:

1. The high rate of symptoms in the lowest socioeconomic stratum indicates transient responses to the relatively frequent and severe stress situations that characterize the lower-class environment.

2. Insofar as these symptoms are not transient, they are perpetuated by secondary gain rather than by environmentally induced personality fects.

In stating these propositions, we are making an assumption about the direction of the relation between stressful events and psychological symptoms. Specifically, we are assuming that symptoms associated with stressful events are consequences of these events, not the other way around. The alternative relationship, in which symptoms precede stressful events, would imply that one consequence of persistent psychological disorder is the presence of self-induced stressful events in the life history.

The problem of whether the victim brings the stressful event on himself does not arise, of course, in the case of "an act of God," such as an earthquake, or even of some obviously man-made disasters, such as the bombing of civilian populations. It is an issue, however, for many stressful events of civil life, including not only obvious examples such as loss of a job but also less obvious instances such as development of cancer (e.g., Bahnson & Bahnson, 1966; Greene, 1966; Hagnell, 1966b; Le Shan, 1966; Muslin, Gyarfas, & Pieper, 1966; Schmale & Iker, 1966).

To deal with this ambiguity in the relation between stressful events and psychological symptoms, we need data on a community population from at least two points in time. At the first point, psychological symptoms would be measured. At the second point, data would be collected on stressful events occurring after the first symptom measure, and a second symptom measure would be taken. To the extent that the symptoms are produced by the events, we should find no relation between frequency of stressful events and symptom levels before the onset of the events. Furthermore, the occurrence of stressful events should be followed by elevation of symptom levels. Alternatively, to the extent that these events are consequences of psychological disorder, level of prior symptoms should be positively related to the frequency of their occurrence and symptom level might not rise following the onset of the event.

To test these alternatives, let us examine data collected from a community sample of Irish, Jewish, Negro, and Puerto Rican respondents studied at two points in time. The general procedures of this study were described in Chapter 6.

Both the first and second interviews included the 22 Midtown items. The second interview also included questions about changes occurring between the two interviews, especially changes in work and physical health. The relevant questions about intervening events were as follows:

Let's see, a Columbia University interviewer first visited your family to ask about health matters in   That was about   months ago.

Have you had any serious illness or health problems since then?

(If yes:) What is (was) the matter?

What were you doing most the past   months?

(For males:) Working, looking for work, or something else?

(For females:) Working, looking for work, keeping house, or something else?

Has there been any change in your work or job status since the time of the first interview   months ago?

(If yes:) What change was that? Why did you change?

The responses to these questions were classified into the following categories of intervening events.

Unfavorable events:

1. Poor physical health of respondent; that is, physical illness, injury, accident, etc., which seems current in negative consequences either because the respondent says so or because it seems inherently so.
2. Poor physical health of respondent's spouse.
3. (For male main earner:) Socioeconomic deterioration; that is, demotion, business failure, unemployment, etc.
4. (For female spouses:) Economic deterioration; that is, demotion, business failure, unemployment, etc., of male main earner.

Favorable events:

5. (For male main earners:) Socioeconomic improvement; that is, promotion, raise, "better job," etc.
6. (For female spouses:) Socioeconomic improvement; that is, promotion, raise, "better job," etc., for male main earner.
7. Birth of one or more children.

Unknown:

8. Events related to the above whose current consequences could not be ascertained.
9. Other events which were mentioned adventitiously, that is, not in response to specific questions.
10. No evidence of an intervening event.

The classification was made independently by a psychiatrist and a sociologist who had no information about respondents' psychological symptoms. They disagreed on 14 of the 74 events classified by either one or the other in the favorable and unfavorable categories listed above. None of these disagreements involved the question of whether an event was favorable or unfavorable.

Utilizing these data, let us consider first the question of whether stressful events happened more often to people who already showed signs of possible psychological disorder. Table 8-4 shows the relation between prior symptom level and the occurrence of favorable as against unfavorable events. The symptom score has been divided into categories of less than

Table 8-4. Relation of Level of Prior Psychological Symptoms to
Quality of Subsequent Events in Respondents' Lives[a]

	Number of Symptoms on 22-Item Midtown Measure	
Quality of Events	Less than Four (%)	Four or More %
Unknown and mixed	61.3	57.6
Known favorable or unfavorable	38.7	42.4
Total per cent	100.0	100.0
Number of respondents	106	33
Favorable	53.7	57.1
Unfavorable	46.3	42.9
Total per cent	100.0	100.0
Number of respondents	41	14[b]
Events Likely to Be Controlled by Respondent		
	(%)	(n)
Favorable	57.1	4
Unfavorable	42.9	4
Total per cent	100.0	
Number of respondents	28	8
Events Not Likely to Be Controlled by Respondent		
	(%)	(n)
Favorable	46.2	3
Unfavorable	53.8	2
Total per cent	100.0	
Number of respondents	13	5

[a] The number of respondents is less than the total subsample of 15 because of wives not included in the first interview.

[b] One respondent who reported two favorable events, one likely and one not likely to be under his control, is excluded from the remainder of the table.

Table 8-5. Direction of Symptom Change in Relation to Quality of Events Impinging on Respondents at Time of Second Interview[a]

Symptom Change	Quality of Events		
	Favorable (%)	Unfavorable (%)	Unknown and Mixed (%)
Fewer symptoms on second interview	65.0	22.2	55.5
More symptoms on second interview	35.0	77.8	44.4
Total per cent	100.0	100.0	100.0
Number of respondents	20[b]	18	55
$\chi^2 = 5.39$; df $= 1$; $p < .05$			
Number of respondents not changing	(n)	(n)	(n)
Same number of symptoms on both interviews	4	5	13
No symptoms on either interview	6	2	12
Total number of respondents	30	25	80

	Events Likely to be Controlled by Respondent	
	(%)	(%)
Fewer symptoms on second interview	61.5	15.4
More symptoms on second interview	38.5	84.6
Total per cent	100.0	100.0
Number of respondents	13	13
$\chi^2_y = 4.06$; df $= 1$; $p < .05$		
	Events Not Likely to Be Controlled by Respondent	
	(n)	(n)
Fewer symptoms on second interview	4	2
More symptoms on second interview	2	3
Number of respondents	6	5

[a] Number of respondents is 3 less than subsample of 151 because of wives not included in first interview and breakoffs who did not give symptom data on second interview.

[b] One respondent who reported two favorable events, one likely and one not likely to be under his control, is excluded from the remainder of the table.

four and four or more on the basis of Langner's finding (Langner, 1962) that this division was useful in discriminating between respondents evaluated by Midtown psychiatrists as psychiatrically "impaired" and those judged psychiatrically "well." Furthermore, events have been divided into those over which the respondent was less likely to have had some control (categories 2, 4, and 6 in the list of events above) and those over which the respondent was more likely to have had some control (categories 1, 3, 5, and 7).

We see that, regardless of the respondent's probable degree of control, there is no relation between prior symptoms and frequency of onset of unfavorable events. Thus these data provide no support for the position that stressful events of these types are consequences of psychological disorder.

The alternative possibility, that stressful events produce psychological symptoms, is tested in Table 8-5. Here we find a significant relation, in the expected direction, between the quality of events and the direction of symptom changes. Furthermore, the direction of the relationship remains the same whether or not the respondent was likely to have had some control over the events.

This test of the directionality of the relation between stressful events and symptoms is limited in terms of both the events and the symptoms included. It may be that some types of symptoms are more likely to be induced by stressful events than others, or that certain types of symptoms predict subsequent self-induced stressful events. Thus wider tests will be needed to determine the generality of the relationships found here. However, with this caveat, the evidence available seems sufficient to justify further investigation of the social environmental hypothesis we have specified.

SUMMARY

In order to develop a nomological net for the construct of psychological disorder, studies of the relation between unfavorable social environments and psychological symptoms are reviewed. A considerable number of studies showed that psychological symptoms associated with stressful events disappeared spontaneously even when the event involved a permanent loss. At the same time, studies of experimental neuroses in animals, of long-term reactions to imprisonment in German concentration camps, and of stimulus and maternal deprivation of both animal and human infants all suggest that unfavorable social environments can cause irreversible psychological disorder. However, the conditions that seem to produce this effect appear to be more extreme than any likely to be found in the environment of the lower class in twentieth century, technologically advanced societies, where most epidemiological studies have been done. This review and analysis of the literature leads to a set of propositions specifying the social environmental etiological hypothesis. Evidence is presented to support the assumption, underlying one of these propositions, that stressors of civil life produce symptoms rather than the other way around.

CHAPTER 9

Frequency and Severity of Stress Situations in Different Status Groups

Two propositions about the relative frequency and severity of stress situations in different status groups are implied by the social environmental hypothesis developed in Chapter 8. The first proposition concerns class differences. The consistent observation in epidemiological studies of high rates of symptoms in the lowest social class, together with our hypothesis that environmentally induced symptoms are responses to stress situations, leads to the prediction that stress situations will be more frequent and more severe in the lower-class environment.

The second proposition is that, within a socioeconomic stratum, stress situations will be found to be more frequent and more severe among members of disadvantaged than among members of advantaged ethnic groups. Thus, for example, low-income Negroes should experience harsher stress situations than low-income white Anglo-Saxon Protestants. This proposition is basic to our strategy for testing our social causation hypothesis against an alternative genetic explanation of the consistent empirical finding of a high rate of psychological symptoms in the lowest socioeconomic stratum.

Although these predictions concerning ethnic and class differences appear plausible, let us examine the available evidence to see whether it supports them.

ETHNIC AND CLASS GROUPS TO BE STUDIED

The most extensive social psychological literature on ethnic differences concerns comparisons between Negroes and whites. This concentration in the literature reflects the fact that the Negro-white contrast is the most important ethnic basis for status in most societies where the two groups are found in sizable numbers. Thus the decision to limit our investigation

131

to Negroes and whites, although based on the availability of literature, also leads to our focusing on disadvantaged and advantaged ethnic statuses of wide import. In addition to its importance as a basis for status, race offers a distinct methodological advantage. As a characteristic ascribed at birth, race, in contrast to language and religion as bases for ethnic identification, anchors our analysis to a factor clearly antecedent to stress situations.

In the case of class, we will make only the gross distinction between middle and lower class. Although important intraclass differences may exist in factors related to exposure to stress situations, the available data do not permit a consistent breakdown at this more refined level, particularly since we will have to distinguish between classes within races. Moreover, the contrasts between middle and lower classes are sufficiently complex and extensive to justify the grosser analysis even if some intraclass differences are lost.

CONCEPTUAL FRAMEWORK FOR INVESTIGATION OF FREQUENCY AND SEVERITY OF STRESS SITUATIONS

The framework that we propose to use to investigate the frequency and severity of stress situations is based on Selye's paradigm of the stress response, translated into social and psychological terms (B. P. Dohrenwend, 1961). Selye views stress as a state of the organism that underlies both its adaptive and maladaptive reactions. His paradigm of the stress response contains four main elements: antecedent *stressor,* defined as any agent that produces stress, frequently a poison or electric shock in his physiological research with animals; antecedent *mediating factors* that increase or decrease the impact of the stressor, such as climate or diet; the *adaptation syndrome,* indicating an intervening state of stress in the organism, for example, nonspecific chemical changes; and consequent *adaptive* or, when there has been "derailment" of the mechanisms underlying the adaptation syndrome, *maladaptive* responses, such as, in Selye's examples, high blood pressure or diseases of the heart and kidneys.

Our concern is with status-related sources of stress. Our focus, therefore, will be on the antecedent elements of the stress paradigm, stressors and mediating factors, as these are associated with the social status of the individual.

Major Social Stressors

Koos (1946), on the basis of his analysis of what "trouble" meant to respondents from a small sample of low-income families in New York City, made a distinction that partially anticipates our translation of Selye's formulation into social and psychological terms. "Troubles" are " . . .

situations outside the normal pattern of life . . . situations which block the usual patterns of activity and call for new ones" (p. 9). Such situations were distinguished from "exigencies" of life such as a month-to-month struggle to pay the rent.

We agree with much of Koos's formulation, since we define major social stressors as objective events that disrupt or threaten to disrupt the individual's usual activities. Unlike Koos's formulation, however, ours contains no necessary negative implication. Nor does the notion of stressors, as we use it, necessarily imply the subjective upset of "crisis" as used by such theorists as Lindemann (1944), Caplan (1964, especially pp. 39–40), and the Cummings (J. Cumming and E. Cumming, 1962, especially pp. 54–55). For example, an event that would be a small problem for most people may be a "crisis" for a psychiatric patient, as it arouses subjective distress. For present purposes, whether a stressor induces a "crisis" is an empirical question. We limit the term "stressor" to objective events. Moreover, we concentrate on *major* social stressors, that is, on those that are likely to disrupt the customary activities of all or most normal individuals exposed to them.

Some stressors are relatively rare and are restricted to limited populations—for example, natural disasters such as floods and tornadoes. Such events occur without reference to social status. They will, therefore, not concern us here.

In contrast, stressors such as marriage and the birth of a first child are experienced by most people. Much has been written about the role of such stressors in "developmental crises" (e.g., Erikson, 1959). And we would expect their impact to be strongly affected by mediating factors associated with social status.

Another class of stressors is related to the fact, discussed in Chapter 5, that in our society upward mobility is the norm. The progression of ethnic groups over succeeding generations is from positions of lower to those of higher social status. Within the life span of any given individual, however, the obstacles to such mobility may be greater or lesser, depending on such characteristics as race and class. Given our interest in status-linked sources of stress, therefore, it seems meaningful to distinguish between stressors that exert pressure on the individual to change from his customary activities to a new set of higher-status activities, in contrast to events that exert pressure on him to change his customary activities to a new set of lower-status activities. The former we shall term "achievement-related" events, for example, promotion. The latter we shall call "security-related" events, for example, losing a job.

Since the same event can be classified both in terms of whether it is developmental or nondevelopmental, and in terms of whether it is achievement-related or security-related, we can start with the typology of

Table 9-1. Examples of Four Types of Social Stressors

	Developmental	Nondevelopmental
Achievement	Finish regular schooling Obtain first adult job Leave parental home Marriage Birth of first child Birth of later child Marriage of child Birth of grandchild	Training for new skills Job promotion or business expansion Assignment of nonjob leadership responsibilities Move to more prestigious neighborhood Nonroutine vacation
Security	Unable to finish regular schooling Unable to obtain first adult job Loss of job Jilted Divorce Death, illness, or injury of breadwinner Miscarriage Illness, injury, or death of child Divorce of child Illness, injury, or death of grandchild	Failure in training course Job demotion or business failure Deprivation of nonjob leadership responsibilities Move to less prestigious neighborhood

major stressors shown in Table 9-1. There are no a priori grounds for attributing greater intrinsic severity to one rather than another of the four types of major social stressors set forth in Table 9-1. Instead, it seems likely that any given stressor can be more or less severe, depending upon the context in which it occurs. Such context we referred to earlier as being supplied by the antecedent mediating factors associated with a particular stressor.

Antecedent Mediating Factors

To avoid confusion with the conditioning concepts of learning theory, we have substituted the term "mediating factors" for Selye's "conditioning factors" in our translation of the paradigm of the stress response. Selye discussed two different types of such factors: "internal," that is, those that have become part of the body through heredity, past experience, etc., and "external," that is, those acting from without, such as climate, which influence the response to a physical stressor such as a poison or electric shock that is simultaneously acting on the organism. In changing from Selye's focus on physical and chemical aspects of stress responses to their social and psychological aspects, we have maintained his basic distinction between *internal mediating factors* and *external mediating factors.*

Under internal mediating factors we include such characteristics of the individual as his abilities, drives, values, and beliefs. External mediating factors consist of more or less adequate material resources such as savings and health facilities, as well as social support from primary groups, consisting of family and friends (e.g., Hamburg & Adams, 1967).

We shall be concerned with mediating factors both as they increase or decrease the impact of stressors, and as they increase or decrease the duration of the effects of this impact on different status groups. Thus among external mediating factors we shall be concerned, for example, not only with level of savings and other factors that define the person's situation at the time, say, of the impact of unemployment, but also with factors such as social support that could mediate the duration of the emotional effects of unemployment. Similarly, among internal mediating factors we shall be concerned not only with the individual's values, which determine the extent of the loss or gain resulting from the stressor, but also with his abilities, and his beliefs concerning his own abilities, which may determine the effectiveness of his response and hence the duration of the effects of a stressor.

STRESSORS

Social Class

We have hypothesized that stressors are more common in the lower class. Evidence from census data concerning developmental security stressors seems to support this suggestion. The shorter life expectancy in the lower class (Mayer & Hauser, 1950; Moriyama & Guralnick, 1956; Tuckman, Youngman, & Kreizman, 1965) implies that families in this group are more likely to be disrupted by the premature death of a parent (e.g., Langner & Michael, 1963, p. 161). The inverse relation between social class and rate of marital breakdown by divorce or separation (Bernard, 1966; Hollingshead, 1953; Udry, 1966) indicates that, even when both parents survive, the lower-class family is less likely to remain intact.

Lower-class members are also likely to experience more developmental achievement stressors because of their relatively high birth rate. Although higher birth rates in higher-income groups have been reported, this finding may not be generalizable, for example, beyond the special conditions found in the university town that was the setting for one such study (Dice, Clark, & Gilbert, 1964). The more general finding is that the highest birth rate is in the lowest social class (e.g., Duncan, 1964; Notestein, 1953). Furthermore, this stressor is more likely in the lower class to take the form of premature birth (Menchaca, 1964; World Health Organization, 1961).

Nondevelopmental stressors do not present an equally clear picture of relatively high rates in the lower class. For nondevelopmental security stressors, the evidence is mixed. Job loss or layoff is more likely to be the lot of the lower-class hourly-wage worker than of the middle-class salaried worker. Moreover, physical health is more often disrupted in lower-class persons by some diseases, such as cervical cancer (e.g., Paloucek & Graham, 1966), and by accidents and injuries to both adults (Haddon, Valien, McCarroll, & Umberger, 1964; Sanders, 1964) and children (Deutsch, 1961). On the other hand, many types of cancer (e.g., Paloucek & Graham, 1966), as well as disorders of the circulatory system (Marks, 1967), are no more common in the lower than in the middle class.

Furthermore, most nondevelopmental achievement stressors are probably almost entirely outside the experience of most lower-class members. Job promotions and business expansions are by their very nature almost exclusively middle-class stressors. In addition, it is characteristically the middle-class member who seeks or has thrust on him responsibilities for community organizations and activities. Even vacations, particularly when they involve extensive travel or other radical changes from usual living patterns, are more likely to impose stressors on the middle than the lower class.

On balance, the evidence concerning the relation between social class and rates of stressors of all types is equivocal. Although some types of stressors are more common in the lower class, others are equally common in all classes, and still others appear to be more frequently experienced by persons in higher class positions. In order to determine precisely how to weight these different patterns it would be necessary to have data on the actual rates of the various types of stressors. One would, for instance, have to determine the frequency of layoffs in the lower class as against promotions and business expansions in the middle class. In the absence of such figures, the most reasonable conclusion seems to be that there is no firm evidence that the overall rate of stressors varies with social class.

Race

Previous writers have pointed out that many comparisons between whites and Negores fail to control social class (e.g., Dreger & Miller, 1968; Pettigrew, 1964, p. 70). Since Negroes are on the whole poorer than whites, such uncontrolled comparisons may reveal differences that are entirely due to the class difference between the races. Moreover, our prediction concerning frequency of stressors concerns ethnic differences within social classes. Therefore we shall limit our review to comparisons of Negroes and whites in which the necessary class controls are available.

In his review of the literature on race differences, Pettigrew presented evidence that the higher rate of physical illness and the shorter life expectancy among Negroes, although due primarily to the difference in average class status of Negroes and whites, cannot be explained entirely in these terms (1964, pp. 97–99). In particular, when the physical health of Negroes and whites in the lowest occupational groups is compared, Negro laborers are found to have relatively high rates of illness.

Lower-class Negroes also experience higher rates of several other stressors, when compared to lower-class whites. Security is more often threatened not only by ill health but also, according to U.S. government statistics, by loss of employment (Shanahan, 1966), which is likely to be prolonged (Aiken & Ferman, 1966), and by disruption of marriage through divorce or separation (Bernard, 1966; Udry, 1966; Udry, 1967). Moreover, lower-class Negroes more often suffer the developmental achievement stressors of premature or abnormal birth (Pasamanick, Knobloch, & Lilienfeld, 1965). On the other hand, there appears to be no major category of stressor in which the rate for lower-class whites is higher than that for lower-class Negroes.

The same generalization appears to be true for middle-class Negroes with respect to their white class counterparts. Although there is no evidence of areas in which middle-class Negroes experience fewer stressors, they have higher rates of divorce and separation than their white class counterparts (Udry, 1966) and higher rates of premature and abnormal births (Pasamanick et al., 1956). The evidence suggests that both lower-class and middle-class Negroes experience stressors more frequently than their white class counterparts.

EXTERNAL MEDIATING FACTORS

Social Class

Insofar as the lower-class person attempts to deal with stressors by manipulation of objective conditions, he is disadvantaged with respect to external mediating factors, since his relatively small income makes him less able than a member of the middle class to command needed goods and services. For example, medical services available to the lower-class person are likely to be less adequate than those available to the middle-class person (e.g., Langner, 1966; Marden, 1966). Faced with the stressor of forced residential relocation, the lower-class person is likely to be offered less satisfactory alternative living quarters (B. P. Dohrenwend, 1961). Similarly, in almost any stressor situation, the lower-class person is likely to find that his leverage on agencies which might provide help is relatively weak.

Whether the lower-class person is also disadvantaged with respect to external factors that directly mediate his ability to adjust emotionally to a stressor is not so obvious. The question here is whether there is any evidence of a class difference in the availability of social support to mediate the impact of a stressor. The data on shorter life expectancy (Mayer & Hauser, 1950) and relatively high rates of broken marriages in the lower class (Bernard, 1966; Hollingshead, 1953; Udry, 1966), cited earlier in discussing stressors, are also relevant here. Not only is the family disruption itself a stressor, but also the lower-class person is more likely to face other stressors in the setting of a family in which one parent is missing. Even when the marriage is not broken, it appears that lower-class husbands and wives tend to behave toward each other in such a way as to provide relatively little mutual psychological support (e.g., Komarovsky, 1962, pp. 144–147, 156–159, 170–171; Rainwater, 1965). Furthermore, the lower-class person is less likely to be involved in voluntary organizations that might provide extrafamilial supportive relationships (Cohen & Hodges, 1963; Wright & Hyman, 1958).

Race

The overriding issue here is the extent to which the disadvantaged group status of Negroes mediates the impact of stressors. Does racial prejudice, for instance, tend to alter the relations among the various components of class? For example, do Negroes who are at comparable levels with whites with respect to indicators of class other than income also have the same income levels? In general, the occupations in which there are relatively high proportions of Negroes tend to yield low income (R. W. Hodge & P. Hodge, 1965; A. F. Taeuber, K. E. Taeuber, & Cain, 1966). Furthermore, there is evidence that at any level of education below college Negroes' incomes are markedly lower than those of whites (Blau & Duncan, 1967; B. P. Dohrenwend, 1966; Hare, 1965; Levenson & McDill, 1966).

A second question concerning the external factors that mediate the impact of stressors on Negroes is whether, given a comparable income, a Negro can buy as much in goods and services as a white person. With respect to many types of goods and services, the middle-class Negro is probably not particularly handicapped in most sections of the United

States. However, a study of nine Negro families who moved into white middle-class suburbs of Boston indicates that this statement cannot be made with regard to housing (Hughes & Watts, 1964). Although all were able to make the move, even a strong Massachusetts law against discrimination did not prevent some families from experiencing long delays, a factor that could prove a severe handicap if the move were a nonvoluntary consequence of a stressor such as forced relocation for slum clearance. Moreover, middle-class Negroes have been found to live in more crowded conditions than their white class counterparts (Tulkin, 1968), and the general trend in the United States seems to be toward a heightening of the barriers excluding Negroes from nonghetto residential areas (Schnore & Evenson, 1966; Farley & Taeuber, 1968). Thus it appears unreasonable to assume that even middle-class Negroes, if faced with a stressor that required a change of residence, would not be more handicapped than their white class counterparts.

The middle-class Negro is also relatively handicapped with respect to the availability of social support to ameliorate the impact of stressors. The finding, based on recent U.S. census data, of a relatively high rate of family instability among middle-class Negroes (Bernard, 1966; Udry, 1966), implies that the Negro is more likely to face a stressor in the context of a family from which one spouse is absent.

Lower-class Negroes also appear to be relatively handicapped, compared to their white class counterparts, by external factors that mediate the impact of stressors, except in one respect. Relative disadvantage for the Negro is implied, for example, by lower levels of income at comparable levels of education below graduation from college (e.g., B. P. Dohrenwend, 1966), by severe and increasing restrictions on residential choice (Schnore & Evenson, 1966; Farley & Taeuber, 1968), and by relatively high rates of marital breakdown (Bernard, 1966; Udry, 1966). On the other hand, there is evidence from both local and nationwide studies that lower-class Negroes have more extrafamilial sources of social support than lower-class whites. They are more likely to belong to organizations and to participate more actively in the organizations to which they belong than their class counterparts among whites (Orum, 1966; Rainwater, 1965, p. 232). Furthermore, some of these organizations characterizing the Negro lower class are specifically designed to deal with the stressor of death in the family (e.g., Davis & Dollard, 1940, pp. 53–54). However, this one area of advantage does not seem sufficient to counterbalance the lower-class Negro's relative disadvantage with respect to material conditions and familial stability. Therefore, lower-class Negroes are probably more handicapped overall than lower-class whites by external factors that mediate the impact of stressors.

INTERNAL MEDIATING FACTORS

To investigate the question of whether class and racial groups differ with respect to internal mediating factors, we will draw on the extensive literature on group differences in abilities, motives, and values, with two restrictions First, because we cannot assume long-term stability in either class differences (e.g., Bronfenbrenner, 1958) or race differences, we will emphasize recent work.

The second restriction arises from the fact that many studies comparing social class and racial groups use school children as subjects. If we were to extrapolate the results of these studies to adults, our conclusions would probably be in error for one of two reasons. In order to use studies whose subjects were young enough so that the entire population was in school, we would have to assume stability of both social class and personality from childhood to adulthood. At least for recent years in the United States, this does not appear to be a reasonable assumption (e.g., Haan, 1964, p. 598). If, on the other hand, we were to try to minimize the amount of extrapolation by choosing studies whose subjects were students close to adulthood, we would have a selected population that excluded school drop-outs (e.g., Empey, 1956, p. 705). For these reasons, we will rely as much as possible, and except where otherwise noted, on studies using adult subjects.

Social Class

Let us consider first the internal mediating factors that influence the likelihood of the individual being effective in manipulating objective conditions. One factor of this type is intellectual ability. Because of the difficulty of obtaining reliable and representative measures of adult intelligence, studies of school children have to be relied on for information on this question.

In recent years a number of questions have been raised about the well-known finding of lower average measured intelligence in lower-class children. The first question is whether the tests used to measure intelligence yield a spuriously low estimate of the intelligence of lower-class children because the test content is more familiar to middle-class children. Studies designed to investigate the effect of this bias showed that a relatively unbiased test still yielded results favoring middle-class children (Eells, Davis, Havighurst, Herrick, & Tyler, 1951; Haggard, 1954) and that the scores on this type of test were not as closely related to success in school work as other intelligence scores (Eells et al., 1951). Therefore it is not possible to dismiss the observed class difference on this count when one is concerned with predicting level of intellectual performance.

Another question about the class difference in intelligence scores is whether it is an artifact produced by the nature of the incentives offered to children in the test situation. It has been argued from experimental evidence that lower-class children respond more favorably to personal reinforcement than to task-oriented reinforcement (Zigler & Kanzer, 1962) and that they require more tangible rewards than middle-class children (Haggard, 1954; Zigler & de Labry, 1962). Since the intelligence tester typically offers nontangible, verbal rewards that are frequently task-oriented, the implication is that the intelligence scores of lower-class children are invalid. However, the finding of a difference in response to personal as against task-oriented reinforcement has failed to replicate (Rosenhan & Greenwald, 1965). Furthermore, direct evidence showing that class differences remain significant even when money is offered challenges the argument concerning tangible rewards (Klugman, 1944). In addition, the finding that some performance scores differ little among social classes (Cropley, 1964) suggests that ineffective incentives cannot explain the discrepancies that are found.

The class difference in verbal intelligence scores appears to be substantial (Cropley, 1964; Haywood & Dobbs, 1964; Karp & Silberman, 1966) even when performance scores are matched (Jahoda, 1964). Moreover, this difference between classes increases with age from 10 to 14 (Jahoda, 1964), indicating that it is reasonable to extrapolate to adults the class difference observed in children. Since problems as diverse as getting a good job and obtaining skilled psychiatric care (e.g., Hollingshead & Redlich, 1958, Ch. 9) are related to verbal skill, the implication of this difference is that lower-class individuals are handicapped in trying to deal with stressors by manipulation of objective conditions.

Another factor that could affect the likelihood of success in manipulating objective conditions is an individual's confidence in his ability to do so. The relevant finding is that members of the lower class are more likely than those of the middle class to see themselves as powerless to manipulate their environment in their own interest (e.g., Archibald, 1953; Bell, 1957; Dean, 1961; Lefcourt, 1966; Mechanic, 1965, p. 449; Simpson & Miller, 1963). Consistent with this class difference is the finding that lower-class persons tend to devalue mastery over nature (Schneiderman, 1964).

Whether this tendency of lower-class persons toward resigned acceptance of their lot is, on balance, disadvantageous or not is, however, a matter of controversy. One view emphasizes ". . . the vitally important survival value of this life-style under the actual conditions of life for the impoverished" (Schneiderman, 1964, p. 17), with the implication of a situation so hopeless that the impoverished person, like an animal in a trap, will only injure himself by struggling. Recognizing that some external as well as internal mediating factors tend to make it difficult for the lower-class person to manipulate his environment effectively, we nevertheless question whether the contribution made by resignation toward psychic adjustment to the disadvantaged situation outweighs the fact that this attitude of helplessness further impedes dealing with stressors by manipulation of objective conditions. The answer seems to lie in historical as well as current cases suggesting that resignation has never proved more than a temporary palliative for the individual, since it has serious consequences in ordinary situations (e.g., Deasy, 1956; Koos, 1954) and disastrous results in the face of severe stressors (e.g., Lukas, 1966). Therefore, recognizing that we are, in the view of some social commentators, adopting a class-tied value position, we interpret the attitude of resignation on balance as aggravating rather than ameliorating the impact of stressors on the lower class.

It is important to distinguish between the attitude of hopelessness about being able to get what one wants and an internalized value that defines certain goals as more desirable than others. The latter may indeed serve to protect lower-class individuals from the impact of certain stressors. In particular, the lower-class emphasis on economic security rather than achievement, insofar as the two are opposed (Centers & Bugental, 1966; Gunderson & Mahan, 1966; Hyman 1953; Larson & Sutker, 1966; Rosen, 1959), appears to be such a protective value. Evidence that it is not simply a rationalization for lack of ability is found in studies showing that the lower-class preference for security holds in junior high school (Wylie, 1963) and high school students (Sewell, Haller, & Straus, 1957) even when intelligence is controlled, and that it is found among the parents of gifted children in their aspirations for their children (Frierson, 1965).

There is, however, another question: Should this valuation of security be interpreted as a rationalization based on veridical perception of the *limited opportunities* open to the lower-class person rather than as an internalized value (e.g., Merton, 1957; W. B. Miller, 1958)? We could find no evidence that permits a clear choice between these much-debated alternatives. Pearlin and Kohn (1966) have argued plausibly, however, that related differences in the valuation of self-direction versus obedience to external authority can be traced to differences in the structural requirements of middle-class as opposed to working-class occupations. On these grounds, it would also seem plausible to interpret the lower-class adult's expressed preference for economic security as a learned value rather than to assume that it represents a rationalization of unresolved chronic conflict about frustrated achievement needs. This interpretation is also indirectly supported by evidence that aspirations for achievement are in some cases directed toward the children of lower-class persons (Chinoy, 1952), indicating one way in which potential conflicts concerning one's own achievement may have been avoided.

An experiment comparing reactions of unemployed males of higher and lower status is suggestive of the way in which the security value may mediate the impact of the unemployment stressor (Goodchilds & Smith, 1963). The results showed that, whereas higher-status subjects tended to perform worse in group problem solving and to give lower self-ratings with longer periods of unemployment, lower-status subjects were likely to improve in both performance and self-ratings with longer unemployment. A difference in values between low- and high-status subjects could explain these results; that is, since the subjects were receiving unemployment insurance, economic security was, at least for the time, not threatened, whereas achievement was threatened by the very fact of unemployment. Thus the psychological loss from unemployment for the security-oriented lower-status subjects would have been less than for the achievement-oriented higher-status subjects. This interpretation of these results must be considered highly speculative, however, particularly since the index of status was composed of four elements, two of which—age and marital status—are not indicators of social class.

Although the available evidence is far from decisive, we suggest, on the basis of the observed class difference in valuation of economic achievement and security, that nondevelopmental achievement stressors would have more severe impact on members of the middle class, and nondevelopment security stressors on members of the lower class. In a fully developed welfare state in which a firm floor had been constructed to provide basic security for the lowest social class, this class difference in aspirations would leave the middle class more vulnerable to stressors insofar as their impact is mediated by values. Where such a floor has not been established, however, neither class would seem to be clearly advantaged by the way in which its values mediate the impact of stressors.

Race

Let us first compare lower-class Negroes and lower-class whites. With respect to intelligence the general finding is that, on the average, Negroes score lower than whites (e.g., de Neufville & Conner, 1966; Dreger & Miller, 1968; Pettigrew, 1964, p. 131; Shuey, 1966; Tulkin, 1968). However, the Negro deficit is not necessarily uniform for all intellectual abilities (e.g. Dreger & Miller, 1968) or for all age and sex groups. A recent study showed, for example, that by age 14, as Negro girls improved and white boys declined somewhat in verbal skill relative to their age norms, these two subgroups approached the same level (Baughman & Dahlstrom, 1968, p. 52).

A further difficulty in generalizing about race differences is that many studies do not control for class. Furthermore, even when controls are attempted, the lower-class Negro is frequently found to be more disadvantaged than the lower-class white with respect to some factors associated with class position (e.g., Dreger & Miller, 1968, p. 9). This fact, together with the finding that the difference between Negro and white average intelligence scores is sharply reduced when the two groups are approximately equally deprived (Pettigrew, 1964, pp. 118–120), has been used to argue against drawing any conclusions about the comparative intelligence of lower-class whites and Negroes. However, this argument holds only if one is interested in determining why Negroes score lower. Our question, in contrast, is whether lower-class Negroes are disadvantaged, for whatever reason, by poorer development of intellectual abilities. Their lower average intelligence scores suggest that this is the case.

Before drawing a conclusion, however, we must consider the argument that the lower Negro scores are an artifact of the testing situation. In particular, it has been shown that Negro subjects respond better to Negro testers (e.g., Klugman, 1944; Pettigrew, 1964, p. 117). Nevertheless, the evidence to date does not suggest that this factor can explain fully the race difference in scores (e.g., Dreger & Miller, 1968, pp. 18–19).

Although it appears that lower-class Negroes probably do score lower on general intelligence tests even when possible artifacts are allowed for, some recent studies indicate that this finding cannot be generalized to all types of intellectual performance. For example, one study of creativity showed that, particularly in the older student group compared, ranging from 5 to 9 years old, Negroes scored as high as whites or higher on the Unusual Uses Test (Iscoe & Pierce-Jones, 1964), and another study revealed that creativity scores of Negro and white first and sixth graders generally did not differ (Singh, 1968). Second, an investigation of the effects of impulsivity among fifth-grade students on errors on the Matching Familiar Figures Test found the Negro students were significantly less impulsive and made significantly fewer errors than white students (Coyle, 1967).

Thus there is no decisive evidence that, overall, either Negro or white lower-class members are handicapped by intellectual abilities, relative to each other, in manipulating objective conditions in response to stressors. However, to the extent that intelligence test scores themselves are a factor in manipulating these conditions, as, for example, in obtaining certain types of jobs, the fact that lower-class Negroes probably score below their white class counterparts on the more conventional measures of intellectual ability puts them at a disadvantage (e.g., de Neufville & Conner, 1966).

Lower-class Negroes also appear to be handicapped relative to their white class counterparts by less confidence in their ability to manipulate their environment in their own interests (e.g., Hammonds, 1964; Lefcourt, 1966; Lefcourt & Ladwig, 1965; Pettigrew, 1964, p. 19). The nature of this handicap is indicated by evidence that Negroes' lack of self-confidence is particularly acute when they are interacting with whites (e.g., Pettigrew, 1964, p. 50). What we may be seeing here are negative effects on self-confidence stemming from the relative deprivation felt by the Negroes when called upon to compare themselves with whites (Stouffer, Suchman, DeVinney, Star, & Williams, 1949). This inference is supported by the finding that Negroes, when competing with whites, gained if their status in the situation was defined with reference to a group having high prestige among Negroes (Lefcourt & Ladwig, 1965).

Thus it appears that lower-class Negroes are more handicapped by internal factors than lower-class whites in dealing with stressors by manipulation of objective conditions. Although this handicap stems partly from lack of self-confidence in situations involving whites, this specificity has little practical significance since, despite efforts of Negro separatists, the numerical minority status and economic weakness of the Negro community probably mean that there are few stressors with which a lower-class Negro can deal effectively without any involvement with whites.

We face two problems in comparing lower-class Negroes and lower-class whites with respect to values that mediate the impact of stressors by affecting the severity of subjective loss from the stressor. The first problem is that almost all of the relevant studies use school children as subjects. Since the school drop-out rate is particularly large among lower-class students, conclusions drawn from such studies may be limited to a subgroup of upwardly mobile lower-class youth.

The second problem is how to interpret complex results. Studies have reported that lower-class Negro mothers (Bloom, Whiteman, & Deutsch, 1965; Rosen, 1959) and lower-class Negro students have higher educational (Gottlieb, 1964; Wylie, 1963) and higher occupational aspirations (Brown, 1965) than comparable whites, as well as higher levels of aspiration in a test of skill (Boyd, 1952). Two studies contradict these results, however, by showing that Negro high school students are less likely to aspire to occupations requiring graduate or professional training (Gottlieb, 1964) and that Negro mothers' occupational aspirations for their sons are lower than those of white mothers (Rosen, 1959). At the same time, it has been reported that Negro and white students' realistic educational and occupational expectations do not differ (Gist & Bennett, 1963), and that the discrepancy between aspirations and realistic expectations is greater for Negroes than for whites (Gottlieb, 1964). The problem is to determine what these findings indicate about the value placed on achievement by lower-class Negroes.

A lead is found in studies showing that in game situations subjects with relatively low levels of need achievement tend to choose plays with either a very high or a very low probability of success (McClelland, 1961, p. 212). Such a relationship between extreme goal setting and relatively low need achievement was predicted by Atkinson from his theory of risk-taking behavior, on the assumption, supported by independent evidence, that low need achievers are concerned more with fear of failure than with hope for success (Atkinson, 1966). Atkinson argued that low need achievers ". . . are setting their aspiration level either *defensively* high or *defensively* low" (p. 20). If this interpretation is correct, it suggests that the high levels of aspiration assessed as unrealistic by lower-class Negroes indicate a high degree of ego involvement and anxiety with respect to failure, and hence vulnerability to achievement stressors. It appears, therefore, that there may be a subgroup of lower-class Negroes, represented by students who do not drop out of school, who are more vulnerable than their white class counterparts to achievement stressors.

With regard to middle-class Negroes, the evidence is that they do not differ from their white class counterparts in average intelligence (Pettigrew, 1964, p. 119; Tulkin, 1968). In this respect, therefore, they suffer no handicap in ability to manipulate objective conditions in reaction to stressors. The evidence is less clear, however, about their confidence in their ability to manipulate their environment. The relevant data come both from studies comparing middle-class with lower-class Negroes and from experimental studies comparing middle-class Negro college students with their white class counterparts.

The most extensive study comparing Negro middle- and lower-class subjects surveyed 1119 respondents in cities in the North and the South (Marx, 1967). This investigation found that Negroes who held more militant attitudes on civil rights were more self-confident (p. 90) and that attitudes were more militant among middle- than among lower-class Negroes (p. 63). This direct relationship between social class and militant attitudes is consistent with two studies of civil rights activity which showed that activism was associated with middle-class status in both the South (Weinstein & Geisel, 1962) and the North (Hughes & Watts, 1964). However, one study, possibly because of a relatively narrow range on the socioeconomic variable, reported no such relationship among a group of Southern subjects (Gore & Rotter, 1963), while another study showed that lower-class Negroes were more active than middle-class Negroes in school desegregation, possibly as the result of a "prolonged and intense desegregation movement" (Luchterhand & Weller, 1965, p. 88). Inconsistency is also found in studies of the relation between social status and self-hate, a characteristic that appears to be particularly incapacitating in Negroes (Roen, 1960). A study of Philadelphia Negroes showed that self-hate is greater in higher socioeconomic groups (Parker & Kleiner, 1964), and a study of Negroes in Georgia and California cities revealed a negative association between self-hate and social class (Noel, 1964).

Experimental evidence suggests, however, that, like lower-class Negroes, middle-class Negro students suffer particularly from lack of self-confidence in situations that require interaction with their white class counterparts (Katz & Benjamin, 1960; Katz, Goldston & Benjamin, 1958). The dynamics of this reaction appears to be that the white person represents a threat so that his presence leads to emotional arousal, and that level of arousal in turn influences performance as predicted from the inverted U function (Katz & Greenbaum, 1963). Thus, in a situation that is otherwise not arousing, the Negro subject will probably perform better in the presence of a white person, but in a situation that is otherwise threatening the heightening of arousal by the presence of a white leads to poorer performance. If this model of the reaction is correct, it suggests that the middle-class Negro would be most likely to be disadvantaged by interaction with whites when the severity of the stressor and the nature of other mediating factors highlighted the Negroes' perception of relative deprivation and hence made the situation a particularly threatening one.

The extent to which a stressor is threatening depends on external mediating factors and on the relation of the consequences of the stressor to the individual's values. In regard to levels of aspiration, insofar as student subjects can be taken as representative, the picture for middle-class Negroes does not differ from that for lower-class Negroes. That is, levels of aspiration are higher than those of white class counterparts in tests of skill (Boyd, 1952) and for education (Gottlieb, 1964) and occupation (Brown, 1965), with the possible exception that whites are more likely to aspire to highly prestigious professional occupations (Gottlieb, 1964). Furthermore, the finding of greater discrepancy between aspirations and realistic expectations among Negroes than among whites seems to apply to the middle class (Gist & Bennett, 1963). These findings, together with the argument presented earlier with respect to lower-class Negroes, imply that middle-class Negroes also have relatively low levels of need achievement and the associated high levels of fear of failure.

Direct comparisons of Negro and white students' levels of need achievement suggest, however, that this generalization may apply only to certain subgroups among middle-class Negroes. Specifically, these comparisons reveal both regional and sex differences, with Negroes showing higher

levels of need achievement than whites in the North (Rosen, 1959) but
not in the South (Brazziel, 1964; Grossack, 1957), and Negro females
displaying higher levels than white females at the same time that either
Negro and white males do not differ (Grossack, 1957) or Negro males
show lower levels than white males (Brazziel, 1964). Thus it appears
that middle-class Negro students vary considerably in their levels of need
achievement relative to whites.

ASSESSMENT OF FREQUENCY AND SEVERITY OF STRESS SITUATIONS

The data available on stressors, external mediating factors, and internal
mediating factors in different class and ethnic groups have proved far
from definitive. With the aid of some simplifying assumptions, however,
they do provide a basis for assessment of the plausibility of hypotheses
about class and ethnic differences in relation to stress situations. Accordingly, Table 9-2 presents the hypotheses that seem most plausible in light
of the evidence. The first line of the table shows that, with respect to
stressors,

1. The evidence is inconsistent and does not indicate, overall, that the
rate of exposure to stressors varies with class.
2. Negroes appear to be exposed to a higher rate of stressors than
their class counterparts among whites.

Table 9-2. Comparison of Frequency and Severity of Stress Situations
Experienced in Contrasting Class and Ethnic Groups
(Question mark indicates that the evidence does not suggest
a difference between groups)

	Social Class Groups	Ethnic Groups within:	
		Middle Class	Lower Class
Frequency of exposure to stressors	Middle ? lower	White < Negro	White < Negro
Severity			
As a function of external mediating factors	Middle < lower	White < Negro	White < Negro
As a function of internal mediating factors	Middle < lower	White ? Negro	White < Negro
As a function of combined external and internal mediating factors	Middle < lower	White < Negro	White < Negro

Concerning external mediating factors, the second line of the table indicates that

1. Lower-class persons are disadvantaged in comparison to middle class persons.
2. Negroes are disadvantaged in comparison to whites of comparable class.

The third line of the table indicates that, taking together all types of internal mediating factors, the most reasonable generalizations appear to be that

1. Lower-class persons are disadvantaged in comparison to middle-class persons.
2. The evidence is inconsistent and does not indicate, overall, that middle-class Negroes are disadvantaged in comparison to middle-class whites.
3. Lower-class Negroes are disadvantaged in comparison to lower-class whites.

The fourth line is based on lines 2 and 3 and indicates that, taking into account all the evidence concerning both external and internal mediating factors, the severity of the impact of stressors will differ for all groups compared:

1. Lower-class persons are disadvantaged in comparison to middle-class persons.
2. Middle-class Negroes are disadvantaged in comparison to middle-class whites.
3. Lower-class Negroes are disadvantaged in comparison to lower-class whites.

Thus the evidence for Negroes as against whites seems to support our proposition concerning the experience of stress situations in disadvantaged and advantaged ethnic groups within the same socioeconomic stratum, indicating that both the frequency and the severity of stress situations are greater for Negroes than for their white class counterparts. However, comparison across classes suggests that the impact of stress situations is more severe in the lower than in the middle class, but that there may not be a difference in the frequency of stress situations experienced in the two classes.

In sum these ethnic and class differences lend plausibility to the social environmental hypothesis about social class and situationally specific symptomatology. Moreover, the results of this analysis lay the groundwork for incorporating this hypothesis into our strategy for a crucial test of the etiological issue.

SUMMARY

Using a conceptualization of stress situations derived from Selye, we survey the literature to investigate hypotheses concerning class differences, and differences between Negroes and whites within classes, with respect to the frequency and severity of stress situations experienced. This review indicates that stress situations are both more frequent and more severe for Negroes than for their white class counterparts, and that stress situations are more severe, though not more frequent, for lower- than for middle-class persons, lending plausibility to the social environmental hypothesis developed in Chapter 8 and paving the way for its incorporation into our strategy for a crucial test of the etiological issue.

CHAPTER 10

The Probability of Secondary Gain or Loss in Different Status Groups

In Chapter 6 we reviewed evidence that sanctions directed at an individual may perpetuate symptoms of psychological distress beyond the termination of the precipitating stressor. Most striking are the instances in which the individual profits materially or socially from his symptoms despite their apparent unpleasantness. This problem, described, for example, in connection with programs of financial compensation for battle-induced disabilities (e.g., Kardiner & Spiegal, 1947), involves what is usually designated by the term "secondary gain." A related phenomenon, which may also serve to perpetuate symptoms, has been reported in a number of studies of institutional processes associated with mental hospitals (e.g., Goffman, 1961; Scheff, 1966; Wing & Brown, 1961). It has been observed that, once an individual is labeled mentally ill, he may be punished for not behaving appropriately and thus may adopt and continue to display psychological symptoms as a means of escaping punishment.

To investigate the full range of effects of sanctions on psychological symptoms, we must not overlook the reverse of the situations just described, that is, the case in which the individual suffers secondary loss as a consequence of his symptoms. If secondary gain helps to preserve symptoms, secondary loss would seem to mitigate against their continuation. For our purposes, there are two reasons for paying special attention to secondary loss as well as secondary gain. First, where we can demonstrate that a particular type of secondary loss is highly probable, we can infer a low probability of secondary gain from the same source, an important consideration since for the most part it is easier to estimate the probability of secondary loss than of secondary gain. Second, we may find that the probability of secondary loss varies with social status, a matter of central importance for the social environmental hypothesis we have proposed.

We will start, then, with two propositions concerning status differences in probability of secondary gain or, conversely, secondary loss, as a consequence of psychological symptoms. First, in partial explanation of the relatively high prevalence of psychological symptoms consistently found in the lowest social stratum, we propose that secondary gain is more likely, and/or secondary loss less likely, in the lower class than in higher classes. That is, lower-class prevalence rates may be elevated not only by the relatively large number of individuals developing symptoms, but also by a tendency for symptoms to persist longer once they have developed in a person in the lower class, as a function of the presence of secondary gain or absence of secondary loss associated with the symptoms.

Our second proposition is implied by our strategy for testing the social environmental versus the genetic hypothesis. This strategy rests on the assumption that environmental pressures that have etiological significance for psychological symptoms are greater for disadvantaged than for advantaged ethnic groups within a given social class. Therefore, insofar as secondary gain perpetuates symptoms, it follows that the probability of such gain should be greater for disadvantaged than for advantaged ethnic groups within a given social class. Conversely, insofar as secondary loss tends to terminate symptoms, the probability of secondary loss should be greater for the relatively advantaged ethnic groups.

Secondary gains or losses may be either material or social. Material gain is exemplified by financial compensation, and material loss by income reduction because of disability. Social gain may be realized in the form of sympathy, and social loss as criticism or rejection.

SOCIAL GAINS OR LOSSES

In the case of social gains or losses, we shall assume that the most powerful sanctions are likely to be administered by the primary group of family and friends. On this assumption, the attitudes of representative members of different class and ethnic groups toward persons with psychological symptoms should indicate the probability of social gain or loss from symptoms in these class and ethnic groups. Actually, since these attitudes are frequently rejecting and at best neutral (e.g., E. Cumming & J. Cumming, 1957), they tell us most directly about the probability of loss. We infer that the probability of gain is low or nonexistent where attitudes are highly rejecting.

Procedure

In the study of a subsample of 151 Irish, Jewish, Negro, and Puerto Rican residents of the Washington Heights area, described in Chapter 6, respondents were asked questions about six brief case descriptions, originally developed for attitude research by Star with psychiatric consultation (1955). These case descriptions, in the order in which they were presented, are as follows.

1. I'm thinking of a man—let's call him Frank Jones—who is very suspicious; he doesn't trust anybody, and he's sure that everybody is against him. Sometimes he thinks that people he sees on the street are talking about him or following him around. A couple of times, now, he has beaten up men who didn't even know him. The other night, he began to curse his wife terribly; then he hit her and threatened to kill her because, he said, she was working against him, too, just like everyone else.

2. Now here's a young woman in her twenties, let's call her Betty Smith. She has never had a job, and she doesn't seem to want to go out and look for one. She is a very quiet girl, she doesn't talk much to anyone—even her own family, and she acts like she is afraid of people, especially young men her own age. She won't go out with anyone, and whenever someone comes to visit her family, she stays in her own room until they leave. She just stays by herself and daydreams all the time, and shows no interest in anything or anybody.

3. Here's another kind of man; we can call him George Brown. He has a good job and is doing pretty well at it. Most of the time he gets along all right with people, but he is always very touchy and he always loses his temper quickly if things aren't going his way, or if people find fault with him. He worries a lot about little things, and he seems to be moody and unhappy all the time. Everything is going along all right for him, but he can't sleep nights, brooding about the past, and worrying about things that *might* go wrong.

4. How about Bill Williams? He never seems to be able to hold a job very long, because he drinks so much. Whenever he has money in his pocket, he goes on a spree; he stays out till all hours drinking, and never seems to care what happens to his wife and children. Sometimes he feels very bad about the way he treats his family; he begs his wife to forgive him and promises to stop drinking, but he always goes off again.

5. Here's a different sort of girl—let's call her Mary White. She seems happy and cheerful; she's pretty, has a good job, and is engaged to marry a nice young man. She has loads of friends; everybody likes her, and she's always busy and active. However, she just can't leave the house without going back to see whether she left the gas stove lit or not. And she always goes back again just to make sure she locked the door. And one other thing about her: she's afraid to ride up and down in elevators;

she just won't go any place where she'd have to ride in an elevator to get there.

6. Now, I'd like to describe a twelve-year-old boy—Bobby Grey. He's bright enough and in good health, and he comes from a comfortable home. But his father and mother have found out that he's been telling lies for a long time now. He's been stealing things from stores and taking money from his mother's purse, and he has been playing truant, staying away from school whenever he can. His parents are very upset about the way he acts, but he pays no attention to them.

Following the presentation of each case, the respondent was asked whether he thought anything was wrong and, if so, whether he thought the problem was one of mental illness. Unless he thought that there was nothing wrong, he was then also asked a series of questions concerning what kind of help or treatment the subject of the case description needed. Responses to this series of questions were coded into the following categories:

1. Nothing wrong.
2. Believes individual can get over it by himself.
3. Miscellaneous mild reactions, for example, needs vacation.
4. Needs help from family and friends or similar recommendation.
5. Needs help from professional person not specifically concerned with mental health, such as clergyman or general practitioner.
6. Needs outpatient help from mental health professional.
7. Needs mental hospitalization.

The first two of these responses imply that no sanctions are to be applied to the individual for the behavior in question. The third category includes the mildest sanctions, and the fourth indicates somewhat more severe criticisms of the individual's behavior.

A study by Phillips (1964) indicates that the fifth, sixth, and seventh recommendations represent increasingly severe levels of sanctioning of the persons in the case descriptions. Phillips presented a community sample of adult women with the first four of the Star descriptions reproduced above, plus a description of a normal person, and added for each case varied indications of the source of help to whom the person had gone:

> None.
> Clergyman.
> Physician.
> Psychiatrist.
> Mental hospital.

Each case was followed by a set of social distance items designed to measure the respondent's degree of rejection or acceptance of the individual. The results for all cases combined showed significant variation in degree of rejection, from least for "none" to most for "mental hospital." These results suggest that the first four of our help or treatment categories, which seem to be the equivalent of "none" in Phillips' study, represent less severe sanctioning than the last three. Phillips' data also show that these last three vary in severity of rejection in the order in which we have listed them, with mental hospitalization resulting in most severe rejection.

Respondents in our study were also asked to agree or disagree with seven items indicating varying degrees of social distance from former patients in a mental hospital. These items formed a Guttman scale, in the order of rejection shown in Table 10-1. Reproducibility of this scale is .909, and scalability is .602. These data will be used to examine social distance attitudes toward former mental hospital patients in different social classes.

Table 10-1. Percentage Willing to Accept a Former Mental Hospital Patient on Seven Social Distance Items

Social Distance Item	Response	Per Cent ($N = 150$)
It would be wise to discourage former patients of a mental hospital from entering your neighborhood.	Disagree	82.0
It would be unwise to encourage the close friendship of someone who had been in a mental hospital.	Disagree	72.0
You would be willing to sponsor a former patient of a mental hospital for membership in your favorite club or society.	Agree	67.3
If you were a personnel manager, you would be willing to hire a former patient of a mental hospital.	Agree	62.0
If you were responsible for renting apartments in your building, you would hesitate to rent living quarters to someone who had been in a mental hospital.	Disagree	54.0
You should strongly discourage your children from marrying someone who was formerly in a mental hospital.	Disagree	37.3
It would be unwise to trust a former mental hospital patient with your children.	Disagree	26.7

Results by Social Class

Using education as the indicator of social class, Table 10-2 shows the distribution of recommended actions given by our respondents for each of the six case descriptions. The cases have been grouped here according to the three larger diagnostic categories into which they fall (American Psychiatric Association Committee on Nomenclature and Statistics, 1952): schizophrenia, neurosis, and personality disorder, in order to relate these results to epidemiological findings reported in Chapter 2.

Reactions to the two cases of neurosis were highly tolerant at all educational levels, with the exception of the tendency of college graduates to recommend outpatient treatment by a mental health professional for the anxiety neurotic. This general lack of class differentiation in attitudes is congruent with our finding that epidemiological studies revealed no consistent relation between social class and rates of neuroses.

By contrast, responses to the descriptions of types of personality disorder revealed consistent attitudinal difference between educational levels. In both cases, respondents at lower educational levels, although showing some disagreement among themselves, reported relatively tolerant attitudes, compared to respondents with more education. Recall that our analysis of epidemiological studies showed that rates of personality disorder were consistently highest in the lowest social class. Combining this finding with the present attitudinal results suggests that the rates of prevalence of personality disorder may be determined in part by the lesser probability in the lower class and the greater probability in the middle class of rejection of individuals showing symptoms of this type of disorder. That is, once the symptoms develop they may persist longer in the lower-class person because of lack of negative social sanctions from family or friends.

This pattern of persistence in the lower class might also be expected for the shy, withdrawn behavior illustrating simple schizophrenia. Again the difference in class attitudes, although not as sharp as in the two cases of personality disorder, indicates greater tolerance in lower- than in higher-class groups. Thus this result is consistent with epidemiological findings of higher rates of schizophrenia in the lower class.

Note, however, that for the paranoid case the lower-class respondents did not show more tolerant attitudes. In fact, they were somewhat more likely than the higher-class respondents to recommend the most drastic action—hospitalization. However, given another lower-class attitude, this finding does not necessarily imply that paranoid symptoms should terminate more rapidly in the lower class than in higher strata.

In particular, the recommendation of hospitalization made in this case raises the issue of possible secondary effects of institutionalization. That

Table 10-2. Recommended Treatment of Fictitious Cases According to Education of Respondent
(Cutting points for χ^2's, indicated by broken lines, chosen to avoid expected cell frequencies of less than 5)

Type of Disorder Represented by Case	Recom- mendation[a]	Years of Education			
		0–7 (%)	8–11 (%)	12–15 (%)	16+ (%)
Schizophrenia[b]					
Paranoid	1	10.5	8.5	4.6	0.0
	2	0.0	2.1	1.5	0.0
	3	0.0	0.0	3.1	0.0
	4	5.3	2.1	3.1	0.0
	5	21.1	31.9	36.9	53.3
	6	63.2	55.3	50.8	46.7

$$\chi^2 = 1.25; \text{df} = 3; p > .50$$

Simple	1	21.1	21.3	7.7	0.0
	2	5.3	0.0	6.2	0.0
	3	26.3	17.0	10.8	6.7
	4	15.8	6.4	9.2	20.0
	5	21.1	46.8	55.4	66.7
	6	10.5	8.5	10.8	6.7

$$\chi^2 = 8.81; \text{df} = 3; p < .05$$

Neuroses	1	57.9	55.3	56.2	33.3
Anxiety neurotic	2	5.3	0.0	4.7	6.7
	3	5.3	4.3	6.2	6.7
	4	10.5	10.6	4.7	0.0
	5	15.8	27.7	25.0	53.3
	6	5.3	2.1	3.1	0.0

$$\chi^2 = 2.95; \text{df} = 3; p < .50$$

Compulsive phobic	1	68.4	72.3	58.5	60.0
	2	0.0	2.1	1.5	0.0
	3	5.3	6.4	1.5	0.0
	4	15.8	10.6	3.1	0.0
	5	10.5	8.5	35.4	40.0
	6	0.0	0.0	0.0	0.0

$$\chi^2 = 2.55; \text{df} = 3; p < .50$$
$$\Sigma\chi^2(\text{neuroses}) = 5.50; \text{df} = 6;$$
$$p < .50$$

Table 10-2. (Continued)

Type of Disorder Represented by Case	Recom-mendation[a]	Years of Education			
		0–7 (%)	8–11 (%)	12–15 (%)	16+ (%)
Personality disorder					
Alcoholic	1	57.9	31.9	16.9	6.7
	2	5.3	10.6	9.2	13.3
	3	5.3	4.3	3.1	0.0
	4	21.1	12.8	12.3	0.0
	Alcoholics Anonymous	5.3	17.0	18.5	6.7
	5	5.3	21.3	29.2	73.3
	6	0.0	2.1	10.8	0.0
	$\chi^2 = 20.73$; df $= 3$; $p < .001$				
Juvenile character disorder	1	26.3	36.2	23.1	20.0
	2	10.5	0.0	4.6	0.0
	3	26.3	19.1	12.3	0.0
	4	10.5	14.9	7.7	6.7
	5	21.1	27.7	46.2	73.3
	6	5.3	2.1	6.2	0.0

$$\chi^2 = 8.92; df = 3; p < .01$$
$$\Sigma\chi^2(\text{pers. disorder}) = 29.65;$$
$$df = 6; p < .001$$

Number of respondents		19	47	65[c]	15

[a] Recommendations: 1. Nothing wrong or will get over by self.
2. Mildest sanctions.
3. Friends or family help.
4. Non-mental-health professional.
5. Mental health professional.
6. Mental hospital.
[b] Directed χ^2 test not applied because direction of difference among groups for paranoid schizophrenic is indeterminate.
[c] Number of respondents for anxiety neurotic is 64.

these effects may vary with social class is suggested by the finding, shown in Table 10-3, that lower-class respondents tended to express greater social distance in relation to ex-mental patients than higher-class respondents. Although the relationship shown in Table 10-3 is statistically weak because of the small number of respondents at the educational extremes, we are inclined to take it serious since it is consistent with the results of other investigators (e.g., E. Cumming & J. Cumming, 1957; Myers & Bean,

Table 10-3. Social Distance toward Former Mental Hospital Patient
According to Respondent's Education
(Values in per cent)

	Years of Education			
	0–7	8–11	12–15	16+
Former mental patient accepted in no situations or in neighborhood only	31.6	19.2	15.4	6.7
Number of respondents	19	47	65	15
			$\chi^2 = 4.04$; df $= 3$; $p < .30$	

1968, pp. 185, 192, 193) and with our own larger analysis of the problem of relations between social status and tolerance of deviance (B. P. Dohrenwend & Chin-Shong, 1967). It seems plausible, therefore, to interpret this lower-class attitude of rejection toward ex-patients as a factor in the well-documented tendency of lower-class schizophrenics to remain longer in mental hospitals than higher-class patients (Hollingshead & Redlich, 1958; Myers & Bean, 1968). The implication is that extreme rejection by family and friends forces the lower-class patient to become dependent on the institution. Within the institution, there is a greater probability that the lower-class schizophrenic's symptoms will be tolerated, since he is far more likely than his higher-class counterpart to reach a point of receiving only custodial care (Hollingshead & Redlich, 1958). It is possible, therefore, that even for schizophrenia the higher prevalence rate in lower-class groups is due at least in part to a greater persistence of symptoms as a function, direct or indirect, of sanctions from primary group members.

Results by Ethnicity within Social Class

The relatively advantaged ethnic groups included in the attitudinal study are the Jews and the Irish, and the relatively disadvantaged ethnic groups the Negroes and the Puerto Ricans. In comparing these ethnic groups within educational levels, we will limit ourselves to the two middle educational levels included in Table 10-2 because of the grossly uneven distribution of ethnic groups at the highest and lowest levels. Only one of our respondents with less than eighth-grade education was from an advantaged ethnic group, and only two respondents from disadvantaged ethnic groups were college graduates.

Table 10-4 shows that there is no basis for expecting rates of neurosis

Table 10-4. Recommended Treatment of Fictitious Cases According to Ethnicity and Education of Respondent
(Cutting points for χ^2's, indicated by broken lines, chosen to avoid expected cell frequencies of less than 5)

Type of Disorder Represented by Case	Recommenda-tion[a]	Years of Education			
		8–11		12–15	
		Disad-vantaged Ethnic Groups (%)	Advan-taged Ethnic Groups (%)	Disad-vantaged Ethnic Groups (%)	Advan-taged Ethnic Groups (%)
Schizophrenia					
Paranoid	1	17.4	0.0	7.7	2.6
	2	0.0	4.2	3.8	0.0
	3	0.0	0.0	7.7	0.0
	4	0.0	4.2	7.7	0.0
	5	39.1	25.0	26.9	43.6
	6	43.5	66.7	46.2	53.8
		$\chi^2 = 2.55$; df = 1; $p < .20$		$\chi^2 = 0.37$; df = 1 $p > .50$	
Simple	1	30.4	12.5	15.4	2.6
	2	0.0	0.0	3.8	7.7
	3	13.0	20.8	19.2	5.1
	4	8.7	4.2	11.5	7.7
	5	39.1	54.2	38.5	66.7
	6	8.7	8.3	11.5	10.3
		$\chi^2 = 1.02$; df = 1; $p < .50$ $\Sigma\chi^2$(schizophrenia) $= 3.57$; df = 2; $p < .20$		$\chi^2 = 5.05$; df = 1; $p < .05$ $\Sigma\chi^2$(schizophrenia) $= 5.42$; df = 2; $p < .10$	
Neuroses					
Anxiety neurotic	1	52.2	58.3	65.4	50.0
	2	0.0	0.0	7.7	2.6
	3	8.7	0.0	7.7	5.3
	4	13.0	8.3	0.0	7.9
	5	26.1	29.2	19.2	28.9
	6	0.0	4.2	0.0	5.3
		$\chi^2 = 0.18$; df = 1; $p > .50$		$\chi^2 = 1.27$; df = 1; $p < .30$	
Compulsive phobic	1	69.6	75.0	57.7	59.0
	2	4.3	0.0	0.0	2.6
	3	8.7	4.2	3.8	0.0
	4	13.0	8.3	7.7	0.0

Table 10-4. (Continued)

Type of Disorder Represented by Case	Recommendation[a]	Years of Education			
		8–11		12–15	
		Disadvantaged Ethnic Groups (%)	Advantaged Ethnic Groups (%)	Disadvantaged Ethnic Groups (%)	Advantaged Ethnic Groups (%)
Compulsive Phobic (Continued)	5	4.3	12.5	30.8	38.5
	6	0.0	0.0	0.0	0.0
		$\chi^2 = 0.17$; df = 1; $p > .50$		$\chi^2 = 0.01$; df = 1; $p > .50$	
		$\Sigma\chi^2$(neuroses) = 0.35; df = 2; $p > .50$		$\Sigma\chi^2$(neuroses) = 1.28; df = 2; $p > .50$	
Personality disorder Alcoholic	1	43.5	20.8	19.2	10.3
	2	8.7	12.5	7.7	10.3
	3	0.0	8.3	3.8	2.6
	4	17.4	8.3	11.5	12.8
	Alcoholics Anonymous	17.4	16.7	11.5	23.1
	5	13.0	29.2	30.8	33.3
	6	0.0	4.2	15.4	7.7
		$\chi^2 = 1.87$; df = 1; $p < .20$		$\chi^2 = 0.27$; df = 1; $p > .50$	
Juvenile character disorder	1	39.1	33.3	7.7	33.3
	2	0.0	0.0	3.8	5.1
	3	17.4	20.8	19.2	7.7
	4	21.7	8.3	11.5	5.1
	5	17.4	37.5	46.2	46.2
	6	4.3	0.0	11.5	2.6
		$\chi^2 = 1.39$; df = 1; $p < .30$		$\chi^2 = 0.50$; df = 1; $p < .50$	
		$\Sigma\chi^2$(pers. disorder) = 3.26; df = 2; $p < .20$		$\Sigma\chi^2$(pers. disorder) = 0.77; df = 2; $p > .50$	
Number of respondents		23	24	26	39[b]

[a] Recommendations: 1. Nothing wrong or will get over by self.
2. Mildest sanction.
3. Friends or family help.
4. Non-mental-health professional.
5. Mental health professional.
6. Mental hospital.
[b] Number of respondents for anxiety neurotic is 38.

161

to differ between advantaged and disadvantaged ethnic groups as a function of primary group sanctions. All groups show a high level of tolerance for the symptoms described in these cases.

The results for the two case descriptions of schizophrenia, although not entirely consistent, suggest less tolerance in advantaged than in disadvantaged ethnic groups. Among less educated respondents, there is a tendency for members of advantaged ethnic groups to express less tolerance for the symptoms of both paranoid and simple schizophrenia. Among better educated respondents, there is no difference in reactions to the paranoid case description, but the advantaged ethnic group members show considerably less tolerance for the shy, withdrawn behavior illustrating simple schizophrenia. Thus these results suggest the possibility that symptoms of schizophrenia would be tolerated somewhat more among members of disadvantaged than among members of advantaged ethnic groups and might therefore be expected to persist longer in the former groups.

The same pattern of differences between ethnic groups holds for both cases of personality disorder. Although better educated respondents of both types of ethnic groups tended to express rejecting attitudes, less educated respondents from disadvantaged ethnic groups were somewhat more tolerant than less educated members of advantaged groups. Thus these results suggest that social tolerance would tend to produce more persistent symptoms and thus higher rates of personality disorder in disadvantaged ethnic groups within lower but not within higher social strata.

MATERIAL GAINS OR LOSSES

What of secondary material gains or losses? Are these also more likely to be factors in the persistence of symptoms in lower- than in higher-class persons, and in lower-class persons from disadvantaged as opposed to advantaged ethnic groups?

We have no data from our own studies on this question, nor are we aware of investigations by others that bear decisively on the issue. Several considerations suggest that it is not implausible, however, to think that the answers are affirmative, at last for symptomatology that proves disabling in work.

Unlike the higher-class person who has savings and material possessions that he stands to lose if he must use them to pay expenses while unable to work, the lower-class individual in disabling circumstances actually stands to gain from systems of state aid. As Ferman (1964) pointed out,

"The worker may be under less pressure from creditors when he is unemployed than when he is working. While working, the worker who has not met his financial obligations may be under the constant threat of garnishment of wages. While he is unemployed, the worker is insulated from this threat: first, by the loan company's reluctance to press for payment when money is scarce, and second, by the legal sanctions which forbid garnishment of relief payments" (p. 509).

Moreover, the low-income worker in unstable job markets may derive actual material gain from being unemployed:

"Receiving a regular payment from a state agency (unemployment compensation or public welfare payments) makes economic expenditures and payments more predictable. While working, income may fluctuate owing to periodic unemployment and underemployment. Landlords very often express satisfaction with the unemployment status of their tenants, since it means regular payment of rent direct from the government agency. Shopkeepers may also extend credit readily to the unemployed because (a) the dole is considered more *predictable* and *regular* income than income from work; and (b) relief checks are administered through the woman in the household, who is regarded as being more dependable in paying bills" (p. 509).

In general, then, the lower the income and the more unstable the employment conditions in a person's usual occupation, the greater the likelihood would seem to be that material secondary gains from state aid will reinforce disabling symptoms.

For members of disadvantaged ethnic groups, such as Negroes and Puerto Ricans, incomes tend to be less, for a given level of education and type of job, than for members of more advantaged ethnic groups (e.g., Blau & Duncan, 1967; A. F. Taeuber, K. E. Taeuber, & Cain, 1966). Also, discriminatory practices often render the economic circumstances of these persons more unstable than those of their class counterparts in more advantaged ethnic groups. Hence the chances for material gains from more stable forms of income from state aid seem likely to be relatively greater for members of disadvantaged ethnic groups than for members of advantaged ethnic groups of lower-class status.

SUMMARY

Two propositions concerning status differences in probabilities of secondary gain or loss from psychological symptoms are related to our research problem and strategy:

1. Secondary gain is more likely or secondary loss less likely in the lowest social stratum than in higher strata.

2. The probability of secondary gain is greater and the probability of secondary loss less in disadvantaged ethnic groups, compared to advantaged ones, within a given social class.

Data on the degrees and types of sanctioning indicated by attitudes toward various types of fictitious psychiatric cases were used to investigate the relative probability of social loss or gain from such symptoms in different status groups. No evidence was found that class or ethnic differences in rates of neuroses would be expected as a function of differential probabilities of social loss or gain. Differences in reactions to two case illustrations of personality disorder did suggest greater tolerance for these symptoms in the lower class and, when a limited range of educational levels was compared, greater tolerance among disadvantaged than among advantaged ethnic groups in the lower stratum but not in the higher stratum.

There was a tendency for members of disadvantaged ethnic groups to show greater tolerance for the symptoms described in the case illustrations of schizophrenia. In addition, greater tolerance for the symptoms of simple schizophrenia was expressed by lower- than by higher-class groups. At the same time, a high rate of recommendation of hospitalization for the paranoid schizophrenic, together with a tendency to express extreme social distance from former mental hospital patients, suggests that lower-class attitudes may account in part for the relatively long hospital stays of lower-class schizophrenic patients.

General considerations of occupational and personal financial conditions in different status groups suggest that the lower class in general, and members of disadvantaged ethnic groups in this class in particular, may experience relative material gain from psychological symptoms that interfere with employment.

CHAPTER 11

Summary and Conclusions

The empirical starting point for our inquiry was provided by 44 studies that have attempted to assess the "true prevalence" of psychological disorder in community populations. Our analysis of these studies shows that their most consistent result is an inverse relation between social class and reported rate of psychological disorder. We find that this relationship holds not only for overall measures of disorder but also for two major subtypes: schizophrenia and personality disorder.

THE ETIOLOGICAL ISSUE

The central issue raised by these findings showing an inverse relationship between social class and psychological disorder is the one posed by Faris and Dunham and their critics 30 years ago. For this relationship can be explained with equal plausibility as evidence of social causation, with the environmental pressures associated with low social status causing psychopathology, or, by contrast, as evidence of social selection, with pre-existing psychological disorder leading to low social status. The latter interpretation is compatible with the position that genetic factors are more important than social environmental factors in etiology.

The problem of finding a basis for determining the relative importance of social environmental and genetic factors has proved persistent. Obstacles are found in the nature of community epidemiological surveys that, with a single exception, were conducted at one point in time and without experimental controls. Causality is inherently difficult to demonstrate in such studies.

Nor have genetically oriented investigations resolved the problem. Studies of twins have pointed to the hypothesis that heredity and environment interact in the etiology of schizophrenia and probably some other major types of psychological disorder, without establishing their relative importance in the interaction.

Of the three types of studies that have aimed at determining the relative importance of heredity and social environment, the most common uses a design involving investigation of the social mobility history of lower-class cases of psychological disorder, usually schizophrenia. These studies, however, have encountered problems in the measurement of social mobility and have failed, for the most part, to provide information about family history with respect to psychological disorder. Thus their results remain inconclusive with regard to the etiological issue.

By and large, genetically oriented investigators have paid little attention to the kinds of environmental factors that are associated with differences in social class. Similarly, environmentally oriented investigators have given little attention to the control of genetic factors in their research. As a consequence, investigators of the role of social environmental factors and investigators of the role of genetic factors have not confronted each others' ideas and findings directly in the bulk of their research.

A STRATEGY FOR A CRUCIAL TEST OF THE ETIOLOGICAL ISSUE

Although it is possible to conceive in the abstract of straightforward approaches such as the experimental manipulation of social class or prospective surveys over several generations of a large sample of families originating from contrasting class backgrounds, there are crucial ethical and practical obstacles to such research strategies. We have, therefore, developed an alternative strategy in the form of a quasi-experimental design based on processes of ethnic group assimilation in open-class societies. Our main illustration of these processes of ethnic assimilation is drawn from the social history of diverse ethnic groups in New York City.

Our strategy is based on three assumptions:

1. There is an almost universally shared norm in open-class societies that upward social mobility is desirable.

2. Serious psychological disorder involves disability that decreases the probability of upward social mobility and increases the probability of downward social mobility.

3. There is greater downward social pressure on members of disadvantaged ethnic groups than on their social class counterparts in more advantaged ethnic groups.

On the basis of these assumptions, it is possible to derive from the opposing social environmental and genetic theoretical orientations alternative predictions about rates of psychological disorder in different ethnic groups *within the same social class*.

The Social Environmental Prediction

If the rate of psychological disorder in a particular social class is a function of the strength of the social pressures experienced by members of this class, we should find higher rates of disorder among persons in disadvantaged ethnic groups. In other words, the greater social pressure exerted on these relatively disadvantaged groups (e.g., Negroes and Puerto Ricans in New York City) would be expected to produce an increment in psychopathology over and above that produced by the lesser social pressure, at any particular class level, on members of more advantaged ethnic groups, such as White Anglo-Saxon Protestants and Jews in New York City.

The Genetic Prediction

By contrast, from a genetic point of view we would expect just the opposite. For if psychological disorder is mainly an outcome of genetic endowment then we would expect the rate in a given class to be a function of social selection processes, whereby the able tend to rise or maintain high status and the disabled to drift down from high status or fail to rise out of low status. Since the downward social pressure is greater on disadvantaged ethnic groups such as Negroes and Puerto Ricans, we would expect more of their healthier members to be kept in low status, thereby diluting the rate of disorder. In contrast, with less pressure to block them, the tendency of healthy members of more advantaged ethnic groups to rise would leave a residue of disabled persons among the lower-class members of these advantaged ethnic groups, thereby inflating the rate of disorder. Thus social selection should function to give a lower rate of disorder in disadvantaged ethnic groups than in advantaged ethnic groups, social class held constant.

Further Specification of Opposing Predictions

Since the evidence from the community studies suggests that class shows a stronger relationship to psychological disorder than ethnic status, it is possible to specify these opposing predictions further. Table 11-1 summarizes the relative magnitudes of the rates of psychological disorder for four ethnic-class status groups, as they would be predicted from the opposing social environmental and genetic orientations to etiology, within the framework of assumptions we have set forth.

These predictions can be tested for any types of disorder that pose the problem of the relative etiological importance of social environment and of heredity. For example, the results of epidemiological studies suggest

Table 11-1. Hypothetical Support for Social Selection Hypothesis as against Social Causation Hypothesis in Relative Rates of Disorder According to Class and Ethnic Status
(1 = lowest rate of disorder; 4 = highest rate of disorder)

	Ethnic Group Status	
Class Status	Advantaged	Disadvantaged
Support for Social Selection Hypothesis		
Higher	2	1
Lower	4	3
Support for Social Causation Hypothesis		
Higher	1	2
Lower	3	4

that not only overall psychological disorder but also schizophrenia and personality disorder raise this issue by dint of their consistently high rates in the lowest social class. Results for the various types of disorder thus investigated could differ, thereby providing specification of the effects of social environmental pressure and genetic endowment. Furthermore, replication of the quasi experiment with different advantaged and disadvantaged ethnic groups in varied national and cultural settings could provide a powerful test.

STATE OF THE EVIDENCE

We have, then, a major substantive issue that could turn on what deceptively appear to be simple questions of fact—for example, what are the rates of psychological disorder among Negroes and Puerto Ricans relative to the rates for their class counterparts in more advantaged ethnic groups in New York City? Since we ruled out, for the most part, data from studies that measured psychological disorder solely in terms of admission to psychiatric treatment as inappropriate for research on our problem, we find that relevant data from previous studies are scarce.

We concentrate, therefore, on data from our own research in Washington Heights, a section of New York City containing about 270,000 people. Unlike the area studied previously by the Midtown researchers, our area has sizable numbers of Negroes and Puerto Ricans, along with members of more advantaged ethnic groups such as Jews and Irish. Potentially, therefore, this research setting is well suited for the investigation of our problem. The studies reported here used interview procedures similar to those of the Midtown Study and the Stirling County Study. As in Midtown and Stirling, the interviewers were not clinicians. The subjects consisted of probability samples of adults aged 21 to 59—about 1300 for a first interview and about 150 for a follow-up—and also a group of about 100 psychiatric outpatients attending various clinics in the area.

Taken at face value, the results from our own and others' studies tend to support the social environmental alternative. This is due mainly to the strong and consistently higher rates of symptoms on all measures reported by Puerto Ricans relative to their class counterparts in more advantaged ethnic groups. However, results for Negroes were not always consistent with those for Puerto Ricans. Although both Negroes and Puerto Ricans tended to score higher than their class counterparts in more advantaged ethnic groups on items designed to measure paranoid tendencies (e.g., "It is safer to trust nobody") and items designed to measure sociopathic tendencies (e.g., "Most people are honest for fear of being caught"), Negroes and Puerto Ricans differed markedly on a 22-item screening instrument from the Midtown Study that relied heavily on psychophysiological items such as "headaches," "cold sweats," and "personal worries that get one down physically." In sharp contrast with Puerto Ricans, Negroes tended to report fewer symptoms on this measure than their class counterparts in more advantaged ethnic groups—a result that is more consistent with the social selection explanation of the inverse relation between social class and psychological disorder and hence provides support for the genetic alternative.

When we subject our results to an intensive methodological analysis, moreover, it becomes clear that they can no longer be accepted at face value. Thus, for example, differences in rating of the social desirability of the symptoms by the different ethnic groups in Washington Heights are consistent with differences in the rates of these symptoms reported by members of the different ethnic groups. Moreover, there are indications that the ethnic groups differed in tendency to yeasay (high for lower educated Negroes on some items) and naysay (high for Irish on some items). These problems of response set suggest that some of the symptom items themselves had different meanings and hence different implications for persons in the different subcultures.

Perhaps the most compelling reason for questioning the face value of the results is provided by a comparison of the patient and nonpatient samples from Washington Heights. In the nonpatient samples, as was noted above, Puerto Ricans scored higher than Jewish, Irish, or Negro respondents on the 22-item screening measure from the Midtown Study. When we look at the results in the patient groups, however, the finding is the same: higher scores for the Puerto Ricans. The fact that the patients

were selected to match on types of disorder strongly suggests that this
ethnic difference indicates more about subcultural contrast in modes of
expressing distress than about differences in underlying psychological disorder. We are forced to conclude that the consistently high rates of symptoms among Puerto Ricans on the measures we used could not validly
be interpreted as evidence of higher rates of psychological disorder.

THE PROBLEM OF VALIDITY IN MEASURING
PSYCHOLOGICAL DISORDER

Our attempt to determine the rates of psychological disorder among
Negroes and Puerto Ricans relative to the rates for their class counterparts
in more advantaged ethnic groups uncovered a host of measurement problems. Underlying all of them is the basic question of validity; that is,
what measures would provide us with the true rates of psychological disorder in these contrasting class and ethnic groups? In our search for
an answer, we examine the evidence provided by epidemiological studies
for the validity of the measures used.

In these studies, the total rates of disorder summed across all subtypes
ranged from a low of less than 1 per cent to a high of 64 per cent.
There is no way to account for this great variability on substantive
grounds. Rather, the differences are found to be related to differences
in thoroughness of data collection procedures and, even more, to contrasting conceptions of what constitutes a "case."

Nor is it possible to determine which of these rates is the most valid,
since none of the studies provided adequate evidence for the validity of
the measures that were used. Clinical judgment was the tool relied upon
for case identification in almost all of the studies. The validity of the
results is assumed to be implicit in the diagnostic process, a dubious
assumption in light of World War II experience with psychiatric screening.

In most studies neither the information available to the judge nor the
criteria on which diagnoses were based are reported in detail. Exceptions
are some of the more recent studies, for example, the Midtown Manhattan
Study and the Stirling County Study, both of which used structured questionnaires, thereby providng a standard set of data for psychiatric assessment. Because these studies are more explicit about their methods than
most, they provide the main points of departure for our analysis of how
best to approach the problem of validity.

After considering each of the major types of validity for which evidence
could have been sought in these studies, we conclude that, with no generally accepted criteria available and no universe of content agreed upon,
construct validity assumes central importance. Our problem, then, is to

develop a theoretical framework or "nomological net" within which validation can be sought for measures of psychological disorder in the course
of resolving the etiological issue that is our main concern.

PERSISTENT DISORDER VERSUS SITUATIONALLY
SPECIFIC SYMPTOMS

One of the startling things about the more recent community studies
is the high rates of psychological disorder they report. The 28 studies
published after 1950 yield a median rate of 15.6 per cent compared to
a median of only 2.1 per cent for the 16 studies published in 1950 or
before. Some of the later investigations, such as the Midtown Study with
a rate of 23.4 per cent, and the Stirling County Study with a rate of
over 50 per cent, reported that only very small minorities of the "cases"
had ever been in psychiatric treatment. The investigators claimed, however,
that the untreated cases resembled cases seen in psychiatric treatment,
thereby attributing to them the quality of persistence and intransigence
that clinicians emphasize in describing experience with psychiatric patients.
This claim is made despite the fact that these studies were conducted
at only one point in time.

Questioning this interpretation, Tyhurst (1957) suggested that the presence of symptoms was not necessarily an indication of the presence of
disorder. Rather, symptoms reported might be transient responses to life
crises. Such considerations led Tyhurst to remark that, if symptom prevalence "is not close to 100 per cent in such surveys, this is probably because
the survey has been incomplete in some way or the memories of informants
were faulty" (p. 161).

It appears, then, that the determinations of psychological disorder
made in community studies, including our own research in Washington
Heights, can no longer be accepted at face value. To do so would require
acceptance of claims that untreated "cases" in the general population
show the same types of stereotyped and repetitive symptomatology as
has been observed in patients over long courses of treatment, without
any direct information about the duration of an individual's symptoms
over time and in different situational contexts.

Moreover, not only is the problem of the possible situational specificity
of much of the symptomatology observed in these studies of general populations important in its own right, but also it seems to be a useful starting
point for developing a nomological net that would include the construct
of psychological disorder and would be relevant to the issue of social
environmental versus genetic etiology. To this end, we review the relevant
literature, organizing our inquiry around two questions: What social condi-

tions produce symptoms of psychological distress in persons exposed to them? Under what conditions do these symptoms persist?

Social Conditions That Produce Symptoms of Psychological Distress

Our review of studies of a wide range of stressful events shows that virtually the entire gamut of psychological symptoms can be produced in previously normal persons by contemporary circumstances. Included, for example, are studies of reactions to combat, civilian bombing, loss of a loved one, and loss of a home resulting from forced urban relocation. A particularly poignant illustration of the impact of the contemporary situation was provided by a nationwide interview study by Sheatsley and Feldman (1964) after the assassination of President Kennedy. Eighty-nine per cent of the respondents said that during the 4 days following the assassination they experienced one or more of fifteen physical and emotional symptoms such as "Didn't feel like eating," "Had headaches," "Had an upset stomach," "Had trouble getting to sleep," and "Felt nervous and tense." These symptoms are very similar to the core symptoms asked about in the Midtown Study, the Stirling County Study, and a number of other recent community studies, including our own in Washinngton Heights.

Conditions under Which Situationally Induced Symptoms Persist

Further analysis of these studies of stress situations indicates, however, that for most persons who experience even such severe situations as combat and civilian bombing the symptom reactions are transient; that is, the symptoms tend to disappear when the situation that induced them is altered. There is, however, evidence that symptoms will persist beyond the situation that produced them if they become associated with secondary gain.

Secondary Gain. The most striking evidence that potentially transient symptoms become fixed if they are rewarded is provided by the experience of the U.S. Army in the early years of World War II, when removal from combat areas and later compensation programs were found to perpetuate symptoms of combat fatigue and traumatic war neurosis. As Kardiner and Spiegal (1947) concluded, " . . . the most important of all [external factors] that tend to render the neurosis chronic is compensation for the resulting disability" (p. 392).

Extreme Environmental Conditions. Our analysis of studies of reactions to stressful situations would hardly be complete without consideration of the literature on experimental neuroses in animals, and of research on stimulus and maternal deprivation with regard to both animal and human infants. The analysis would also be incomplete if it did not take into account research on long-term reactions to imprisonment in Nazi concentration camps during World War II. These lines of investigation have shown that extremely unfavorable social environments can cause irreversible psychological disorder in the absence of secondary gain. It is highly unlikely, however, that stressful events in the lower-class social environment, either singly or in combinations, come close to approximating the conditions that produced persistent psychological symptoms in the absence of secondary gain in concentration camp victims or in experimental animals subjected to stimulus and maternal deprivation.

THE PROBLEM OF ETIOLOGY OF SYMPTOMS THAT PERSIST IN THE ABSENCE OF CONTINUING STRESS SITUATIONS OR SECONDARY GAIN

The rather surprising inference that we draw from this comparison of lower-class environment with extreme situations in concentration camps or with experimental studies of deprivation is that lower-class social conditions do not produce self-perpetuating symptoms in otherwise normal persons. If, therefore, we find symptoms that persist in the absence of secondary gain, we must infer some cause other than the social environment. Although the biological environment might be involved, the lack of positive evidence of exogenous biological psychopathogenic factors in most types of psychological disorder, together with evidence from studies of twins and foster children of the existence of a genetic factor in a variety of types of disorder, makes the latter alternative seem the more probable. We posit, therefore, that symptoms that persist in the absence of stress situations or secondary gain in everyday life are genetic in origin.

STRESS SITUATIONS IN CONTRASTING CLASS AND ETHNIC GROUPS

What evidence do we have that the excess of symptoms in the lowest social stratum might consist of reactions to stressful situations? We have considerably more data on massive events such as combat and civilian bombing, and on unusual circumstances such as concentration camp experience, than we do on the more usual events that disrupt the activities of most individuals at one time or another—a death in the family, the birth of a first child, and so on. And we know very little about the differential frequency and severity of such stress situations in contrasting class and ethnic groups. Nevertheless, several things seem likely from our analysis of the available literature. Specifically, stressful events appear to be more severe for lower- than for middle-class persons, and within classes both more frequent and more severe for Negroes than for whites, the only ethnic comparisons available.

SECONDARY GAIN IN DIFFERENT CLASS AND ETHNIC GROUPS

Turning to secondary gain, we consider the question of whether the gain from symptomatology was likely to be greater in lower- than in higher-class groups, and within classes among members of disadvantaged as opposed to advantaged ethnic groups. Our data for this investigation come from a study in Washington Heights of public attitudes toward various types of fictitious psychiatric cases and toward ex-mental patients.

Analysis of these attitudinal data suggests that, in general, symptoms characteristic of schizophrenia and of personality disorder would be more likely to be perpetuated by social gain or absence of loss in lower-class groups and, especially within the lower class, by disadvantaged than by advantaged ethnic groups. In addition, general considerations of occupational and personal financial conditions in different status groups suggest that the lower class in general, and members of disadvantaged ethnic groups in this class especially, may experience relative material gain from psychological symptoms that interfere with employment.

PROPOSITIONS

Our assessment of the available evidence, then, leads us to five main propositions as a basis for further investigation:

1. The results of 44 community studies of the "true prevalence" of psychological disorder indicate that there is an inverse relationship between social class and psychological symptoms.
2. Social environmental pressures in normal civil life, even in the lowest social class, produce symptoms that persist only as long as the situational pressure continues or in the presence of secondary gain; symptoms that persist regardless of the social situation and in the absence of secondary gain are probably genetic in origin.
3. Therefore, psychological symptoms in community populations are of two main types.
   A. Mainly generated by social situations and (1) transient in the absence of secondary gains or (2) persistent when supported by secondary gain.
   B. Mainly generated by personality defect, which is probably genetic in origin, and persistent even in the absence of secondary gain.

4. Despite unreliable measures, higher rates of psychological disorder are consistently found in the lowest social class because all of the main types and subtypes described above are likely to be inversely related to social class.
    A. The transient, situationally induced symptoms, because stress situations are harsher in lower- than in higher-class environments.
    B. The situation-induced symptoms that persist with the support of secondary gain, both because the stress situations are harsher and because secondary gain is more probable in the lower class.
    C. The persistent, defect-generated symptoms, because social selection processes are operating.
5. The relative proportions of these types of symptoms in lower-class groups are unknown. Therefore the relative importance of genetic and social environmental factors in the etiology of psychological symptoms also remains unknown.

REFORMULATION OF THE ETIOLOGICAL ISSUE

On basis of these propositions, it is possible to develop further the framework from which we derived our strategy for a crucial test of the etiological issue. In doing so, the construct "psychological disorder" is drawn into the web of hypotheses, thereby placing it in a nomological network in terms of which construct validation can be sought. In Table 11-2 our quasi-experimental strategy for testing the etiological issue is extended and specified on the basis of our propositions about the relation of social environmental and genetic factors to three types of psychological symptomatology.

FUTURE RESEARCH

The test described in Table 11-2 involves three coordinated procedures: sampling of subjects in contrasting status groups, measurement of stress situations and secondary gain, and measurement of psychological symptoms. These procedures should incorporate certain types of controls whose need was indicated by the findings of research to date.

Sampling of Subjects in Contrasting Status Groups

It will be necessary to secure samples from general populations that permit comparisons between advantaged and disadvantaged ethnic groups with social class controlled. This requirement implies probability sampling designs that will make it possible to overrepresent rare categories of respondents, such as middle-class Puerto Ricans and lower-class white Anglo-Saxon Protestants residing in the northeastern United States.

Table 11-2. Proposed Test of the Social Environmental as Against the Genetic Hypothesis in a Quasi-Experimental Design

	Primary Propositions	
	Social Environmental Hypothesis	Genetic Hypothesis
1. Relative level of symptoms within socioeconomic strata ranging from higher to lower	Disadvantaged higher than advantaged ethnic groups	Disadvantaged lower than advantaged ethnic groups
2. Psychological symptoms absent in the absence of stress situations except in cases covered by #3	Yes	No
3. Psychological symptoms present in the absence of stress situations always provide secondary gain	Yes	No

	Secondary Propositions Based on Primary Propositions from Social Environmental Hypothesis	
	Within a Socioeconomic Stratum:	
	Disadvantaged Ethnic Groups	Advantaged Ethnic Groups
4. Given propositions 1 & 2: relative frequency and severity of stress situations	Higher	Lower
5. Given propositions 1 & 3: relative probability of secondary gain from psychological symptoms	Higher	Lower

The indicator of social class must take into account the different results obtained when, for example, education rather than occupation is the class indicator in studies of social mobility. Therefore it will be necessary to keep separate various indicators of class in tests of the social causation and genetic hypotheses.

Furthermore, it will be important to pay special attention to relations among the different indicators, especially as these relationships provide evidence of differential downward social pressure on the members of the various ethnic groups. In analogy with checks to verify the effectiveness of an experimental manipulation, this will make it possible to specify the extent to which the historical situation has created greater downward pressure on the particular disadvantaged groups being studied compared to members of more advantaged groups. One such check, revealing the lower family income of Negroes and Puerto Ricans compared with more advantaged ethnic groups of comparable education in Washington Heights, was reported earlier. Other checks should be made on occupational mobility between generations and on income changes over a period of several years for added evidence of differential downward social pressure.

Measurement of Stress Situations and Secondary Gain

Distinguishing the various types of symptoms in contrasting class and ethnic groups will involve, first, assessing stress situations in everyday life. It will be necessary to determine the incidence of the stressors in contrasting class and ethnic groups and to follow their impact over time so that the direction of the relationships between stressors and symptomatology can be validated. The definitive test of whether a symptom is situation induced or is a result of personality defect could be its disappearance after the stress situation is altered. As Bradburn (1966) has suggested, however, stress situations of everyday life may be pervasive in low-status groups, occurring as they do in the context of widespread and persistent social discrimination. In some cases, therefore, the test may require repeated follow-ups over extended periods of time to detect situational changes.

We will also need data on attitudes in different status groups specifically designed to show how primary groups either contribute to secondary gain associated with an individual's symptoms or preclude it. Furthermore, these primary group attitudes, as well as material circumstances leading to gain or loss, will need to be assessed over time for individual subjects to determine their relationship to the subjects' symptomatology.

Measurement of Psychological Symptoms

The symptoms sampled must represent the population of symptoms characteristic of the nosological categories to be studied. However, they must also take into account the fact that the same degree of distress may be expressed differently by persons from different subcultural backgrounds. Furthermore, since sheer number of symptoms of subjective distress cannot be taken as an indicator of severity in a comparison across subcultures, the problem of how symptoms of subjective distress relate to disability in role functioning is critical. Obtaining measures of such impairment that are not inherently associated with social status will present difficulties that, to be overcome, will require normative data on role functioning in different status groups.

Moreover, the symptoms that appear to be most characteristic of low-status groups are not only those of the psychophysiological variety, which can be confused with physical illness, but also behaviors similar to those described under the heading "Personality Disorders" in the *Diagnostic and Statistical Manual* of the American Psychiatric Association (1952). Both types of symptoms—those that may be confounded with physical illness and those that involve antisocial acting out—are difficult to assess with personal interview techniques alone.

These problems are difficult but not, we think, insurmountable. The use of trained clinicians, preferably psychiatrists given the problems of relations between some types of symptoms and physical illness, may provide leads. Such leads would be enhanced if different types of interviews were used on an experimentally controlled basis to counter problems of response set that may be associated with subcultural differences in modes of expressing distress. The use of criterion groups with known disabilities in role functioning, including known records of antisocial behavior, and of criterion groups, such as community leaders, with histories of above-average effectiveness in role functioning, should also help.

EPILOGUE

The future research we envision, then, would be directed at testing the relative strengths of social environmental and genetic factors in psychological symptomatology through the quasi-experimental strategy of comparing the distribution of situation-generated symptoms with that of defect-generated symptoms in advantaged versus disadvantaged ethnic groups, with social class controlled. These tests would be replicated in diverse settings and with diverse advantaged and disadvantaged ethnic groups.

*   *   *

In the best of all possible worlds, the outcomes would make it possible for future investigators to proceed further along at least two lines of investigation, pinning down the precise nature of the processes whereby, on the one hand, social environmental factors produce situation-generated symptoms and, on the other hand, genetic factors produce defect-generated symptoms. The first line of research would belong mainly to behavioral scientists; the second, primarily to geneticists and biochemists. The fork in the road, however, would be clear to both groups on the basis of the results produced by the program outlined above.

References

Aiken, M., & Ferman, L. A. The social and political reactions of older Negroes to unemployment. *Phylon,* 1966, **27,** 333–346.

Akimoto, H., Shimazaki, T., Okada, K., & Hanasiro, S. Demographische und psychiatrische Untersuchung über abgegrenzte Kleinstadtgevölkerung. *Psychiatria et Neurologia Japonica,* 1942, **47,** 351–374.

American Psychiatric Association Committee on Nomenclature and Statistics. *Diagnostic and Statistical Manual: Mental Disorders.* Washington, D.C.: American Psychiatric Association, 1952.

Archibald, K. Status orientations among shipyard workers. In R. Bendix & S. M. Lipset (Eds.), *Class, Status and Power.* New York: The Free Press, 1953. Pp. 395–403.

Atkinson, J. W. Motivational determinants of risk-taking behavior. In J. W. Atkinson & N. T. Feather (Eds.), *A Theory of Achievement Motivation.* New York: John Wiley & Sons, 1966. Pp. 11–29.

Bahnson, C., & Bahnson, M. B. Role of the ego defenses: denial and repression in the etiology of malignant neoplasm. *Annals of the New York Academy of Sciences,* 1966, **125,** 827–845.

Baughman, E. E., & Dahlstrom, W. G. *Negro and White Children: A Psychological Study of the Rural South.* New York: Academic Press, 1968.

Bell, W. Anomie, social isolation, and the class structure. *Sociometry,* 1957, **20,** 105–116.

Bellin, S. S., & Hardt, R. H. Marital status and mental disorders among the aged. *American Sociological Review,* 1958, **23,** 155–162.

Bernard, J. Marital stability and patterns of status variables. *Journal of Marriage and the Family,* 1966, **28,** 421–439.

Blau, P. M., & Duncan, O. D. *The American Occupational Structure.* New York: John Wiley & Sons, 1967.

Bloom, R., Whiteman, M., & Deutsch, M. Race and social class as separate factors related to social environment. *American Journal of Sociology,* 1965, **70,** 471–476.

Blum, R. H. Case identification in psychiatric epidemiology: methods and problems. *Milbank Memorial Fund Quarterly,* 1962, **40,** 253–288.

Blumenthal, M. D. Sex as a source of heterogeneity in a mental health survey. *Journal of Psychiatric Research,* 1967, **5,** 75–87.

Böök, J. A. A genetic and neuropsychiatric investigation of a north Swedish population, with special regard to schizophrenia and mental deficiency. *Acta Genetica et Statistica Medica,* 1953, **4,** 1–100.

Böök, J. A. Genetical aspects of schizophrenic psychoses. In D. D. Jackson (Ed.), *The Etiology of Schizophrenia.* New York: Basic Books, 1960. Pp. 23–36.

Booth, C. *Life and Labour of the People,* Vol. I. London: Williams & Norgate, 1889.

Boyd, G. F. The levels of aspiration of white and Negro children in a non-segregated elementary school. *Journal of Social Psychology,* 1952, **36,** 191–196.

Braatoy, T. Is it probable that the sociological situation is a factor in schizophrenia? *Acta Psychiatrica Scandinavica,* 1937, **12,** 109–138.

Bradburn, N. Discussion of "A study of untreated psychiatric disorder in samples of urban adults" by B. P. Dohrenwend. Presented at Symposium on Social Pscyhological Approaches to the Conceptualization and Measurement of Psychological Disorder, Annual meeting of the American Psychological Association, New York City, September, 1966.

Brazziel, W. F. Correlates of southern Negro personality. *Journal of Social Issues,* 1964, **20,** No. 2, 46–53.

Bremer, J. A social psychiatric investigation of a small community in northern Norway. *Acta Psychiatrica et Neurologica Scandinavica,* 1951, Supplementum 62.

Bronfenbrenner, U. Socialization and social class through time and space. In E. E. Maccoby, T. M. Newcomb, & E. L. Hartley (Eds.), *Readings in Social Psychology,* Third Edition. New York: Henry Holt, 1958. Pp. 400–425.

Bronfenbrenner, U. Early deprivation in animals and man. In G. Newton (Ed.), *Early Experience and Behavior.* Springfield, Ill.: Charles C Thomas, 1968. Pp. 627–764.

Brown, R. G. A comparison of the vocational aspirations of paired sixth-grade white and Negro children who attend segregated schools. *Journal of Educational Research,* 1965, **58,** 402–404.

Brugger, C. Versuch einer Geisteskrankanzählung in Thüringen. *Zeitschrift für die gesamte Neurologie und Psychiatrie,* 1931, **133,** 352–390.

Brugger, C. Psychiatrische Ergebnisse einer medizinischen, anthropologischen, und soziologischen Bevölkerunguntersuchung. *Zeitschrift für die gesamte Neurologie und Psychiatrie,* 1933, **146,** 489–524.

Brugger, C. Psychiatrische Bestandaufnahme im Gebeit eines medizinish-anthropologischen Zensus in der Nähe von Rosenheim. *Zeitschrift für die gesamte Neurologie und Psychiatrie,* 1937, **160,** 189–207.

Caplan, G. *Principles of Preventive Psychiatry.* New York: Basic Books, 1964.

Caro, F. G., & Pihlblad, C. T. Aspirations and expectations: a re-examination of the bases of social class differences in the occupational orientations of male high school students. *Sociology and Social Research,* 1965, **49,** 465–475.

Cartwright, A. The effect of obtaining information from different informants on a family mobidity inquiry. *Applied Statistics,* 1957, **6,** 18–25.

Casler, L. Perceptual deprivation in institutional settings. In G. Newton (Ed.), *Early Experience and Behavior.* Springfield, Ill.: Charles C Thomas, 1968, Pp. 573–626.

Centers, R., & Bugental, D. E. Intrinsic and extrinsic job motivations among different segments of the working population. *Journal of Applied Psychology,* 1966, **50,** 193–197.

Child, I. L., & Whiting, J. W. M. Determinants of level of aspiration: evidence from everday life. *Journal of Abnormal and Social Psychology,* 1949, **44,** 303–314.

Chinoy, E. The tradition of opportunity and the aspirations of automobile workers. *American Journal of Sociology,* 1952, **57,** 453–459.

Clausen, J. A. Mental disorders, In R. K. Merton & R. A. Nisbet (Eds.), *Contemporary Social Problems.* New York: Harcourt, Brace & World, 1961. Pp. 127–180.

Clayton, P., Desmarais, L., & Winokur, G. A study of normal bereavement. *American Journal of Psychiatry,* 1968, **125,** 168–178.

Cohen, A. K., & Hodges, H. M., Jr. Characteristics of the lower-blue-collar class. *Social Problems,* 1963, **10,** 303–334.

Cohen, B. M., & Fairbank, R. Statistical contributions from the mental hygiene study of the Eastern Health District of Baltimore. II. Psychosis in the Eastern Health District in 1933. *American Journal of Psychiatry,* 1938, **94,** 1377–1395.

Cohen, B. M., Fairbank, R., & Greene, E. Statistical contributions from the Eastern Health District of Baltimore. III. Personality disorder in the Eastern Health District in 1933. *Human Biology,* 1939, **11,** 112–129.

Cole, N. J., Branch, C. H. H., & Orla, M. Mental illness. *A. M. A. Archives of Neurology and Psychiatry,* 1957, **77,** 393–398.

Couch, A., & Keniston, K. Yeasayers and naysayers: agreeing response set as a personality variable. *Journal of Abnormal and Social Psychology,* 1960, **60,** 151–174.

Coyle, P. J. Differences in reflection-impulsivity as a function of race, sex, and socio-economic class. *Dissertation Abstracts,* 1967, **27** (12-B), 4549.

Crandell, D. L., & Dohrenwend, B. P. Some relations among psychiatric symptoms, organic illness, and social class. *American Journal of Psychiatry,* 1967, **123,** 1527–1538.

Cronbach, L. J., & Meehl, P. E. Construct validity in psychological tests. *Psychological Bulletin,* 1955, **52,** 281–302.

Cropley, A. J. Differentiation of abilities, socioeconomic status, and the WISC. *Journal of Consulting Psychology,* 1964, **28,** 512–517.

Cumming, E., & Cumming, J. *Closed Ranks: an Experiment in Mental Health Education.* Cambridge, Mass.: Harvard University Press, 1957.

Cumming, J., & Cumming, E. *Ego and Milieu.* New York: Atherton Press, 1962.

Dahlstrom, W. G., & Welsh, G. S. *An MMPI Handbook*. Minneapolis: University of Minnesota Press, 1960.

Davis, A., & Dollard, J. *Children of Bondage: the Personality Development of Negro Youth in the Urban South*. Washington, D.C.: American Council on Education, 1940.

Davis, A., Gardner, B. B., & Gardner, M. R. The class system of the white caste. In E. E. Maccoby, T. M. Newcomb, & E. L. Hartley (Eds.), *Readings in Social Psychology*, Third Edition. New York: Henry Holt, 1958. Pp. 371–379.

Dean, D. G. Alienation: its meaning and measurement. *American Sociological Review*, 1961, **26**, 753–758.

Deasy, L. C. Socio-economic status and participation in the poliomyelitis vaccine trial. *American Sociological Review*, 1956, **21**, 185– 191.

de Neufville, R., & Conner, C. How good are our schools? *American Education*, 1966, **2**, 1–7.

Deutsch, M. Socio-developmental considerations in children's accidents. In *Behavioral Approaches to Accident Research*. New York: Association for the Aid of Crippled Children, 1961. Pp. 90–102.

Dice, L. R., Clark, P. J., & Gilbert, R. K. Relation of fertility to occupation and to income in the male population of Ann Arbor, Michigan, 1951–1954. *Eugenics Quarterly*, 1964, **11**, 154–167.

Dobzhansky, T. *Mankind Evolving*. New Haven, Conn.: Yale University Press, 1962.

Dohrenwend, B. P. The social psychological nature of stress: a framework for causal inquiry. *Journal of Abnormal and Social Psychology*, 1961, **62**, 294–302.

Dohrenwend, B. P. Social status and psychological disorder: an issue of substance and an issue of method. *American Sociological Review*, 1966, **31**, 14–34.

Dohrenwend, B. P., & Chin-Shong, E. Social status and attitudes toward psychological disorder: the problem of tolerance of deviance. *American Sociological Review*, 1967, **32**, 417–433.

Dohrenwend, B. P., & Dohrenwend, B. S. The problem of validity in field studies of psychological disorder. *Journal of Abnormal Psychology*, 1965, **70**, 52–69.

Dohrenwend, B. S., Colombotos, J., & Dohrenwend, B. P. Social distance and interviewer effects. *Public Opinion Quarterly*, 1968, **32**, 410–422.

Dohrenwend, B. S., & Dohrenwend, B. P. Field studies of social factors in relation to three types of psychological disorder. *Journal of Abnormal Psychology*, 1967, **72**, 369–378.

Dohrenwend, B. S., & Dohrenwend, B. P. Sources of refusals in surveys. *Public Opinion Quarterly*, 1968, **32**, 74–83.

Dreger, R., & Miller, S. Comparative psychological studies of Negroes and whites in the United States: 1958–1965. *Psychological Bulletin Monograph Supplement*, 1968, **70**, No. 3, Part 2.

Dube, K. C. Mental disorder in Agra. *Social Psychiatry*, 1968, **3**, 139–143.

Duncan, O. D. Residential areas and differential fertility. *Eugenics Quarterly*, 1964, **11**, 82–89.

Dunham, H. W. Current status of ecological research in mental disorder. In A. M. Rose (Ed.), *Mental Health and Mental Disorder*. New York: W. W. Norton, 1955. Pp. 168–179.

Dunham, H. W. Social structures and mental disorders: competing hypotheses of explanation. In *Causes of Mental Disorders: A Review of Epidemiological Knowledge, 1959*. New York: Milbank Memorial Fund, 1961. Pp. 227–265.

Dunham, H. W. *Community and Schizophrenia: an Epidemiological Analysis*. Detroit, Mich: Wayne State University Press, 1965.

Dunham, H. W., Phillips, P., & Srinivasan, B. A research note on diagnosed mental illness and social class. *American Sociological Review*, 1966, **31**, 223–227.

Eaton, J. W., & Weil, R. J. *Culture and Mental Disorders*. Glencoe, Ill.: The Free Press, 1955.

Edwards, A. L. *The Social Desirability Variable in Personality Assessment and Research*. New York: Dryden Press, 1957.

Eells, K., Davis, A., Havighurst, R. J., Herrick, V. E., & Tyler, R. W. *Intelligence and Cultural Differences*. Chicago, Ill.: University of Chicago Press, 1951.

Eitinger, L. *Concentration Camp Survivors in Norway and Israel*. London: Allen & Unwin, 1964.

Elinson, J., & Loewenstein, R. *Community Fact Book for Washington Heights, New York City, 1960–1961*. New York: Columbia University School of Public Health and Administrative Medicine, 1963.

Empey, L. T. Social class and occupational aspiration: a comparison of absolute and relative measurement. *American Sociological Review*, 1956, **21**, 703–709.

Erikson, E. H. Identity and the life cycle. *Psychological Issues Monograph*, 1959, No. 1.

Essen-Möller, E. Psychiatrische Untersuchungen an einer Serie von Zwillingen. *Acta Psychiatrica Scandinavica*, 1941, Supplementum 23.

Essen-Möller, E. Individual traits and morbidity in a Swedish rural population. *Acta Psychiatrica et Neurologica Scandinavica*, 1956, Supplementum 100.

Essen-Möller, E. Twin research and psychiatry. *International Journal of Psychiatry*, 1965, **1**, 466–475.

Fabrega, H., Rubel, A. J., & Wallace, C. A. Some social and cultural features of working class Mexican psychiatric outpatients. *Archives of General Psychiatry*, in press.

Faris, R. E. L. Comments on "Alternative hypotheses for the explanation of some of Faris' and Dunham's results" by Mary Bess Owen. *American Journal of Sociology*, 1941, **47**, 51–52.

Faris, R. E. L., & Dunham, H. W. *Mental Disorders in Urban Areas: an Ecological Study of Schizophrenia and Other Psychoses.* Chicago: Chicago University Press, 1939.

Farley, R., & Taeuber, K. E. Population trends and residential segregation since 1960. *Science,* 1968, **159,** 953–956.

Feldman, R. S., & Green, K. F. Antecedents to behavior fixations. *Psychological Review,* 1967, **74,** 250–271.

Felix, R. H., & Bowers, R. V. Mental hygiene and socio-environmental factors. *Milbank Memorial Fund Quarterly,* 1948, **26,** 125–147.

Ferman, L. A. Sociological perspectives in unemployment research. In A. B. Shostak & W. Gomberg, *Blue-Collar World: Studies of the American Worker.* Englewood Cliffs, N.J.: Prentice-Hall, 1964. Pp. 504–514.

Field, M. J. *Search for Security.* Evanston, Ill.: Northwestern University Press, 1960.

Fink, R., Shapiro, S., Goldensohn, S. S., & Daily, E. F. The "Filter-Down" process to psychotherapy in a group practice medical care program. *American Journal of Public Health,* 1969, **59,** 245–257.

Fremming, K. H. *The Expectation of Mental Infirmity in a Sample of the Danish Population.* London: Eugenics Society, 1951.

Fried, M. Grieving for a lost home. In L. J. Duhl (Ed.), *The Urban Condition.* New York: Basic Books, 1963. Pp. 151–171.

Frierson, E. C. Upper and lower status gifted children: a study of differences. *Exceptional Children,* 1965, **32,** 83–90.

Gerth, H. H., & Mills, C. W. (Eds.). *From Max Weber: Essays in Sociology.* New York: Oxford University Press, 1946.

Gillis, L. S., Lewis, J. B., & Slabbert, M. *Psychiatric Disturbance and Alcoholism in the Coloured People of the Cape Peninsula.* Cape Town: University of Cape Town, Department of Psychiatry, 1965.

Ginzberg, E., Anderson, J. K., Ginsburg, S. W., & Herma, J. L. *Patterns of Performance.* New York: Columbia University Press, 1959. (a)

Ginzberg, E., Anderson, J. K., Ginsburg, S. W., & Herma, J. L. *The Lost Divisions.* New York: Columbia University Press, 1959. (b)

Gist, N. P., & Bennett, Jr., W. S. Aspirations of Negro and white students. *Social Forces,* 1963, **42,** 40–48.

Glass, A. J. Psychotherapy in the combat zone. In *Symposium on Stress.* Washington, D.C.: Army Medical Service Graduate School, 1953. Pp. 284–294.

Glazer, N., & Moynihan, D. P. *Beyond the Melting Pot.* Cambridge, Mass.: M.I.T. Press, 1963.

Gnat, T., Henisz, J., & Sarapata, A. A psychiatric-socio-statistical study of two Polish towns. Paper read at First International Congress of Social Psychiatry, London, August, 1964.

Goffman, E. *Asylums.* New York: Doubleday-Anchor, 1961.

Goldberg, E. M., & Morrison, S. L. Schizophrenia and social class. *British Journal of Psychiatry*, 1963, **109**, 785–802.

Goodchilds, J. D., & Smith, E. E. The effects of unemployment as mediated by social status. *Sociometry*, 1963, **26**, 287–293.

Gore, P. M., & Rotter, J. B. A personality correlate of social action. *Journal of Personality*, 1963, **31**, 58–64.

Gottesman, I. I., & Shields, J. Schizophrenia in twins: 16 years' consecutive admissions to a psychiatric clinic. *British Journal of Psychiatry*, 1966, **112**, 809–818.

Gottlieb, D. Goal aspirations and goal fulfillments: differences between deprived and affluent American adolescents. *American Journal of Orthopsychiatry*, 1964, **34**, 934–941.

Greene, W. A. The psychosocial setting of the development of leukemia and lymphoma. *Annals of the New York Academy of Sciences*, 1966, **125**, 794–801.

Grossack, M. Some personality characteristics of Negro college students. *Journal of Social Psychology*, 1957, **46**, 125–131.

Gruenberg, E. M. Problems of data collection and nomenclature. In C. H. H. Branch, E. G. Beier, R. H. Anderson, & Carroll A. Whitmer (Eds.), *The Epidemiology of Mental Health*. Brighton, Utah: Departments of Psychiatry and Psychology, University of Utah and Veterans Administration Hospital, Fort Douglas Division of Salt Lake City, Utah, 1955. Pp. 63–70.

Gruenberg, E. M. Comments on "Social structures and mental disorders: competing hypotheses of explanation" by H. W. Dunham. In *Causes of Mental Disorders: a Review of Epidemiological Knowledge, 1959*. New York: Milbank Memorial Fund, 1961. Pp. 265–270.

Gunderson, E. K., & Mahan, J. L. Cultural and psychological differences among occupational groups. *Journal of Psychology*, 1966, **62**, 287–304.

Gurin, G., Veroff, J., & Feld, S. *Americans View Their Mental Health*. New York: Basic Books, 1960.

Haan, N. The relationship of ego functioning and intelligence to social status and social mobility. *Journal of Abnormal and Social Psychology*, 1964, **69**, 594–605.

Haddon, Jr., W., Valien, P., McCarroll, J. R., & Umberger, C. J. A controlled investigation of the characteristics of adult pedestrians fatally injured by motor vehicles in Manhattan. In W. Haddon, Jr., E. A. Suchman, & D. Klein (Eds.), *Accident Research: Methods and Approaches*. New York: Harper & Row, 1964.

Häfner, H. Psychological disturbances following prolonged persecution. *Social Psychiatry*, 1968, **3**, 79–88.

Haggard, E. A. Social status and intelligence: an experimental study of certain cultural determinants of measured intelligence. *Genetic Psychology Monographs*, 1954, **49**, 141–186.

Hagnell, O. *A Prospective Study of the Incidence of Mental Disorder.* Stockholm: Svenska Bokförlaget Norstedts-Bonniers, 1966. (a)

Hagnell, O. The premorbid personality of persons who develop cancer in a total population investigated in 1947 and 1957. *Annals of the New York Academy of Sciences,* 1966, **125,** 846–855. (b)

Hamburg, D. A., & Adams, J. E. A perspective on coping behavior. *Archives of General Psychiatry,* 1967, **17,** 277–284.

Hammonds, A. D. Socio-economic status and anomia: an interpretation and specification of the relationship. *Dissertation Abstracts,* 1964, **24,** 4833.

Hare, E. H., & Shaw, G. K. *Mental Health on a New Housing Estate.* New York: Oxford University Press, 1965.

Hare, N. Recent trends in the occupational mobility of Negroes, 1930–1960: an intracohort analysis. *Social Forces,* 1965, **44,** 166–173.

Hastings, D. W. Psychiatry in Eighth Air Force. *Air Surgeon's Bulletin,* 1944, **I** (8), 4–5.

Haywood, H. C., & Dobbs, V. Motivation anxiety in high school boys. *Journal of Personality,* 1964, **32,** 371–379.

Heath, R. G. Discussion of "Biochemical theories of schizophrenia" by S. S. Kety. *International Journal of Psychiatry,* 1965, **1,** 433–437.

Heilbrun, A. B., Jr. Social-learning theory, social desirability, and the MMPI. *Psychological Bulletin,* 1964, **61,** 377–387.

Helgason, T. Epidemiology of mental disorders in Iceland. *Acta Psychiatrica Scandinavica,* 1964, Supplementum 173.

Helweg-Larsen, P., Hoffmeyer, H., Kieler, J., Thaysen, E. H., Thaysen, J. H., Thygesen, P., & Wulff, M. H. Famine disease in German concentration camps. *Acta Psychiatrica et Neurologica Scandinavica,* 1952, Supplementum 83.

Henry, A. F., & Short, J. F. *Suicide and Homicide.* New York: The Free Press, 1954.

Heston, L. L. Psychiatric disorders in foster home reared children of schizophrenic mothers. *British Journal of Psychiatry,* 1966, **112,** 819–825.

Hodge, R. W., & Hodge, P. Occupational assimilation as a competitive process. *American Journal of Sociology,* 1965, **71,** 249–264.

Hollingshead, A. B. Class differences in family stability. In R. Bendix & S. M. Lipset (Eds.), *Class, Status, and Power.* New York: The Free Press, 1953.

Hollingshead, A. B., & Redlich, F. C. *Social Class and Mental Illness.* New York: John Wiley & Sons, 1958.

Hughes, H. M., & Watts, L. G. Portrait of the self-integrater. *Journal of Social Issues,* 1964, **20,** No. 2, 103–114.

Hyde, R. W., & Chisholm, R. M. The relation of mental disorders to race and nationality. *New England Journal of Medicine,* 1944, **231,** 612–618.

Hyde, R. W., & Kinglsey, L. V. Studies in medical sociology: the relation of mental disorder to the community socioeconomic level. *New England Journal of Medicine,* 1944, **231,** 543–548.

Hyman, H. H. The value systems of different classes: a social psychological contribution to the analysis of stratification. In R. Bendix & S. M. Lipset (Eds.), *Class, Status, and Power*. New York: The Free Press of Glencoe, 1953.

Hyman, H., Cobb, W. J., Feldman, J. J., Hart, C. W., & Stember, C. H. *Interviewing in Social Research*. Chicago, Ill.: The University of Chicago Press, 1954.

Inouye, E. Similarity and dissimilarity of schizophrenic twins. *Proceedings of the Third World Congress of Psychiatry*, Montreal, 1961, **1**, 524–530.

Iscoe, I., & Pierce-Jones, J. Divergent thinking, age, and intelligence in white and Negro children. *Child Development*, 1964, **35**, 785–797.

Jackson, D. D. A critique of the literature on the genetics of schizophrenia. In D. D. Jackson (Ed.), *The Etiology of Schizophrenia*. New York: Basic Books, 1960. Pp. 37–87.

Jahoda, G. Social class differentials in vocabulary expansion. *British Journal of Educational Psychology*, 1964, **34**, 321–323.

Janis, I. L. *Air War and Emotional Stress*. New York: McGraw-Hill Book Company, 1951.

Joint Commission on Mental Illness and Health. *Action for Mental Health*. New York: Basic Books, 1961.

Kadushin, C. Social class and the experience of ill health. *Sociological Inquiry*, 1964, **34**, 67–80.

Kaila, J. Uber die Durchschnittshäufigkeit der Geisteskrankheiten und des Schwachsinns in Finnland. *Acta Psychiatrica et Neurologica*, 1942, **17**, 47–67.

Kallmann, F. J. *The Genetics of Schizophrenia: A Study of Heredity and Reproduction in the Families of 1,087 Schizophrenics*. New York: J. J. Augustin, 1938.

Kallmann, F. J. The genetic theory of schizophrenia: an analysis of 691 schizophrenic twin index families. *American Journal of Psychiatry*, 1946, **103**, 309–322.

Kallmann, F. J. *Heredity in Health and Mental Disorder*. New York: W. W. Norton, 1953.

Kardiner, A., & Spiegal, H. *War Stress and Neurotic Illness*. New York: Paul B. Hoeber, 1947.

Karp, S. A., & Silberman, L. Field dependence, body sophistication, and socio-economic status. *Research Reports, Sinai Hospital of Baltimore*, 1966, **1**, 17–25.

Katz, I., & Benjamin, L. Effects of white authoritarianism in biracial work groups. *Journal of Abnormal and Social Psychology*, 1960, **61**, 448–456.

Katz, I., Goldston, J., & Benjamin, L. Behavior and productivity in bi-racial work groups. *Human Relations*, 1958, **11**, 123–141.

Katz, I., & Greenbaum, G. Effects of anxiety, threat, and racial environment on task performance of Negro college students. *Journal of Abnormal and Social Psychology*, 1963, **66**, 562–567.

Kellert, S., Williams, L. K., Whyte, W. F., & Alberti, G. Culture change and stress in rural Peru. *Milbank Memorial Fund Quarterly,* 1967, **45,** 391–415.

Kety, S. S. Biochemical theories of schizophrenia. *International Journal of Psychiatry,* 1965, **1,** 409–430.

Klugman, S. The effect of money incentives versus promise upon the reliability and obtained scores of the revised Stanford-Binet test. *Journal of General Psychology,* 1944, **30,** 255–269.

Kohn, M. L. Social class and schizophrenia: a critical review. *Journal of Psychiatric Research,* 1968, **6,** (Supplement 1), 155–173.

Kolb, L. C., Bernard, V. W., & Dohrenwend, B. P. (Eds.), *Urban Challenges to Psychiatry.* Boston: Little, Brown, and Company, in press.

Kole, D. M. A cross-cultural study of medical-psychiatric symptoms. *Journal of Health and Human Behavior,* 1966, **7,** 162–173.

Komarovsky, M. *Blue-Collar Marriage.* New York: Random House, 1962.

Koos, E. L. *Families in Trouble.* New York: Kings Crown Press, 1946.

Koos, E. L. *The Health of Regionville.* New York: Columbia University Press, 1954.

Kringlen, E. Schizophernia in male monozygotic twins. *Acta Psychiatrica Scandinavica,* 1964, Supplementum 178.

Kringlen, E. Twin study in schizophrenia. *Proceedings of the First International Congress of Psychosomatic Medicine,* Excerpta Medica International Congress Series No. 134, 1966, pp. 119–122.

Kringlen, E. *Heredity and Environment in the Functional Psychoses: An Epidemiological-Clinical Study.* Oslo: Universities forlaget, 1967.

Lange, J. *Crime as Destiny.* London: Allen & Unwin, 1931.

Langer, E. Medicine for the poor: A new deal in Denver. *Science,* 1966, **153,** 508–512.

Langner, T. S. A twenty-two item screening score of psychiatric symptoms indicating impairment. *Journal of Health and Human Behavior,* 1962, **3,** 269–276.

Langner, T. S. Psychophysiological symptoms and women's status in Mexico. In J. M. Murphy & A. H. Leighton (Eds.), *Approaches in Cross-Cultural Psychiatry.* Ithaca, N.Y.: Cornell University Press, 1965. Pp. 360–392.

Langner, T. S., & Michael, S. T. *Life Stress and Mental Health.* New York: Free Press of Glencoe, 1963.

Larson, R. F., & Sutker, S. S. Value differences and value consensus by socioeconomic levels. *Social Forces,* 1966, **44,** 563–569.

Lefcourt, H. M. Internal versus external control of reinforcement: a review. *Psychological Bulletin,* 1966, **65,** 206–220.

Lefcourt, H. M., & Ladwig, G. W. The effect of reference group upon Negroes [*sic*] task persistence in a biracial competitive game. *Journal of Personality and Social Psychology,* 1965, **1,** 668–671.

Leighton, A. H. *My Name Is Legion.* New York: Basic Books, 1959.

Leighton, A. H., Lambo, T. A., Hughes, C. C., Leighton, D. C., Murphy,

J. M., & Macklin, D. B. *Psychiatric Disorder among the Yoruba.* Ithaca, N.Y.: Cornell University Press, 1963.

Leighton, A. H., Leighton, D. C., & Danley, R. A. Validity in mental health surveys. *Canadian Psychiatric Association Journal,* 1966, **11,** 167–178.

Leighton, D. C., Harding, J. S., Macklin, D. B., Macmillan, A. M., & Leighton, A. H. *The Character of Danger.* New York: Basic Books, 1963.

Lemkau, P. *Mental Hygiene in Public Health.* New York: McGraw-Hill Book Company, 1949.

Lemkau, P., Tietze, C., & Cooper, M. Mental hygiene problems in an urban district. *Mental Hygiene,* 1942, **26,** 100–119.

Le Shan, L. An emotional life-history pattern associated with neoplastic disease. *Annals of the New York Academy of Sciences,* 1966, **125,** 780–793.

Levenson B., & McDill, M. S. Vocational graduates in auto mechanics: a follow-up study of Negro and white youth. *Phylon,* 1966, **27,** 347–357.

Liddell, H. S. A comparative approach to the dynamics of experimental neurosis. *Annals of the New York Academy of Sciences,* 1953, **56,** 164–170.

Lin, T. A study of the incidence of mental disorder in Chinese and other cultures. *Psychiatry,* 1953, **16,** 313–336.

Lindemann, E. Symptomatology and management of acute grief. *American Journal of Psychiatry,* 1944, **101,** 141–148.

Lipset, S. M., & Zetterberg, H. L. Social mobility in industrial societies. In S. M. Lipset & R. Bendix, *Social Mobility in Industrial Society.* Berkeley, Calif.: University of California Press, 1959. Pp. 11–75.

Llewellyn-Thomas, E. The prevalence of psychiatric symptoms within an island fishing village. *Canadian Medical Association Journal,* 1960, **83,** 197–204.

Loewenstein, R., Colombotos, J., & Elinson, J. Interviews hardest-to-obtain in an urban health survey. *1962 Proceedings of the Social Statistics Section of the American Statistical Association.* Pp. 160–166.

Luchterhand, E., & Weller, L. Social class and the desegregation movement: a study of parents' decisions in a Negro ghetto. *Social Problems,* 1965, **13,** 83–88.

Lukas, J. A. Village of hunger and lethargy. *New York Times Magazine,* October 2, 1966, pp. 30–31, 88–109.

Luxenburger, H. Vorläufiger Bericht über psychiatrischen Serienuntersuchungen an Zwillingen. *Zeitschrift für die gesamte Neurologie und Psychiatrie,* 1928, **116,** 297–326.

Luxenburger, H. Untersuchungen an Schizophrenen Zwillingen und ihren Geschwistern zur Prüfung der Realität von Manifestationsschwankungen. *Zeitschrift für die gesamte Neurologie und Psychiatrie,* 1936, **154,** 351–394.

Maier, N. R. F. Frustration theory: restatement and extension. *Psychological Review,* 1956, **63,** 370–388.

Malzberg, B. *Social and Biological Aspects of Mental Disease.* Utica, N.Y.: State Hospital Press, 1940.

Manis, J. G., Brawer, M. J., Hunt, C. L., & Kercher, L. C. Validating a mental health scale. *American Sociological Review,* 1963, **28,** 108–116.

Manis, J. G., Brawer, M. J., Hunt, C. L., & Kercher, L. C. Estimating the prevalence of mental illness. *American Sociological Review,* 1964, **29,** 84–89.

Marden, P. G. A demographic and ecological analysis of the distribution of physicians in metropolitan America, 1960. *American Journal of Sociology,* 1966, **72,** 290–300.

Marks, R. U. A review of empirical findings. In S. L. Syme & L. G. Reeder (Eds.), *Social Stress and Cardiovascular Disease.* New York: Milbank Memorial Fund, 1967. Pp. 51–108.

Marx, G. T. *Protest and Prejudice: a Study of Belief in the Black Community.* New York: Harper & Row, 1967.

Mayer, A. J., & Hauser, P. Class differentials in expectation of life at birth. *La Revue de L'Institut International de Statistique,* 1950, **18,** 197–200.

Mayer-Gross, W. Mental health survey in a rural area. *Eugenics Review,* 1948, **40,** 140–148.

McClelland, D. C. *The Achieving Society.* Princeton, N.J.: D. Van Nostrand Company, 1961.

Mechanic, D. The influence of mothers on their children's health attitudes and behavior. *Pediatrics,* 1965, **33,** 444–453.

Meehl, P. E. Schizotaxia, schizotypy, schizophrenia. *American Psychologist,* 1962, **17,** 827–838.

Menchaca, F. J. Facteurs sociaux de la prematurité. *Courrier,* 1964, **14,** 76–81.

Merton, R. *Social Theory and Social Structure.* Glencoe, Ill.: Free Press, 1957.

Meyerson, A. Review of "Mental Disorder in Urban Areas: an Ecological Study of Schizophrenia and Other Psychoses." *The American Journal of Psychiatry,* 1940, **96,** 995–997.

Michael, S. T. Psychiatrist's commentary. In L. Srole, T. S. Langner, S. T. Michael, M. K. Opler, & T. A. C. Rennie, *Mental Health in the Metropolis: the Midtown Manhattan Study.* New York: McGraw-Hill Book Company, 1962.

Miller, H. P. New definition of our poor. *New York Times Magazine,* April 21, 1963.

Miller, W. B. Lower class culture as a generating milieu of gang delinquency. *Journal of Social Issues,* 1958, **14,** No. 3, 5–19.

Mintz, N. L., & Schwartz, D. T. Urban ecology and psychosis: community factors in the incidence of schizophrenia and manic-depression among Italians in greater Boston. *International Journal of Social Psychiatry,* 1964, **10,** 101–118.

Mishler, E. G., & Scotch, N. A. Sociocultural factors in the epidemiology of schizophrenia: a review. *International Journal of Psychiatry,* 1965, **1,** 258–293.

Mishler, E. G., & Waxler, N. E. Decision processes in psychiatric hospitalization: patients referred, accepted, and admitted to a psychiatric hospital. *American Sociological Review*, 1963, **28,** 576–587.

Moriyama, I. M., & Guralnick, L. Occupational and social class differences in mortality. *Trends and Differentials in Mortality: Papers Presented at the 1955 Annual Conference of the Milbank Memorial Fund.* New York: Milbank Memorial Fund, 1956. Pp. 61–73.

Murphy, H. B. M. Migration and the major mental disorders. In M. B. Kantor (Ed.), *Mobility and Mental Health.* Springfield, Ill.: Charles C Thomas, 1965. Pp. 5–29.

Murri, A. Delle neurosi da trauma. *La Riforma Medica,* 1912, **28,** 533–540.

Muslin, H. L., Gyarfas, K., & Pieper, W. J. Separation experience and cancer of the breast. *Annals of the New York Academy of Sciences,* 1966, **125,** 802–806.

Myers, J. K., & Bean, L. L. *A Decade Later: a Follow-up of* Social Class and Mental Illness. New York: John Wiley & Sons, 1968.

Nansen, O. *From Day to Day.* New York: G. P. Putnam's Sons, 1949.

Nathan, T. S., Eitinger, L., & Winnik, H. Z. The psychiatric pathology of survivors of the Nazi-holocaust. *Israel Annals of Psychiatry,* 1963, **1,** 113.

New York State Department of Mental Hygiene, Mental Health Research Unit. A mental health survey of older people. *Psychiatric Quarterly Supplement,* 1959, Part I, 45–99.

Noel, D. L. Group identification among Negroes: an empirical analysis. *Journal of Social Issues,* 1964, **20,** No. 2, 71–84.

Notestein, F. W. Class differences in fertility. In R. Bendix & S. M. Lipset (Eds.), *Class, Status and Power.* New York: The Free Press of Glencoe, 1953.

Noyes, A. P., & Kolb, L. C. *Modern Clinical Psychiatry,* Sixth Edition. Philadelphia: W. B. Saunders, 1963.

O'Connor, N. Children in restricted environments. In G. Newton (Ed.), *Early Experience and Behavior.* Springfield, Ill.: Charles C Thomas, 1968. Pp. 530–572.

Ødegaard, Ø. Emigration and insanity: a study of mental disease among the Norwegian-born population of Minnesota. *Acta Psychiatrica et Neurologica,* 1932, Supplementum 4.

Ødegaard, Ø. The incidence of psychoses in various occupations. *International Journal of Social Psychiatry,* 1956, **2,** 85–104.

Opler, M. K. & Singer, J. L. Ethnic differences in behavior and psychopathology: Italian and Irish. *International Journal of Social Psychiatry,* 1956, **2,** 11–22.

Orum, A. M. A reappraisal of the social and political participation of Negroes. *American Journal of Sociology,* 1966, **72,** 32–46.

Owen, M. B. Alternative hypotheses for the explanation of some of the Faris' and Dunham's results. *American Journal of Sociology,* 1941, **47,** 48–51.

Paloucek, F. P., & Graham, J. B. The influence of psychosocial factors in the prognosis in cancer of the cervix. *Annals of the New York Academy of Sciences,* 1966, **125,** 814–816.

Parker, S., & Kleiner, R. J. Status position, mobility, and ethnic identification of the Negro. *Journal of Social Issues,* 1964, **20,** No. 2, 85–102.

Parker, S., & Kleiner, R. J. *Mental Illness in the Urban Negro Community.* New York: The Free Press, 1966.

Pasamanick, B. Discussion. In J. Zubin (Ed.), *Field Studies of the Mental Disorders.* New York: Grune & Stratton, 1961. P. 362.

Pasamanick, B. Thoughts on some epidemiologic studies of tomorrow. In P. H. Hoch & J. Zubin (Eds.), *The Future of Psychiatry.* New York: Grune & Stratton, 1962. Pp. 216–223.

Pasamanick, B., Knobloch, H., & Lilienfeld, A. Socio-economic status and some precursors of neuropsychiatric disorder. *American Journal of Orthopsychiatry,* 1956, **26,** 594–601.

Pasamanick, B., Roberts, D. W., Lemkau, P. W., & Krueger, D. B. A survey of mental disease in an urban population: prevalence by race and income. In B. Pasamanick (Ed.), *Epidemiology of Mental Disorder.* Washington, D.C.: American Association for the Advancement of Science, 1959. Pp. 183–191.

Pauling, L. Orthomolecular psychiatry. *Science,* 1968, **160,** 265–271.

Pearlin, L. I., & Kohn, M. L. Social class, occupation, and parental values: a cross-national study. *American Sociological Review,* 1966, **31,** 466–479.

Pettigrew, T. F. *A Profile of the Negro American.* Princeton, N.J.: D. Van Nostrand Company, 1964.

Phillips, D. L. Rejection of the mentally ill. *American Sociological Review,* 1964, **29,** 679–686.

Phillips, D. L. The "true prevalence" of mental illness in a New England state. *Community Mental Health Journal,* 1966, **2,** 35–40.

Piotrowski, A., Henisz, J., & Gnat, T. Individual interview and clinical examination to determine prevalence of mental disorders. *Proceedings of the Fourth World Congress of Psychiatry, Madrid, September 5–11, 1966,* Excerpta Medica International Congress Series No. 150, pp. 2477–2478.

Plunkett, R. J., & Gordon, J. E. *Epidemiology and Mental Illness.* New York: Basic Books, 1960.

Pollin, W., Stabenau, J. R., & Tupin, J. Family studies with identical twins discordant for schizophrenia. *Psychiatry,* 1965, **28,** 60–78.

Porter, J. The future of upward mobility. *American Sociological Review,* 1968, **33,** 5–19.

Primrose, E. J. R. *Psychological Illness: a Community Study.* London: Tavistock Publications, 1962.

Rainwater, L. *Family Design: Marital Sexuality, Family Size, and Contraception.* Chicago: Aldine Publishing Company, 1965.

Reid, D. D. Precipitating proximal factors in the occurrence of mental disorders: Epidemiological evidence. In *Causes of Mental Disorders: a Review of Epidemiological Knowledge, 1959.* New York: Milbank Memorial Fund, 1961. Pp. 197–216.

Rin, H., Chu, H., & Lin, T. Psychophysiological reactions of a rural and suburban population in Taiwan. *Acta Psychiatrica Scandinavica,* in press.

Rin, H., & Lin, T. Mental illness among Formosan aborigines as compared with the Chinese in Taiwan. *The Journal of Mental Sciences,* 1962, **108,** 134–146.

Robins, L. N. *Deviant Children Grown Up: a Sociological and Psychiatric Study of Sociopathic Personality.* Baltimore: The Williams & Wilkins Company, 1966.

Roen, S. R. Personality and Negro-white intelligence. *Journal of Abnormal and Social Psychology,* 1960, **61,** 148–150.

Rosanoff, A. J. Survey of mental disorders in Nassau County, New York, July-October 1916. *Psychiatric Bulletin,* 1917, **2,** 109–231.

Rosanoff, A. J., Handy, L. M., & Plesset, I. R. The etiology of manic-depressive syndromes with special reference to their occurrence in twins. *American Journal of Psychiatry,* 1935, **91,** 725–762.

Rosanoff, A. J., Handy, L. M., Plesset, I. R., & Brush, S. The etiology of so-called schizophrenic psychoses, with special reference to their occurrence in twins. *American Journal of Psychiatry,* 1934, **91,** 247–286.

Rosanoff, A. J., Handy, L. M., & Rosanoff, I. A. Criminality and delinquency in twins. *Journal of Criminal Law & Criminality,* 1934, **24,** 923.

Rosen, B. C. Race, ethnicity, and the achievement syndrome. *American Sociological Review,* 1959, **24,** 47–60.

Rosenhan, D., & Greenwald, J. A. The effects of age, sex and socio-economic class on responsiveness to two classes of verbal reinforcement. *Journal of Personality,* 1965, **33,** 108–121.

Rosenthal, D., Wender, P., & Kety, S. S. In D. Rosenthal & S. S. Kety (Eds.), *Transmission of Schizophrenia.* London: Pergamon Press, 1968.

Roth, W. F., & Luton, F. B. The mental hygiene program in Tennessee. *American Journal of Psychiatry,* 1943, **99,** 662–675.

Sanders, E. P. Relation between accident incidence and types and levels of job. *Psychological Reports,* 1964, **14,** 670.

Sandifer, M. G., Jr. Social psychiatry 100 years ago. *American Journal of Psychiatry,* 1962, **118,** 749–750.

Scheff, T. J. *Being Mentally Ill: a Sociological Theory.* Chicago, Ill.: Aldine Publishing Company, 1966.

Schmale, A., & Iker, H. The psychological setting of uterine cervical cancer. *Annals of the New York Academy of Sciences,* 1966, **125,** 807–813.

Schneiderman, L. Value orientation preferences of chronic relief recipients. *Journal of Social Work,* 1964, **9,** 13–19.

Schnore, L. F., & Evenson, P. C. Segregation in southern cities. *American Journal of Sociology,* 1966, **72,** 58–67.

Scott, W. A. Research definitions of mental health and mental illness. *Psychological Bulletin,* 1958, **55,** 29–45.

Sewell, W., Haller, A., & Straus, M. Social status and educational and occupational aspirations. *American Sociological Review,* 1957, **22,** 67–73.

Shanahan, E. Negro jobless up—why? *New York Times,* September 11, 1966, 6E.

Sheatsley, P. B., & Feldman, J. The assassination of President Kennedy: public reaction. *Public Opinion Quarterly,* 1964, **28,** 189–215.

Shields, J. Personality differences and neurotic traits in normal twin school children. *Eugenics Review,* 1954, **45,** 213–246.

Shuey, A. M. *The Testing of Negro Intelligence,* Second Edition. New York: Social Science Press, 1966.

Simpson, R. L., & Miller, M. Social status and anomia. *Social Problems,* 1963. **10,** 256–264.

Singh, S. P. A comparison between privileged Negroes and underprivileged Negroes, privileged whites, and underprivileged white children on a test of creativity. *Dissertation Abstracts,* 1968, **28** (7-A), 2569–2570.

Slater, E. The monogenic theory of schizophrenia. *Acta Genetica et Medica,* 1958, **8,** 50–56.

Slater, E., & Shields, J. *Psychotic and Neurotic Illnesses in Twins.* London: H. M. Stationery Office, 1953.

Smith, R. T. A comparison of socioenvironmental factors in monozygotic and dizygotic twins, testing an assumption. In S. G. Vandenberg (Ed.), *Methods and Goals in Human Behavior Genetics.* New York: Academic Press, 1965. Pp. 45–61.

Solomon, R. L. Traumatic avoidance learning: the principles of anxiety conservation and partial irreversibility. *Psychological Review,* 1954, **61,** 353–385.

Srole, L., Langner, T. S., Michael, S. T., Opler M. K., & Rennie, T. A. C. *Mental Health in the Metropolis: the Midtown Study,* Vol. I. New York: McGraw-Hill Book Company, 1962.

Star, S. A. Psychoneurotic symptoms in the army. In S. A. Stouffer, L. Guttman, E. A. Suchman, P. F. Lazarsfeld, S. A. Star, & J. A. Clausen (Eds.), *Studies in Social Psychology in World War II. The American Soldier: Combat and Its Aftermath.* Princeton, N.J.: Princeton University Press, 1949. Pp. 411–455.

Star, S. A. The screening of psychoneurotics in the army: technical development of tests. In S. A. Stouffer, L. Guttman, E. A. Suchman, P. F. Lazarsfeld, S. A. Star, & J. A. Clausen (Eds.), *Measurement and Prediction.* Princeton, N.J.: Princeton University Press, 1950. Pp. 486–547. (a)

Star, S. A. The screening of psychoneurotics: comparison of psychiatric diagnoses and test scores at all induction stations. In S. A. Stouffer, L. Guttman, E. A. Suchman, P. F. Lazarsfeld, S. A. Star, & J. A. Clausen (Eds.), *Measurement and Prediction.* Princeton, N.J.: Princeton University Press, 1950. Pp. 548–567. (b)

Star, S. A. *The Public's Ideas about Mental Illness.* Chicago: National Opinion Research Center, University of Chicago, 1955 (mimeographed).

Stern, C. *Principles of Human Genetics,* Second Edition. San Francisco: W. H. Freeman and Company, 1960.

Stouffer, S. A., Suchman, E. A., DeVinney, L. C., Star, S. A., & Williams,

Jr., R. M. *The American Soldier: Adjustment during Army Life*. Princeton, N.J.: Princeton University Press, 1949.

Strömgren, E. Statistical and genetic population studies within psychiatry: methods and principal results. *Actualités Scientifiques et Industrielles, Congrès International de Psychiatrie, VI, Psychiatrie Sociale.* Paris: Herman & Cie, 1950. Pp. 155–188.

Strotzka, H., Leitner, I., Czerwenka-Wenstetten, G., & Graupe, S. R. Socialpsychiatrische Feldstudie über eine ländliche Allgemeinpraxis. *Social Psychiatry* 1966, **1**, 83–87.

Susser, M. *Community Psychiatry: Epidemiologic and Social Themes.* New York: Random House, 1968.

Szasz, T. S. *The Myth of Mental Illness.* New York: Paul B. Hoeber, 1961.

Taeuber, A. F., Taeuber, K. E., & Cain, G. G. Occupational assimilation and the competitive process: a reanalysis. *American Journal of Sociology,* 1966, **72**, 273–285.

Targowla, R. Les séquelles pathologiques de la déportation dans les camps de concentration allemands pendant la deuxième guerre mondiale. *Presse Médicale,* 1954, **62**, 611–613.

Taylor, Lord, & Chave, S. *Mental Health and Environment.* London: Longmans, Green, 1964.

Throne, J. L., & Gowdey, C. W. A critical review of endogenous psychotoxins as a cause of schizophrenia. *Canadian Psychiatric Association Journal,* 1967, **12**, 159–174.

Tienari, P. Psychiatric illness in identical twins. *Acta Psychiatrica Scandinavica,* 1963, Supplementum 171.

Tienari, P. Schizophrenia in monozygotic male twins. In D. Rosenthal & S. S. Kety (Eds.), *Transmission of Schizophrenia.* London: Pergamon Press, 1968.

Tietze, C., Lemkau, P. V., & Cooper, M. Schizophrenia, manic-depressive psychosis, and social-economic status. *American Journal of Sociology,* 1941, **47**, 167–175.

Trussell, R. E., Elinson, J., & Levin, M. L. Comparisons of various methods of estimating the prevalence of chronic disease in a community—the Hunterdon County Study. *American Journal of Public Health,* 1956, **46**, 173–182.

Tsuwaga, T., Okada, K., Hanasiro, S., Asai, T., Takuma, R., Morimura, S., & Tsuboi, F. Uber die psychiatrische Zensusuntersuchung in einem Stadtbezirk von Tokyo. *Psychiatria et Neurologia Japonica,* 1942, **46**, 204–218.

Tuckman, J., Youngman, W. F., & Kreizman, G. B. Occupational level and mortality. *Social Forces,* 1965, **43**, 575–577.

Tulkin, S. R. Race, class, family, and school achievement. *Journal of Personality and Social Psychology,* 1968, **9**, 31–37.

Turner, R. J. Social mobility and schizophrenia. *Journal of Health and Social Behavior,* 1968, **9**, 194–203.

Turner, R. J., & Wagenfeld, M. O. Occupational mobility and schizophrenia:

an assessment of the social causation and social selection hypotheses. *American Sociological Review*, 1967, **32**, 104–113.

Tyhurst, J. S. The role of transition states—including disasters—in mental illness. In *Symposium on Preventive and Social Psychiatry*. Washington, D.C.: Government Printing Office, 1957. Pp. 149–169.

Uchimara, Y., Akimoto, H., Kan, O., Abe, Y., Takahashi, K., Inose, T., Shimazaki, T., & Ogawa, N. Über die vergleichend psychiatrische und erbpathologische Untersuchung auf einer Japanischen Insel. *Psychiatria et Neurologia Japonica*, 1940, **44**, 745–782.

Udry, J. R. Marital instability by race, sex, education, and occupation using 1960 census data. *American Journal of Sociology*, 1966, **72**, 203–209.

Udry, J. R. Marital instability by race and income. *American Journal of Sociology*, 1967, **72**, 673–674.

U.S. National Health Survey. *Reporting of Hospitalization in the Health Interview, a Methodological Study of Several Factors Affecting the Reporting of Hospital Episodes*. Health Statistics. Series D-4. PHS Publication No. 584-D4. Washington, D.C.: Public Health Service, 1961.

U.S. National Health Survey. *Comparison of Hospitalization Reporting in Three Survey Procedures, a Study of Alternative Survey Methods for Collection of Hospitalization Data from Household Respondents*. Health Statistics. Series D-8. Publication No. 584-D8. Washington, D. C.: Public Health Service, 1963.

Warner, W. L., Low, J. W., Lunt, P. S., & Srole, L. *Yankee City* (one-volume abridged edition). New Haven: Yale University Press, 1963.

Wechsler, H. Community growth, depressive disorders, and suicide. *American Journal of Sociology*, 1961, **67**, 9–16.

Weinstein E. A., & Geisel, P. A. Family decision making over desegregation. *Sociometry*, 1962, **25**, 21–29.

Wilde, W. A. Decision-making in a psychiatric screening agency. *Journal of Health and Social Behavior*, 1968, **9**, 215–221.

Williams, J. A., Jr. Interviewer-respondent interaction: a study of bias in the information interview. *Sociometry*, 1964, **27**, 338–352.

Williams, R. M., Jr. *Strangers Next Door: Ethnic Relations in American Communities*. Englewood Cliffs, N.J.: Prentice-Hall, 1964.

Wilson, R. S. On behavior pathology. *Psychological Bulletin*, 1963, **60**, 130–146.

Wing, J. K., & Brown, G. W. Social treatment of chronic schizophrenia: a comparative survey of three mental hospitals. *Journal of Mental Science*, 1961, **107**, 847–861.

World Health Organization. Public health aspects of low birth weight. Third report of the expert committee on maternal and child health. *Technical Report Series*, 1961, No. 217.

Wright, C. R., & Hyman, H. H. Voluntary association memberships of American adults: evidence from national sample surveys, *American Sociological Review*, 1958, **23**, 284–294.

Wylie, R. C. Children's estimates of their schoolwork ability, as a function of sex, race, and socioeconomic level. *Journal of Personality,* 1963, **31,** 203–224.

Zigler, E., & de Labry, J. Concept-switching in middle-class, lower-class, and retarded children. *Journal of Abnormal and Social Psychology,* 1962, **65,** 267–273.

Zigler, E., & Kanzer, P. The effectiveness of two classes of verbal reinforcers on the performance of middle- and lower-class children. *Journal of Personality,* 1962, **30,** 157–163.

Zitrin, A., Ferber, P., & Cohen, D. Pre- and paranatal factors in mental disorders of children. *Journal of Nervous and Mental Disease,* 1964, **139,** 357–361.

Zubin, J. Classification of the behavior disorders. *Annual Review of Psychology, Vol. 18.* Palo Alto, California: Annual Reviews, Inc., 1967. Pp. 373–406.

Name Index

199

Subject Index